Bill Belich...

Compiled by Pete Smith

Table of Contents

COACHING PHILOSOPHY & ORIGINS 2

PRACTICE PLANNING & FUNDAMENTAL
FOOTBALL 102

GAME PREPARATION 162

    Training Camp 228

    Game Planning for the Super Bowl 271

X'S AND O'S... 284

STRATEGY AND SITUATIONS................................ 312

    Special Teams... 336

    Punt/Punt Return 354

    Kickoff/Kickoff Return.................................. 373

    Two Point Conversions 390

    Red Zone.. 399

1

COACHING PHILOSOPHY & ORIGINS

Q: Are you a combination of all the people you've played for or coached with?

BB: It's hard to say. I think my first five years in the league, it was a different head coach every year with a lot of different assistant coaches in that group, from Baltimore to Detroit to a new coaching staff in Detroit, to Denver, to the Giants, to actually a couple years later a new coaching staff with the Giants when Bill [Parcells] came in and all that. My first few years in the league, different head coaches, different coordinators, different assistant coaches. It was a lot of good things from a lot of them.

I wouldn't say I was overly influenced by one person or another person. There were some people I would say I was influenced to the point of: 'If I ever coached that position or if I'm ever in charge of this, I'm never going to do it that way.' There's some of that, too. There are also plenty of things that I did learn.

It was a little bit like that at Navy. There were different coaches that went through there. Coach [Wayne] Hardin, Coach [Lee] Corso, even after I'd grown up and left there, like Coach [Nick] Saban and people like that that were there, Coach [Paul]

Johnson when he came in and ran all the option stuff. Just being around those people and all, you learn different things, different ways of doing it, different ideas. I was probably influenced a little bit by everybody.

I couldn't really – besides my dad, that was a constant – but there were so many other coaches involved that I had the opportunity to observe or spend time with or be in meetings or on the field with and that kind of thing, football camps. My dad ran a football camp every summer, so there were another dozen coaches there, some of whom were Navy but plenty of other ones were from other colleges and other associations that he had. I've worked with and observed a lot of coaches. I don't know. It's kind of a menagerie.

Q: How did your father influence your career?

BB: I grew up going to Navy practices and meetings that he would have with the team. He scouted Navy's upcoming opponents on Tuesday night's. He would go over to the field house, then the team would come over and he would watch the film with them. Of course, back in those days, players went both ways, offense and defense. You would watch continuous film of offense, defense and special teams. The same guys were out there playing whether you were on offense or defense. I would go over there with them, sit and listen to him talk to the team. He just told them that this is what they're going to do, here's the key, this is the backfield stance, whatever it was. Just talking to the team and preparing the team from a scouting standpoint.

Of course, that gave me a great opportunity to see a number great coaches that were at the Naval Academy. Head coaches like Wayne Harden and good assistant coaches like coach Rozano and coach Corso, Ernie, George, I'll go down the line. There was dozens of them. Joe Bugal, just all the positions. Each guy had a different style and a different way of doing things. I kind of learned that you could be a good coach doing it this way or doing it that way. As it goes back to my dad, I would say hard work and preparation.

To go to a game and watch him scout the game was an unforgettable experience. There would be four or five other scouts in the press box scouting the game. He'd be there with his book and scout it. He would write down the substitutions and the play and would be ready to go for the next play. When it was all over, those plays were the game. You had to wait two days before you had the chance to see the film. You would have other scouts asking what happened on that play. He was just so good at it. When the game would be over and we would be driving home, we would talk about the game but he saw every play. The scheme and the defense, the pattern that they ran, the coverage they were in, who blitzed.

He had a great vision. He taught me what he watched for. How he watched the triangle, the fullback, how to move down to the passing game if the quarterback was off the line of scrimmage. If it was a running play, see the blocking pattern. Before that, he already knew the blocking pattern, the down and distance, the formation on the front. That was already locked in and he just put it together. It was really impressive but I realized that came from not just watching it but knowing where the players were and where they came from. When he would come back, he usually came back Saturday night after the game. Say Navy was playing a home game, he would go scout Penn State or whoever it was and get back Saturday night. Sunday morning coach Rozano, coach George, coach Harden would come over or call him and ask him what happened in the game because they hadn't seen the film yet and he'd tell them.

Those kinds of things really got him ahead on the game plan. Those are some of the things I learned from him. I was fortunate to. He ran a football camp and I had the opportunity to coach in that camp. Not that I was a coach, but it helped me get into it. In college for sure because I wasn't allowed to go to that camp as a player. That was for high school players only. Kind of just getting into coaching even at that level and just understanding coaching meetings, personalities, decisions, techniques and fundamentals. It was good preparation. Long answer to a short question.

Q: You've talked about you guys being a game plan offense. Where was the idea of being a game plan offense born from for you?

BB: I don't know, I guess I've always had that philosophy. You try to do what you think works best against that particular opponent certainly within the framework of what you're comfortable doing, whether that's offense, defense or special teams, it's all the same. [Former Head Coach] Wayne Hardin at Navy maybe, if you want to go back a ways; Detroit, the Giants. I don't know.

Q: Would you agree with the thought that it's an ambitious thing to try to do because you have to be able to execute in all areas, as opposed to majoring in one thing?

BB: I'll just give you this example. When I was in high school at Annapolis, I played for Al Laramore, who was Maryland Coach of the Year, a Hall of Fame high school coach in Delaware and all that. So, he's a pretty good coach. We won a lot of games, we won a ton of games and we ran four plays. We ran four plays: 22 Power, 24 Quick Trap, 28 Counter and Sprint Right and that was it. When we ran them to the other side, we just flipped formation. The whole line flipped and the play went the other way: 22 Power, 24 Quick Trap, 28 Counter and Sprint Left. That was the offense, that was the entire offense and we won a lot of games.

Then the next year when I went to Andover and played for Coach [Steve] Sorota there, who again was a great player, great coach, played with [Vince] Lombardi at Fordham and was one of the most renowned coaches I'd say ever in New England prep school football or maybe high school football period for that matter. The quarterback called his own plays. They didn't send them in; they didn't tell him what to call. They got in the huddle and he may have asked for a suggestion from me or Ernie [Adams] or somebody, but he called whatever he wanted to call and that was the offense.

So, that was about as opposite as you could get it from one year to the next year. We won just as many games. It was totally different, but both were very successful.

So what's the right way to do it? What's the wrong way to do it? I don't know. Whatever works, whatever you believe in. But then it all has to line up that way.

I got to Baltimore with Coach [Ted] Marchibroda, Bert Jones. Bert called all the plays. I want to say it was his second year in the league. He called all the plays. Call timeout, come over to the sideline, fourth-and-one, Burt would say, 'What do you want me to call?' Ted would say, 'We have 24 Hunch, we have 36 Bob, we have Play Pass 37 Y Flag, whatever you feel good about.' 'Alright.' Other players and coaches would come up and say, 'What are we going to run?' 'I don't know, it depends what Burt calls.'

There are other teams, Coach [Ray] Perkins, Coach [Bill] Parcells, those guys, called every play. Not that we wouldn't audible to a play or something but he called every play.

So, what's right and what's wrong? I don't know. It can all work. If you do it right and you have the other things – if you do it one way, you have to have other things that are in place to do that. There's a reason for doing it. There are also some drawbacks to doing it that way. When that happens, you have to have some way to counter it.

That's the same way on defense. When I was with the Broncos and Joe Collier, there were game plans where we had 60 different fronts – fronts. It's hard to imagine 60 different fronts in a 3-4 defense really, but that what it was. It was 60 different alignments, which would include a linebacker that was blitzing so any one of the four linebackers were blitzing so that was part of it.

I got to the Giants when Bill [Parcells] came in, we put in a 3-4 there. We played one front with one adjustment. We reduced the end on the weak side from a four-technique to a three-technique and that's it. Then I'd say 95 percent of the snaps that we played from '81 to '90 that weren't nickel snaps; over 90 percent of them had to be either base or reduced front, maybe 95 percent. It might have been higher than that.

Two good defenses: the Orange Crush, the Broncos defense, that was a great defense. The Giants defense, that was a great defense. The same 3-4, two totally different philosophies. So what's the right way to do it? Both work.

Q: Do you have a go-to list of how you want to approach game-day coaching?

BB: I definitely believe in a process. I don't know that that's the same in every single game. Well, I'd say it's not the same in every single game. It depends on who you're playing and kind of what they do or what you anticipate them doing as to how you want to approach it. It's a great question. It's a very interesting point of discussion. I think there are a lot of things to look at throughout that, but it's all critical in the communication and coordination of processing the information that you get during the game, I'd say it's not easy to do. I'm not saying it's impossible, but it's not easy to do because it comes from a lot of different sources and you definitely want to prioritize it.

I'd say those are some of the components of it. Number one, getting the most important things handled – whatever they are. It could be what you're doing, it could be what they're doing, it could be the weather conditions – whatever the most important things are making sure that you start at the top. And also you don't have all day. You don't even know how long you have. If you're on defense the offense could be out there for a seven-minute drive, they could be out there for a 30-second drive, so you've got to prioritize what you're doing so that you get to the most important things first, so if you're running out of time, you haven't used your time inefficiently. So that's number one.

Number two, there's the, what we're doing versus what they're doing. A lot of times just making sure that you're right is more important than identifying what they're doing. Sometimes identifying what they're doing, until you get that cleared up then you're kind of spinning your wheels in the sand and you're not making any progress because you don't really understand exactly what the issues are. In the game situation that changes all that. You have the information from players, which is they're in the heat of the battle. You have information from the press box, who can get as much of an overview as you can get. You have sideline information. So sometimes that's the same, sometimes information – you don't see it quite the same way. The way one coach sees it, the way the press box sees it, the way the sideline sees it, the way a player on the field sees it, it's not quite all the same way. So you've kind of got to sort all that out. And then there is the balance of fixing what is in the rearview mirror and looking ahead. So like, OK we've got to take care of these problems, here's what happened, but at the same time, you're spending all your time on that, some of that is not even relevant because the next time you go out there, OK what are we going to do? We've corrected those problems, maybe we're going to make a different call or maybe we're going to be in a different situation, how do we handle that? So there is the balancing of new information versus analysis of previous information.

There are a lot of components to that, and I think a good coach, the decision making that they make within all that is what makes him a good coach. What information is important, where do we start, how do we get the most information across in the least amount of time and making sure that we get the information to the right people? Some coverage adjustment, the guard doesn't care about. He doesn't care about what coverage they're running. The receiver doesn't care if the nose is shaded or not shaded. But I'd say that's a very interesting part of game day from a coaching standpoint and one that's important, it's critical, and there are a lot of components to it.

Q: What are some of the bullet points of success when you reflect on why your organization has been able to remain successful for so long?

BB: Well, mainly we have a lot of great players here,

so I think that's always the most important thing. I've been very fortunate to have great players. I have a lot of great coaches here; coaches that have gone on to other opportunities and coaches that are here that have been considered for other opportunities as well. So, we have a number of people who are general managers or are in high personnel positions throughout the league. We have a number of coaches who have been head coaches or have left here to be head coaches.

Q: How important is it not to get caught up in the emotion of the game when trying to make game day decisions?

BB: Again, that's part of it. I think playing emotionless is not good, so there is a balance between I think when you're alert, when you're emotional, when you have a lot of energy that you're on a higher alert, but there's a point where that can go over the edge and be detrimental where its more about that than it is about the execution of your job. So there is a fine line there between poise, composure, decision making and energy and emotion and enthusiasm. And they're all good and they're all important, but there is a balance there. There's got to be a balance in there somewhere. But in terms of decision making I think you've got to try to make decisions based on what's right, not where your heart is, but what's best for the football team. But in terms of talking about or conveying that to your team or to a particular unit, that's discretionary and judgmental.

Q: What would be the scouting report on Bill Belicheck the Wesleyan University football player?

BB: Got a long way to go, buddy. Maybe you outta try coaching. Quite a few people told me that, actually. That's probably good advice. I got that from a couple of coaches. Football and lacrosse. 'Got a better career in coaching than you'll have in playing.'

Q: Did it help you as a younger coach coming up the ranks as a part of a smaller staff where you were able to fulfill more roles and wear several hats in terms of responsibilities on the staff?

BB: Well, it certainly helped me. I'm not sure if I can speak for a lot of other coaches because I don't know what their individual experiences were, but yeah it certainly helped me. I was very fortunate in my first job with Coach [Ted] Marchibroda that the staff they had was small and he had come from a large staff with George Allen in Washington. So honestly, I got to do the work that the Redskins probably had nine other assistants doing so it gave me a lot of experience. I got paid what I deserved. It wasn't about that. But the experience was great and then being able to work in the kicking game, work on special teams at Baltimore, Detroit, Denver and then the Giants. Being able to work on offense at Detroit, being able to work on defense at Baltimore, and Denver and the Giants really gave me exposure to every - literally every player on the team - especially as the special teams coach. Other than the quarterbacks - maybe a couple of situational plays with them - but basically other than the quarterbacks, you're working with every position group and pretty much every player on the roster, so I don't think anything prepared me for being a head coach as well as being a special teams coach did. But, and also I'd say the other thing about a special teams coach, it forces you to learn a lot about strategy and how the kicking game effects situational football.

Not that you don't know that offensively or defensively, but when you're the special teams coach I'd say you understand a little more about the - and sometimes you learn the hard way - a little bit about the strategy and the situational play that's involved there. So, the fact that those staffs were small, the fact that I was able to have those different experiences with those different organizations unquestionably was a big benefit, especially that early in my career to have that. Bruce [Arians] is a head coach. He coached under some of the great coaches like Bear Bryant, Jackie Sherrill, Bill Cowher and so forth. So, he has got a long list of mentors. He has had head coaching experience at the college level, at the professional level, position coach, quarterback coach, coordinator. Mike [Zimmer] had a lot of experience, too. His father is a high school coach; things like that. Pete [Carroll], obviously the same thing; coordinator, positon coach, head coach, college head coach, pro head coach a couple of times, third time in Seattle. So, yeah, I mean it all adds up. Sometimes getting kicked around a little bit early in your career; there are sometimes some benefits to what you learn and experience and then later on at some point maybe it helps you or helps to bring things together a little bit.

Q: You broke into the league right around the time that the Steelers were starting their dynasty there with a handful of Super Bowls.

BB: Yeah, so on that note - in '75 with the Colts, we started out 1-4 and we won the last nine games to go 10-4 and win the division. It was a tremendous turnaround. Then we went to Pittsburgh for the playoffs, and they had a great team. We really had a chance in that game. I think it was like, 17-13, I think it was in the fourth quarter. We drive down, we're on the like five or six-yard line, whatever it was, and they intercepted, ran it back for a touchdown. So instead of going ahead, now we're down by two scores and we end up getting beat. For my first year in the league, the point being for my first year in the league, just seeing how good they were, I mean, they were so good on defense. Every guy was better than the next guy. From [Joe] Greene to [Jack] Lambert, that whole front four, and then the secondary, and offensively - and then at the Giants going against them every year, I mean literally we played them every year in preseason, plus a couple random games here and there in the regular season. They were very - when you're a young coach and you're looking at, ok - who does things in a way that you admire or respect or want to emulate, or what can you take from a good program to help you as a coach, or if you ever get a chance, what would you do that they do? They were one of those teams. Not to cut you off on a question, but yeah, from the first year, the Steelers had a very strong impact from the outside on my philosophy as a coach.

Q: What was it like trying to game plan for those guys on any given week?

BB: Yeah, I was on the defensive side of the ball, so with [Lynn] Swann, [John] Stallworth, [Franco] Harris, [Rocky] Bleir, [Terry] Bradshaw, it was, [Mike] Webster, I mean you could go right down the line, one Hall of Fame guy after another, one All-Pro guy after another. It was a very, very solid team. But again, I would say from going against them in '75 to going against them in the '80s or even into '91 when I was in Cleveland, not a lot changed. They had a very consistent philosophy of what they did. They drafted players into it. Of course that was all before free agency so they kept their players; they built them up in the system. They had a very good training program. That was another thing that was impressive about the Steelers and Coach [Chuck] Noll was in terms of the offseason program and player development and how strong, physically their players were. That was uncommon at that point in time, I would say. I went to the Colts [and] we didn't even have a weight room. We didn't have a weight coach, either, but there was no weight room. There was a little universal gym that had four or five stations and that was it. You could have put the weight room in a corner. That was it. But that wasn't like that in Pittsburgh, and then when I went to Detroit, we had a much - it was a legitimate weight room, it was a legitimate weight program; probably similar to what the Steelers had, but kind of trying to keep up with that. Floyd Reese was the strength coach, so then I saw the difference between no weight program and a weight training offseason conditioning program. But that was all, of course, predated by what the Steelers were doing. Again, there were a lot of things like that that they did that were definitely on the forefront that they did a great job of developing. Younger players, bringing them up through the system, guys that might not play for years one, two, three, whatever it was, but then they get in there and then they're pretty good. So they developed players and they had a very, very well-balanced team. That was another thing about them, too. It didn't matter if it was offense, defense, special teams; they were just good at everything. It wasn't like, 'Well, they're pretty good here but we can take advantage of them there.' There wasn't really much of that.

Q: How much did your upbringing around the Navy football program prepare you to deal with the uncertainty and unexpected circumstances that can surround football?

BB: Probably quite a bit. As you know, growing up and when the team you know the most about is the Navy team, you know those kids have to deal with a lot. Like all colleges, there's no redshirting so they graduate in four years and there's a lot of turnover pretty quickly. Just watching some of the coaches there - Coach [Wayne] Hardin, Coach [George] Welsh, people like that, Coach [Rick] Forzano - had to adapt to different things that happened to the team as just part of the normal course of events and how they handled them. I watched my Dad in some of those situations, being observant, not really being part of any decision or anything, but just listening to them talk about how they made decisions or what their options were and then how to pick the best one, things like that. That was great, a lot of great learning experiences there. I still remember in '64 when [Roger] Staubach was coming off of the Heisman year and hurt his Achilles early in the year and Coach Hardin had to manage that, managing the practices and so forth because of what Staubach wasn't able to do for many of the games, in preparation for the games, each game in the '64 season, just things like that. I'm sure I learned a lot there, probably more than I can even remember.

Q: Well, what is your opinion now about your decision to transition from the Jets to the Patriots?

BB: The situation with the Jets, I just -- at that particular point in time I just felt like I had to make a decision for the football team and the organization, either to make a commitment to the organization or to not make one. It was as simple as that, either make it or don't make it. There were a lot of uncertainties at the time, and I just could not make it so rather than re-hash that whole press conference, I'll just cut it off there at about 30 seconds. (Laughter).

As far as the opportunities to come to New England, I again am thankful and appreciative to Mr. Kraft and the organization for having confidence in me and for doing what they had to do in order to facilitate my moving to New England's. When I left the Jets, I didn't know what was going to happen, I didn't know if I was going to be coaching in 2000 or not, and there was just -- that decision was just one that I felt like I had to make because I thought it was the right thing to do for me and for the football team, and that's -- I don't know if that's a high point or a low point, but it was a transition and obviously that was a big decision in my career.

Q: Teams are putting more pressure coaches nowadays --

BB: Can I tell you -- let me just digress for a second.

I grew up in Annapolis at the Naval academy. When I was young, Navy was a real good football team. They were a perennial power, a couple Heisman Trophy winners, and after that it went south and there were a lot of losses there and I saw a lot of coaches come and go. Believe me, nobody has to tell me about pressure of coaching to win, and nobody has to tell me about coaching not winning and then leaving and losing their jobs. I is saw that firsthand when I was probably 12, 13 years old, and unfortunately I've been seeing it for the next 37 years.

You know, I know there's pressure to win now and there's some instability in coaching. I think it's always kind of been that way.

Q: How much did your upbringing around the Navy football program prepare you to deal with the uncertainty and unexpected circumstances that can surround football?

BB: Probably quite a bit. As you know, growing up and when the team you know the most about is the Navy team, you know those kids have to deal with a lot. Like all colleges, there's no redshirting so they graduate in four years and there's a lot of turnover pretty quickly. Just watching some of the coaches there - Coach [Wayne] Hardin, Coach [George] Welsh, people like that, Coach [Rick] Forzano - had to adapt to different things that happened to the team as just part of the normal course of events and how they handled them. I watched my Dad in some of those situations, being observant, not really being part of any decision or anything, but just listening to them talk about how they made decisions or what their options were and then how to pick the best one, things like that. That was great, a lot of great learning experiences there. I still remember in '64 when [Roger] Staubach was coming off of the Heisman year and hurt his Achilles early in the year and Coach Hardin had to manage that, managing the practices and so forth because of what Staubach wasn't able to do for many of the games, in preparation for the games, each game in the '64 season, just things like that. I'm sure I learned a lot there, probably more than I can even remember.

Q: How much pride do you and the organization take in winning consistency?

BB: A lot. Yeah, a lot. That's what we're here for is to win games. Yeah, we take a lot of pride in it. But, that being said, there's probably another time to talk about that and reflect back on it and so forth. You know, none of those other - however many seasons it was or however many games it was - really makes any difference this week. I mean, nobody cares about that. This is just strictly a matchup between the Patriots and the Bills in 2017, and how these two teams compete against each other is really what it's all about. So, I don't think living in the past is going to help us, and I don't think living in the future is going to help us, either. The best thing we can do is prepare and get ready to play Buffalo in Buffalo, which is always tough, and that will take a lot of work and a lot of preparation and it will have its own unique challenges this week that we haven't faced all year. So, that's a big challenge for us. Whatever did or didn't happen in the past is a matter of record, so I'll leave the commentary on that to you guys. I think we really need to just focus on what we're doing. But, yeah, certainly we take pride in winning and that's important to us, whether it's games, division, conference, whatever. Yeah, sure, of course. That means a lot to us.

Q: What kind of football books do you have?

BB: Football books, strategy and technique books. All of the coaches' books. Bob Zuppke, Knute Rockne, all of those guys, a lot of guys you've never heard of. (Amos Alonzo) Stagg of course, Walter Camp, those are some of the more famous ones that there are books by. Dana Bible. There are books by Chuck Mather about high school coaching in 1955. All the way back, it is pretty interesting. There is a book in 1932 or 1933 by Leroy Mills about punting.

Q: How did you acquire all of these books? Is that the kind of thing you collected, or do you have to go out and look for them?

BB: You can't be that picky about those books, you can't say, "I'm looking for a book in 1930 about the passing game." You have to take whatever they wrote about. It's interesting. The box, the single-wing, the training rules they had – don't take a shower after games, it will zap all of your energy – some of them are comical really, some of the things that were talked about in the teens and 20s.

Q: Were people talking about those things back then?

BB: Yes they were, it's amazing. I'm talking about technical football books, not the fictional football books about Johnny's fourth quarter touchdown pass or whatever it is, but (Knute) Rockne, (Amos Alonzo) Stagg, (Walter) Camp, and (Bob) Zuppke. All of those guys wrote about what they did and how they did it, how they coached it, it is pretty interesting. Obviously it is a totally different game, back then it was all power football. Seven, eight, and nine man fronts, very minimal passing game. Leverage, blocking and schemes, it is all pretty interesting.

Q: Is this open to the public?

BB: No, they have it in their old library, especially some of the old and rarer ones. It is pretty extensive, I'm talking three or four of these rooms full of books. It is not just a stack of books. You could be there for a couple weeks. Then they archive all of the newspaper articles, so you can pretty much research anything.

Q: How many books do you have?

BB: A couple hundred.

Q: Do you collect them?

BB: Yes, I do. My Dad collected them. He threw me some of his leftovers and that kind of got me started. I added a few to it.

Q: Is there one in particular that you draw upon?

BB: No there aren't. There is no bible if that is what you're looking for.

Q: How many of (Bill) Parcells' books do you have?

BB: I try to keep up with some of the more recent ones too. The two (Bill) Walsh books are pretty good ones to read for today's game. Of all of the books written about pro football, contemporary books, Bill's two books are really written for pro coaches. If you're a pro coach, you have to read Bill's books. If there is a bible, it would be the two Bill Walsh books.

Q: I have a historical question for you and while you were in grade school during this period, I'm hoping that you have some insight based on your

study of the game. What was it like for Gino Cappelletti kicking field goals back in the '60s?

BB: Well, yeah, I mean I was – thanking you for not dating me back quite that far. When I first came into the league in 1975, I think we talked about this before, I would say most teams had a kicker. Some teams had a punter, other teams had a guy that played a position and also punted. Then most every team had a position player who was the long snapper, either an offensive lineman or a linebacker or tight end or somebody like that. There were very, just pure long snappers like every team has now. There were, as I said, some punters, probably there were more punters than there were positon players punting, but there was an element of both. I would say the kickers had almost all transitioned at that point. I think one of the big things with kicking, unlike punting, is timing. You have the snapper and the holder and the operation and when the kicker starts a little bit early then that fouls up the timing.

If the kicker starts a little bit late then it doesn't foul up the timing, it just puts you more at risk to have the kick blocked. So, one of the things the kicker deals with is just the timing and some of that is the anticipation. So the more the kicker knows the snapper, the more he can kind of anticipate that mannerism or length of time, anticipation of when the snap is going to occur and then start into his approach to the ball and kick.

Obviously, the better that operation is and the more experience those guys have together, to include the holder, then theoretically the better it will be, the smoother it will be. With a punter, again, there's less of that. I mean, there's some, but there's certainly less of that because that other guy is not involved. Again, a long answer to a short question, but part of the issue in the kicking game in those days was time. So, if you were a kicker, you weren't able to kick until – even if that's all you did, if you were just a pure kicker – you wouldn't be able to kick until the center was available to snap. So the centers would usually come out maybe five, 10 minutes early and maybe snap for the punter and the punters would punt to the punt returners, which again, your punt returners were usually position players, too.

Then let's call it after practice, then that same snapper would snap to the holder and the kicker and that was their practice, those whatever it was, five, 10 minutes at the end of practice and the same thing with the returners. Now you have situations where during the whole practice, as you've seen out there on the field, the snapper, the holder and the kicker or the snapper and the punter work together for extended periods of time. It's not just five minutes at the end of practice after everything else has been done. So the opportunity to be precise and efficient and the execution level on that, obviously, drastically improves. I'd say then where you see the biggest change – so, was it challenging for those kickers? Sure it was. Because a, the field conditions were a lot less than what they are now where it's either great, most fields are pretty good grass or it is turf, which is very consistent. Back in those days, the fields would vary from one end to the other, depending on if you were kicking sometimes on the infield end that was sodded or not sodded, depending on what time of year it was versus the outfield end in the baseball stadiums, which is what most of them were. The conditions weren't as good, the timing wasn't as good, the opportunity to work with those players, with each other wasn't as good.

Then I would say that the biggest difference would be in the punting game when I would say until the mid-'80s, most all teams used at least one end tight, if not both ends tight in punt formation unless they could see that the team was in an obvious return mode and there wasn't a threat to rush, then they would split out both guys. But a lot of times you'd see guys split out and then if the return team threatened, then they'd pull them and they were tight punt formations. So in the mid-'80s, really the whole punting game kind of got revolutionized and changed dramatically with Steve DeOssie in Dallas. When Steve went to Dallas, he was able to snap and block and Dallas went exclusively to a spread punt formation and teams like us – the Giants – because they were in our division, we always felt like…I mean, normally the snapper's responsibility on the punt formation back in those days was just snap the ball. They didn't have any blocking responsibility ever. Then that all changed when DeOssie went to Dallas and he started doing it and so you'd see what you see now, which is two spread guys, eight guys rush, the center will block one of them and the other seven guys block the other seven and they punted the ball.

Once we all saw that, that it was doable and Steve was doing it, then you started looking for, 'OK, can we get a guy to do that?' that enabled you to split the ends out. That's not a kicking conversation, but it's all kind of related there. Then that got to the evolution of how important the snapper was and I would say that teams at that point saw the value of keeping a pure snapper that was able to not only snap the ball consistently, but also snap and block because of the advantages it gave you in the punting game. I would say within probably five years or so, by the early '90s, you rarely saw a team in a tight punt formation, unless it was the end of the game or backed up or a situational type of punt. Almost everybody went to spread punt formations. That was really the result of the snapping situation, in my opinion.

Q: How did Ray Perkins, who coached both in New England and with the Giants, help shape both organizations in your eyes?

BB: Well, on a personal level, Ray had a huge influence on my life and my career. When I went to the Giants in 1979, Ray hired me as the special teams coach. That was really a tremendous opportunity for me and a break in my career at a pretty young age – 27 – to have an opportunity to coach the special teams unit and have the responsibility for coaching players. I did that some in Detroit but the special teams was a bigger responsibility so it was a great opportunity for me. Ray, obviously, played under Coach [Bear] Bryant and Coach [Don] Shula – those great Colts teams and that Alabama team.

He had a very tough, hard-nosed mentality and as a receiver he brought that mentality to coaching. Of course he was very good and knowledgeable about the passing game but he was a tough coach. The receivers blocked. He conditioned the team hard. He practiced hard. He coached the team like he played and he was a real grinder as a player and everybody always remarked about his toughness and competitiveness as a player, and I think that came across in his coaching and he instilled that in his staff and in his players. So it was great for me to work under him. He had, again, a huge influence in my career, not just for giving me the opportunity but I learned a lot from Coach Perkins and he was very supportive of me in the kicking game to give me the time and the ability to use the players that he felt would make a difference in the game.

We used a lot of starters on special teams when I was the coach there, players like Lawrence Taylor and so forth. They had a big impact on the game in the kicking game and Coach Perkins was behind that, so that was a great opportunity for me, as well. I learned a lot about managing a team and handling a team in those four years that I was with him. He was here for a short period of time and then went to San Diego. He was here with Ernie Adams, so between Ernie's connections and Ray's connections to the Patriots – the Giants and then back to the Patriots in Ernie's case, and Ray's case because Ray was here in '96 when I was here – there was an opportunity. He's had a strong influence on both organizations and then helped develop a lot of the coaches that had come up through those systems. Ron [Erhardt] – kind of the same thing. I was in New York when Ron came.

He was still the head coach at the Patriots when Coach [Bill] Parcells came down in '81 and then Bill brought Ron down a couple of years later. So there was obviously a strong connection there. I mean all of the terminology that we use today and the terminology that we used at the Giants, which I would imagine the Giants still probably have a big foundation on that because of Coach [Tom] Coughlin, it all came from Coach [Chuck] Fairbanks and Coach Perkins, Coach Erhardt, Coach [Hank] Bullough, whether it's on the offensive side of the ball or the defensive side of the ball.

With Coach Fairbanks it was all kind of the same, so as those coaches went to other organizations in leadership positions in the team and the league, like

Coach Perkins did, or Coach Erhardt did, and Coach Parcells did, then that nomenclature, terminology and some of the systematic things that were done under Fairbanks at New England traveled with those coaches. As we've come back in New England, Charlies [Weis] and myself, people like that, even Ernie and the scouting system – that was all developed under Fairbanks and Bucko [Kilroy] and so forth even though it kind of – I don't know if it ever really left here – as we and people who grew up in that system and learned it came back, if we needed to change things we probably changed them back, or if they were already in place then we just left them in place, so again, the foundation of those teams, the late 70's through the early 80's – I shouldn't say early – the late 70s all of the way to today is in a way, it's fundamentally from a terminology base and, again, a lot of the systematic things that are done are probably very similar.

That's a great question. I haven't gotten that one in a long time; great question. There's a tremendous connection between those two organizations from the people that have traveled back and forth and who they've brought with them, as well.

Q: Over the last three years the three coaches with the most victories happens to be the three oldest in the league in yourself, Pete Carroll and Bruce Arians. Do you think it is a matter of having so much experience that allows for that success or is

there some other common correlation between experience and success at the head coaching level?

BB: Well, you know, I think, obviously, I have a lot of respect for Pete and Bruce and honestly I'd throw Mike [Zimmer] in there, too. Obviously, he got a late start in Minnesota, but I think Mike is a tremendous coach. He has always been very good. His units have always been very productive every place that he has been. That's another experienced coach that has gone in and done very well with that team and that franchise. I think that you look at those three guys and they've all done a pretty solid job. I'd say they didn't come into great situations. They had to build those up, at least in the early part, the early years when they got there. So, I give a lot of credit to those three guys. But yeah, it's something that doesn't seem like a lot of NFL teams are really that interested in. They seem more interested in different types of coaching hires. Those three have done extremely [well]. Again, I'd throw Mike in there. I know you didn't but I'd throw him in there. I think those guys have done really well. I have a lot of respect for all three of them.

Q: Is that a good nod to the value of having experience? Is that fair to say?

BB: Well, as I've said many times, players win games and games that we've won here are because we've had good players that have gone out and won them. I certainly wouldn't want to take anything away from the great players that we've had here that have won so many games for us. That's really where it starts. I don't care who the coach is; without good players you're not going to win many games at any level, so start with that.

Q: Has a team of yours ever lost a game because of a bad call?

BB: Look, there are a lot of plays in the game, so I don't think any game comes down to one play. I mean, it can come down to one play, but there are a lot of other plays that affect the game. That's why we play 60 minutes.

Q: Is it a coaching challenge to sometime find opportunities to get guys involved?

BB: Yeah, it really is. That's a great point that you brought up there and it's one that we constantly talk about and try to maximize and it's not easy. For me, it went back to kind of my days as the defensive coordinator for the New York Giants. We had a lot of depth at linebacker. Honestly, there were times when we could have played six linebackers, and there were even some passing situations where we did, where we took the defensive line out of the game and put all of the linebackers on the field. But it's hard to do things like that over an extended period of time. Say you have a scheme, and you've worked on that scheme all week, all year, and then to do something that is pretty far off of that, it's okay as a changeup I guess, but then it takes away what you've been working on and what you've been trying to construct. It's hard to feature that. I know I give you guys a hard time every week. You look at the production sheet, carries, receptions, targets, whatever, and there are going to be guys on the top of that and there are going to be guys that have fewer and you always ask what happens to them, what happened to them in this game. Sometimes that is a function of the game, the game plan, or just the way the game played out. But if they're on our team and we put them out on the field, it's because we want them out there, we think they can be productive, they've earned that opportunity, and sometimes they got more opportunities than others and sometimes after a period maybe of lesser activity or fewer opportunities, then those opportunities come and they do well with them, and then it looks different than what it really is, like all of sudden there was some really big improvement and it really is just a question of opportunity. Some of those opportunities you can control as a coach, but a lot of them you can't.

When the ball snaps, we don't know what's going to happen, especially on defensive side of the ball. We don't know where it's going to go or what they are going to do, we just have to react to it. It definitely is a challenge. You want to have guys involved and you want to have them have roles, but each game sometimes the scheme overrides an individual player and you have to be in a particular scheme for a percentage of the time that takes certain players out of play, but you feel like that's what you need to do to be competitive. So, it's definitely a challenge. It's a good problem to have. You're certainly better off having more players, where it's hard to utilize all of them rather than having a few players and it all falls on one guy's shoulders, kind of like when I got here with Troy Brown and 15 passes a game were going to him. I mean, he's a good player, but in part because there weren't a lot of other options. It's better to be in the other position where you have more options and you use the ones that you feel are best for your team, and that's probably something that's helped our team though the years win games is the depth that we've had at positions and how many different players we've had come through in one way or another, whether it be the skill positions or not at the skill positions to help the team win when they were called on. That's part of having a good team. It is definitely a challenge, but you have to, particularly on the defensive side of the ball, you have to stop what they do, and some players on your roster may be better suited to stop certain things than others, as opposed to having the same guys out there for every single play. People my age, your age, that's kind of the way we grew up watching the game. I know when I watched pro football and when I first came into the league, it was basically the same 11 guys out there. It didn't matter if you had the ball on their one-yard line or if you had the ball with five seconds to go in the game, there were two receivers, two backs and a tight end, and the defense was in 4-3. And then it was such a revolutionary step to add a third receiver or put in a nickel back, even though the nickel back really wasn't a nickel back – all he was was a linebacker that was a smaller or more athletic guy. So, you're used to seeing the same people out there. So, that production is more consistent and comparable than what we have now where, so frequently in the league, us and everybody else, at the end of the play, two or three guys run onto the field, and two or three guys run off the field. It's just a different way of getting used to that. I'm not saying it's a bad thing or a good thing, it's just different.

Q: Is a rule of thumb that celebrating and congratulating a teammate on a great play is the way to go, as opposed to trying to get in the head of somebody else on the other team?

BB: Yeah, first of all you never want to ... We don't coach penalties. So, we don't want penalties, we don't coach them, so judgment to do the right thing, whatever it is, tackle a guy, be physical, celebrate – it's all got to be within the rules. That's number one. Like, we're not trying to go beyond any rule ever. But yeah, just in general, I mean, look, these guys work hard, they work hard every day, they work hard all week, they prepare for the game, yeah, if you go out and make a good play you should be excited about it. If anyone else works hard at something and it comes out well, hey, we feel good. We should feel good. And when you do it together as a group, you feel good with your group. The guy who scored feels good for the guys who blocked for him. The guys who blocked for him feel good for the guy who scored and vice versa. You throw a pass, you catch it, somebody had to block, somebody had to run the route, somebody had to throw it, somebody else took the coverage to help somebody else get open or whatever, you intercept a pass, you had a good pass rush, other guys were covered. So there is a lot of team excitement on those plays. You see it on the sidelines. A guy on the field makes a play, you see the bench explode. That emotion comes out with hard work and success naturally. I don't think it's something that you want to restrain. At the same time, there is another play. I mean unless there is a touchdown or a drive-ending play or turnover, but a lot of times there is another play, so one good play, that's fine, but if the next play is a bad play then that offsets it. But again there is a balance there in all that. But I don't think it's good when a team goes out and we make a good play and nobody cares. I don't think that's particularly ... It's not anything that I'm proud of any more than if we make a bad play and we don't care. If we make a bad play we want to get it right. If we make a good play we should feel good about it.

Q: Is every year different to you?

BB: Absolutely. It absolutely is even though fundamentally I think a lot of things are the same; things you have to do in camp in order to prepare for a season, but each year is different. Players are different, teams we play are different, things change in the league, there are some rule modifications, or whatever. Things like that. So, every year is different and the chemistry – each team is different. Even with some of the same players there's still always a little bit of a different mix. We'll just have to see how it all goes. I don't try and predict it. I don't try and control it. It will just work itself out. We've got a lot of snaps out there, a lot of days, a lot of training camp days. It will all take care of itself.

Q: How important is dictating tempo and rhythm to you?

BB: Not as important as points. They name of the game is the score and not giving them up, so that's what's important. So however that happens that's what I'm for.

Q: Does that make it easier for you as an offense to formation to get into a certain matchup that you like?

BB: You could do it that way, sure.

Q: Would you say your program is more predicated on teaching your team how to win games or how to not lose games?

BB: Well, both. You can't win them until you can teach them to not lose them, but you can't dig a hole and win games either. I mean you've got to attack, so both.

Q: Are there any situations on the sideline where you say 'We haven't seen this before or we weren't prepared for this?'

BB: Sure, yeah. I mean, you might have seen it before but maybe you haven't practiced it with this group that happens to be out there. It might have been a different place or different time or that type of thing. Yeah, but look, we know the proverbial 'They could come out with nine foot line splits.' I mean, what are you going to do? We're not going to practice nine foot line splits every week but what if they come out with them? If there's an unexpected situation that comes up then we have a call that we would get to or it could be two calls depending on maybe what personnel we have in the game or something like that to kind of be sound and just play through the down and figure it out.

Q: What goes into your decision to leave a player out there and not pull him and allow him to try to

make an adjustment to a mistake he may have made?

BB: The same thing that goes into everything I do. I try to do what's best for the team, but I would say my advice to you and to the fans to everybody else would be not to be too quick to decide who's right and who's wrong when you don't really know what's going on. And that's hard for me, too. If I watch something on another play or another team I can see there's a mistake. I'm not necessarily sure who made it. Obviously, something wasn't done properly; that's evident. But what went wrong and why it went wrong, what's the background of how it happened, if you're not really part of the team I mean that's a very hard thing to evaluate. I know I respect the experts that are out there, we have a lot of good ones, but I wouldn't - I know it's very hard for me when I see a mistake on film that another team makes to identify exactly what the problem was because it could probably be one of two or three things. Unless you actually know what the call was, what they were taught to do, I don't know if you really know who actually made the mistake.

Q: How much can a young player gain by sitting back and watching the game?

BB: I think it'd be better if he was playing. It'd be better for him and hopefully we can get to that point, but again we have good depth at that position. I mean look, everybody learns something every day, but I'd like for him to be able to play more if the circumstances could work out.

Q: When you travel to a new stadium that you've never coached in before what is one of the first things you'll do upon arrival to get a feel for a new surrounding?

BB: Yeah, I think it's the same every week whether you've been there or not. Of course if you haven't been there [then] there is a newness to it, but even if you have been there at most you're probably playing in that stadium once a year. So just re-familiarizing yourself with the conditions, the sun, the lights, the scoreboard, the 40-second clock. I would say in most of these stadiums, the way they're built, there's a difference in the wind between in the end zone where it's more protected and out at midfield and usually the flags are no indicator of anything other than it's the opposite of whatever they are. The turf, the footing, the consistency of that, if cleats are an issue. [If] it's a turf field then obviously it's not the case, but if it's not then what are the conditions? Cleveland's surface versus, let's just say Arizona's surface - I mean, they couldn't be more different. So each game is different so even if you've been in the stadium before, if it's a day game, if it's a night game, whatever the wind is, whatever the sun is, it's different for that day. I think fundamentally you just always want to go through that process and reacclimate yourself to the specific conditions for that particular game.

Q: Sometimes the cameras will catch you and the staff walking the field hours before kickoff. Is that what you're doing during that period, evaluating the stadium conditions?

BB: Yeah. Yeah, sure. You can get a feel for that then and then I'd say in pregame warmups, you know, again depending on the conditions, but I always talk about the kicking game because the wind will affect the kicking game more than it will affect the passing game. But then how does that affect our overall field goal range, four-down situation, directional kicking, so forth. Walking around is one thing but actually going out there and kicking the ball or throwing the ball is a little bit different. I'd say you have a better gauge on it after pregame warmups. So we kick first so that's the first part of pregame warmups and then we do the rest of it. Maybe if the field is slick in terms of cutting and running certain routes, maybe it's a certain area of the field like we have to be careful of running comebacks on the sideline. We don't want to fall down and throw a pick-six or something like that, so you know, it's just things like that.

Q: Do you ever take a look at the grain of the turf as far as which direction it may be cut or if there is any kind of slickness to the way it is laid out?

BB: Yeah, I'd say through the years there's, you know, I mean things have changed a lot through the years, but yeah, there's some fields that definitely have a slickness to them, if you will. And that could be the way it's cut or whatever, rolled, or whatever they do. Some fields have a softness to them. We're not dealing with this anymore but even not that far long ago was the whole infield situation in Miami, whether it's sodded or infield or whatever, but that was definitely a factor. Like in those games we always tried to in the fourth quarter be kicking on the non-infield end, regardless of what the wind was, as an example. So again, that's something we've got to deal with. The seams and so forth, you know, those old fields like Veterans Stadium that were baseball fields where they would take out the pitcher's mound and put in a square of turf that they would inlay in there, whether there's some bad seam areas in various spots. I mean, definitely players were aware of that. I mean, they're not looking at it; they're playing. But there's some awareness of it. The end zone, a lot of times the sidelines when you have a multi-purpose field there are multiple markings out there. We had that when I was in Denver in the old Mile High Stadium where the Denver Bears played. The first-base line ran not quite parallel to the sideline and so it was lighter but you could still kind of see it and the way it was cut it was clearly there but the sideline was a little bit further. I remember we had a couple of plays out there, one in particular, where a runner thought he was out of bounds and he was still in bounds and he got hit and it was a yard sale; helmet, ear pads, chinstrap. Each stadium has their own little idiosyncrasies and uniqueness.

Q: How do you balance having a player use his own instincts on the field versus having him play within the context of the defense?

BB: I mean I've coached every player I've ever coached the same way. You have an assignment, you have something you're responsible for and then the instincts come after that. As long as you cover your guy, that's your job. You want to cover him off, you want to cover him on, inside technique, outside technique, back pedal, squat, whatever it is. I mean there's a million different ways to do it. If you have him covered I'm going to be happy about it, you're going to be happy about it, right? So that's the bottom line. Now after that then there is an instinctive part to every play, so I've coached players - that's the way I've coached them my whole career. When I was a special teams coach I had different punters, different kickers. They don't all kick it the same way. They kick it far, they kick it high. I'm happy, they're happy, the team is happy. That's good. If they don't then we've got to try and find a better way to do it. I don't see it any differently now than I saw it when I started coaching. I don't see it really much differently from one positon to another. The techniques are different, the assignments are different but a player's instinct and his style of play - that belongs to each of us. We're all different. But there are certain fundamentals that I think as a coach you are obligated to teach the best way that you know how and work with individual players within that framework.

Q: Can a player's intelligence overcome some of his physical deficiencies on the football field?

BB: Maybe the way I see it is if a player understands what you're telling him and he works hard to try to improve on it then he gets better. If he doesn't understand or doesn't want to understand what you're telling him then how does he get better? Even if he works hard he's probably not going in the right direction. Being able to understand what we're doing, how to do it, and then being able to understand how to do it better, how to improve, wherever that is, whether it's in training, in the weight room, technique, preparation, any of those areas, if a player understands what he can do and he works at it then he's going to improve. But I think that's the most important thing to me, not what he can do outside of football on some other occupation. I care about that but I don't really care about that. I care about whether he can do it in a football context.

Q: So, is it just your constant war against human nature?

BB: I don't know if it's that, but I know how we prepare for a regular season game, and I want the preparation to be the same for a preseason game so that it becomes a habit. If you get into a bad habit in the preseason it's just going to take you awhile to get out of that habit in the regular season, and I don't want to encourage anybody to get into that. I understand that this is not the Super Bowl, but if you're a football player you play, if you're a coach you coach. My job as a coach is to get the team ready to play, and whatever situation comes up in the game, I'm going to coach the situation to win. Am I going to pull out every stop? No, I'm not saying that, but if it's third and three, we're going to try and gain three yards. If it's a field goal situation at the end of the game to win, then we'll try to block it. Whatever it is, we're going to play that situation regardless of who is out there playing. I'm not saying our front line best player is going to be out there every single play, that's separate. What the players really need to understand, and the point I'm really trying to drive home, is we're here to win. We are going to do what we need to do to win, and that's the way that the team is going to be coached.

Q: Is it just as important for your coaching staff to get into that game mentality?

BB: Absolutely. There's a lot of us that have a lot of experience, but still it has to be put together, and it's different from the way it has been. I've tried to simulate that in practice in terms of calling plays, and you can see how in practice the last few days the coaches have been further and further away in team periods and the players are more on their own. We have to develop a coaches' communication both on the sideline and from the press box down in terms of making adjustments, handling substitutions, and situationally what do we want to do. This is a time of the year that as a staff we have to start preparing for those situations. We really haven't done that in the last two weeks because it's been the day-to-day training camp where you plan a practice, watch the film, make the corrections, and do it again. We're really starting to get into things like what charts are we going to have in the press box. Who's going to put the stuff on the board at halftime? What's the pregame warm-up? How are we going to handle the communication if a guy gets hurt, and he comes off to the sideline? How are we going to tell how long he is out for, and who is going to tell who? There's a lot of organization. We the coaches have to go through a period too.

Q: How important are those meetings with the captains every week and how long have you been doing it?

BB: I've been doing it since I've been a head coach. I mean, for us it's a good opportunity to, look, I can't meet with every single player. That's really not practical. I rely on those meetings to get feedback from the players or sometimes I explain things to the players that I feel like the team needs to know and let them convey the message in their way or at least understand what the thought process is from my standpoint or the staff's standpoint. But I talk to them and they give me a lot of feedback every week. They do a great job of I'd say not telling you what you think the coach wants to hear but telling you what they think is important, what we need to do, where there's an issue, what we need to address, and then that helps me address it. Most important thing for us is on Sunday is everybody being ready to go, being on the same page, going in there collectively ready to perform our best. Between Friday morning and Sunday afternoon there's still plenty of time to sometimes make some changes, or adjustments, or go back over something, or whatever the situation happens to be and address it. That's very valuable.

Q: You mentioned that being a captain could in a way be inherent of the safety or linebacker position due to the communication required there. Is that a little bit more difficult for a captain like Rob Gronkowski because tight end may not typically be one of those positions?

BB: Yeah, well I mean I'm not saying that those positions have to be captains. I'm just saying those positons are inherent in the communication of that particular unit, just like the personal protector is inherent in handling the communication on the punt team and so forth. We've had captains at other positions. Troy Brown was a receiver. Rob

[Gronkowski] - I don't think that was a prerequisite. I'm just saying when it comes to making communication on the offensive or the defensive side of the ball that basically it starts on the inside and works its way out. You don't have receivers and corners being the primary person in the communication because who's going to be able to communicate with them? The guy next to them and then it's going to have to go from there. Those guys - Rob Ninkovich, Mike Vrabel - those guys have played on the end of the line. I mean, they were great captains and great leaders. Again, I don't think there's a prerequisite for the captain positon.

Q: What does Tom Brady add to the situation as a captain?

BB: Yeah, again, there's another [position]. I mean, the offense runs through him. His input on where the team is offensively on Friday going into the weekend is usually going to have some bearing on what happens the next couple of days and then into Sunday. Again, it's the same thing. If you had 10 people in there you'd have input from probably 10 good people. But I mean it's hard to have a captains meeting with 15 captains. I'm not saying you can't do it, I'm just saying you better decide how you want to set it up. We've usually historically had a couple of guys on each side of the ball, somebody in the kicking game. Our players in the kicking game have been pretty consistent. It was Larry [Izzo] pretty much to

Slate, but you know, obviously we've had other great
leaders there, too. We've had them in the past - the
Tracy White's to Nate Ebner's to the returners and so
forth. However, you set it up we try to get a couple of
guys from each general area, whoever the players
select. I mean, really it's not my choice; it's their
choice.

**Q: How often do things get changed after those
meetings or are those more for establishing the plan
and then executing it throughout the week?**

BB: I'd say they change every week. I mean, if a
player tells me in that meeting 'Look coach, we've
worked on this. We're not really comfortable with it. I
think there's too much confusion here,' [then] throw it
out; no problem. Get rid of it. I don't want that to
happen. Or sometimes it's 'Look, we're having a little
of trouble with this. I think if we just get a couple of
more times I think we've got it. We like it, it's a good
idea, it's going to work, we just don't quite have it
down yet.' Well, maybe we add a couple of plays in
practice that we hadn't planned on having to cover
that situation. Or it could be on the punt team like
'Hey coach, we just need one more look at this rush
that they're running. We've got it but can we just see
it one more time?' Yeah, sure; things like that. Or they
might tell me that 'Hey, this guy is down a little bit. I
think he needs a little confidence. I think if you said
something to him that would really help him.' OK,
good. I wasn't aware of that. I'll definitely do it. I

50 | On Football

mean, it could be a million different things. There's no set formula but it's just about communication and feedback.

Q: Do you ever have to have a conversation with a player when his role might change and could affect his playing time?

BB: Yeah, sure. We always talk about that. It's not an easy conversation because everybody wants to play more but at the same time everybody wants to have a good team and everybody wants to win. Everybody wants to do their role. We all want it to be bigger but sometimes we have to understand the bigger team picture, which I think our players do. Again, that's not always. But you give that up when you play football. You give up some of your individuality. You give up some of your individual preferences or individual control you have to play the great team sport of football. If you want to go out there and run track, or swim, or throw the shotput, or play tennis or whatever it is; great. There's nothing wrong with that and you control everything. You control how you practice. You control when you practice. You control how hard you hit the ball or how soft you hit it or whatever. Play golf. Then you're your own team but when you buy into a team sport, not just defensively but offensively and in the kicking game, practice for the show-team, practice for the other side of the ball, so forth and so on, then you make a commitment to the team. And that's different than playing individual sports. All players, that's something that all players have to deal with but that's part of playing football. But to your point of Logan [Ryan], he does a great job of that. But yeah, do all players want to play more? Do all players want more opportunities? Of course they do. But we have to try to set up a system and a structure that we feel like gives our team the best chance to win and I think everybody respects that.

Q: Would you find it difficult to play against an offense that decided to throw it 90 percent of the time due to their aggressiveness or would it be a relief due to their predictability?

BB: When you coach defense you don't have any control over what the other team calls. You have to just defend whatever they do. You can't really worry about it. If they want to run it every time, they can run it. If they want to throw it every team, they can throw it. If they want to split it in half, they can split it in half. You don't have any control over that. You just have to defend what the situation [is] and the personnel they have in the game.

Q: What's the latest in a season that you've ever made significant changes to your defensive approach?

BB: Every week.

Q: More specifically, have you ever made significant changes to the personnel used at later points in the season?

BB: Yeah. It depends on who you play, what the situation is. I mean in 1990 when I was with the Giants we played the Bears in the first postseason game. We played them in a 4-3 [defense]. The second game we played the 49ers in a 3-4. We played a post-safety coverage game against the Bears and played a split-safety coverage game against the 49ers, and then against Buffalo in the Super Bowl we played a 2-4 and a 3-3-nickel the entire game. Is that changing your defense? I mean, to me it was doing what we thought was best against the team we were playing. You can call it whatever you want to call it. I don't know. To me, that's just an example. I know that's a long time ago but that's the way we look at the game. We try to do what we think is best every week, whatever that is. I don't know. Who's the next game against? What are they doing? What do we have? What's the situation relative to other factors involved in the game? What do we feel like is the best way to play the game? That's the way we're going to play it.

Q: Are turnovers a byproduct of good defense? Do you go into a game not trying to create turnovers and they just happen because you're playing good fundamental defense?

BB: We always try to create turnovers. I mean you always try to play good defense, try to stop the run, try to turn the ball over, try to get off the field on third-down, play good red-area defense. I mean it's just like every time you get the ball on offense. You try to score points. If we weren't trying to score points we'd just send the punt team out there and just give it back to them. If we weren't trying to play good defense, if we weren't trying to stop them every time we go out on the field, what's the point of sending them out there? We might as well send the punt return team out there if that's what it's going to be. Yeah, we're trying to do that every single time we go out on the field. Like why else would the defense go out there? They go out there to stop them. Why else would the field goal team go out there? To score points. Why do we send the offense out there? To move the ball and score points. Why else would you put them out there?

Q: Is there an element of luck involved in recovering fumbles based on the way the ball bounces?

BB: I mean the ball can bounce however it bounces. The more guys you have there then the better chance you have of getting it. Sometimes it could be one against three and it bounces to the one guy and he makes the play. But, you know, you've got to recover it, too. The ball is not easy to get. We've all seen it squirt out. It looks like one players going to get it and somebody else gets it. When we get our chances we just have to capitalize on them.

Q: Your offense focuses on limiting interceptions. What does that say about your quarterback play and how do you feel the production has been from that position?

BB: Well, I think that that's certainly [what] we always strive for, is good ball-security. In particular, when you throw it a decent amount there are things that can go wrong that you have to try to avoid. I think there are a lot of people that deserve a lot of credit for that. It starts with the quarterbacks but the offensive line and the receivers, which includes the tight end and the backs. We've all seen a lot of interceptions occur from quarterbacks as they're throwing, balls getting tipped up in the air, receivers dropping the ball or going off of their hands for interceptions, things like that. It's not just the quarterback but it's the receivers getting open, it's the lineman in pass protection, it's the receivers catching the ball, it's the quarterback making good throws and good decisions, but it's all part of the team execution of the play and if it's good, then there's a pretty good chance you're not going to turn the ball over. And if any part of that is bad then you're getting into risky situations and probably eventually it's going to get you. I think our coaching staff has done a real good job of that and the execution level of the team offensively has been a big part of that as well.

Certainly at the quarterback positon – I'm not taking anything away from that – but all of the other positons as well. As I said, we've all seen a lot of interceptions that you wouldn't put on the quarterback that were kind of caused or the result of something else that happened so avoiding those; that's all part of it, too.

Q: Is there a benefit to the team or the coaching staff from being in close games down the stretch and proving that you can finish games strong?

BB: Well, it's hard to win in this league. I don't agree with the way you look at it. It's hard to answer. Whatever situation we have we compete in. We compete the best we can for 60 minutes every game. Some situations, I mean, we obviously have some control over all of it but whatever it is, it is. We try to do the best that we can with it.

Q: What goes into the decision to use the double-pass as opposed to perhaps saving it like you did back in the 2014 Divisional playoff game?

BB: Well, I think you're always looking for plays that complement other plays. So if you do something in this league you can't just keep doing it all the time. I mean, other teams are too good and they're too well-coached. You've got to have something that comes off of it. I think there's an element to that in most of the plays that we run. Whatever we run there is a complimentary play somewhere that's either a different run from the same formation or a different pass from the same formation or plays that kind of look alike but they're really trying to attack different parts of the defense. I think that's a very important part of an offensive or a defensive system, or special teams system for that matter to have those complementary plays. As far as saving it, I'm not really sure what that means. We're trying to go out there and win a game. If you don't win any games then what are you saving it for? You better find a way to win some games or you'd just be saving it for some other organization that you're coaching for.

Q: What are some of the advantages and disadvantages of going up-tempo?

BB: I think Chip and the Eagles [did] a great job with it. The speed that they go at, it's hard to get much communication in. It forces you to kind of simplify things defensively. You just don't have time to get some of that stuff called or can't get the right group in, or you only want to run it against certain looks, but the time you have to communicate is short. Generally speaking, they're a lot better at it than you are because they do it more than you do. Defensive communication and adjustments and being ready to play at that speed is hard. On top of that, the Eagles have just a tremendous group of skill players. They're literally two deep at every position or more – running back, tight end, quarterback, receiver. I mean, they have two floods of groups of really good skill players at all those positions. That makes it really tough because they have so many good players, so many explosive guys.

Q: Scheme-wise is there anything in particular you have to defend, like tempo?

BB: Tempo is a problem. But I'd say the biggest thing with their offense is they make you defend the whole field. They run from sideline to sideline, they run up the middle, they throw deep, they throw outside, they throw inside, they throw short catch-and-run plays, they throw balls that are over the top behind the defense, they throw the intermediate routes, the over routes, the in-cuts, the outside scissors, sail-type routes. There is really nothing that you can say, 'Well we don't have to worry about this or that.' You do because they run it inside, they run it outside, they throw it short, middle, deep, they have a lot of misdirection plays so you can't over-pursue because they have plays that force you to defend the backside of the plays. I'd say that's really the strength of their offense. On top of that, they go really fast and try to wear the defense down or force the communication issue on defense so if you aren't aligned properly or you aren't able to get your assignments – even if you're aligned right, if you're not able to get your assignments done quickly the way the plays come off, there's space in there, somebody gets free, they do a good job of finding it. They're used to playing fast at that tempo more so than the defenses are because there aren't a lot of teams that do it like that.

Q: What is your perspective on some players around the league deciding to take a knee during the national anthem?

BB: The only team I'm really worried about is our team, the New England Patriots. I can't worry about everybody else or what everybody else in the league is doing. It's not my job and it's not my responsibility. I have enough to handle right here trying to coach and get our team ready to go, so that's what I focus on, the New England Patriots.

Q: Is there a common thread or reaction a player has when he joins the organization? What's the main message you try to give those guys to help them fit in?

BB: We start at the bottom and try to work our way up. Yeah, you'd have to ask them what their thoughts are. We just try to get them caught up to what we're doing, so just don't take anything for granted. Just work from the bottom up.

Q: How do you stay motivated despite so much success?

BB: I don't really see it as work. It's actually beach working. You get to do what you love to do dealing with a lot of great people. I have a great staff. Players work hard and are very cooperative and compliant. They have a great attitude about teamwork, playing unselfishly and working unselfishly. Really doesn't feel like work. Try and give everyone the opportunity to do their job. We have a lot of people that do it very well. A great coaching staff and a great group of players. I have a lot of respect for all of them. I try and stay out of the way and let them do their job. They all do it pretty well.

Q: Would you say you are good at relaxing?

BB: Yep.

Q: If you had to choose, would you go to the beach or play golf?

BB: Well, I'm not going to beach in 60 degrees and 20 mile an hour winds. I mean, you can go to the beach by yourself on that day. Call an audible. Make the decision.

Q: What is your thought process on multiple fourth-and-one opportunities? Is there ever a hesitation to run the same type of play out of fear that they've already seen it or is it more a case of making them stop it?

BB: Right. Well, that's a great question. That's always something to consider as whether to run a play again after they've already seen it kind of with the mentality of 'Make them stop it. Let's see if they've got it figured out,' versus running it again and feeling like not running it again and saying 'Well, they're probably going to make the adjustment to that. Let's move on to something else.' It's a great question. It's always something that you have to take into consideration with your play-calling and the same thing defensively. You run a blitz or you run a punt return or a kickoff return and you hit it. Do you come back with it again or do you, like I said, figure that they're going to stop it and move on to something else? Yeah, and if you do it right then you feel good about it, and if you do it wrong you always feel like you should've done the other thing. That's a good question. You have to sometimes just kind of have a feel for the situation or maybe anticipate if you've seen those types of situations from the team before, figure out what they're going to do with it. Are they going to really adjust if you hurt them with something or are they going to just say 'Well, we didn't play it well. We're going to play it better and keep playing the same thing that we've been playing. We're just going to do a better job of it.' Yeah, that's kind of the pendulum swing on that one. It's an interesting point.

Q: When evaluating a blitz from a defensive back do you judge its success as to whether or not he gets the quarterback on the ground or can it be just as effective to rush him out of the pocket or hurry the throw?

BB: Well, sure. Anything that affects the passing game can be a good thing. As you said, getting pressure, flushing him out. A lot of times, again, it depends on what the rest of the play is and how many people are coming and what the coverage is and so forth. A lot of times when you bring a player from the perimeter it forces one of the eligible receivers, usually the back but it could be a tight end, to stay in and protect and so that is one less receiver you have to cover, which could either free somebody up or the man who's covering could come as a second blitzer so you actually add in to the rush. In a similar fashion, anytime you bring five players, like the Rams did on numerous occasions in the game, I mean all teams do it. We do it. When you bring five rushers and it doesn't keep one of the eligible receivers in, so just five-on-five with the offensive line, then you get all singles on the pass rush. So that creates some opportunities, too. Again, it kind of depends on what you're trying to do. Of course if nobody picks him up that's great. That doesn't always happen but a lot of times you plan those type of plays thinking that if you don't come free you'll force one of the receivers, [Benny] Cunningham or [Lance] Kendricks, to stay in and protect and then that's one less guy you have to cover. There's a lot of different strategies to doing that relative to what's going on in the inside part of the defense, whether you're playing man or zone behind it, kind of which side of the formation you're coming off of, whether it's the passing strength, or to the tight end, or to the back, or away from the back, or away from the tight end or so forth. Pass protections change some matchups and if you can get a favorable one then that's maybe something you want to consider. If it leads too big of a void or creates a problem for you then it's something you don't want to do or maybe you don't want to bring the player off of a certain side or off of a certain receiver because of the way they adjust to it.

Q: How difficult is it to get the offense to perform at a high level when they haven't had a lot of game reps together recently?

BB: Well I mean I don't know. It is what it is. It's the National Football League. Every team has an injury report. I'm sure some of their guys battled through it to be out there. We had guys battling through it to be out there, to be out there and practice. It's the National Football League. We have a lot of tough guys in this room, on this team. Again, they come to work every day. Sometimes they're not able to practice or perform, but they're in there getting treatment, they're in there doing everything they can to get back out there as soon as they can. I think the guys that played today it's a real credit to them and our training staff that they were even back out there. I'm sure we'll have some of those guys in the same boat this week, and I know they'll battle hard to be out there and give us everything they've got.

Q: Do injuries on offense force you to change your offensive philosophy?

BB: We really, every week we talk about what we're going to try to do, how we match up with the team we're playing and so forth. Those conversations take place every week. We just don't go out and run the same plays 16 weeks in a row even if none of our players' change. You've seen us play enough to know that we don't really do that. How we play this week is going to be different than how we played last week for a number of reasons. We have the same conversation every week.

Q: With injuries, do you pull a guy aside and talk to him about the next-man-up mentality or is that something that is expected with the Patriots?

BB: Look, every player that's in that room has a job to do and they have a role on the team and they're all important and they know that. They know that from day one. There's no grey area there. It's black and white. We all have a job to do. That's why we're here. We're not fans. We all have something to contribute to the team. That's being ready to go to do whatever it is that the team needs you to do. It could be something on Wednesday. It could be something on Thursday. It could be something on Sunday. Whatever it is we all need to be ready to do that. Those things may change from week to week, they may change from day to day and that's part of being prepared and being ready.

That's everybody. There is nobody that's not in the category – nobody.

Q: So if a guy ends up having an increased role, you wouldn't pull him aside and talk to him about his new responsibilities?

BB: Oh yeah, absolutely. Look, players' roles change every week. So yeah, sure we talk to them about, 'Look here's what we need you to do this week. These are the most important things that we need you to do.' Because again when you go through a whole week of preparation, there are five thousand things – do this on this play, if they do this we do that, if they do that we do something else, if this happens that happens, if he goes there you go there. You go on the next play, it's the same scenario. You need to get past all that and say, 'Alright look what we really need to do, here's A, B, C, here's the three things you've got to do this week for us to win.' Next guy, look here's what you've got to do. Next guy, here's what you've got to do. Maybe they play the same position but it might be different roles. Whatever it is, each week is different, but those need to be defined for the players. It's not just show up and do whatever you feel like and see how it goes. Each of us has a job to do. Look, my job is different every week. So is every other coach's job, every player's job. Each week brings its own challenges. We have to respond to those challenges and meet them I'd say distinctly. They're different.

Q: What are your thoughts on the importance of downfield blocking and ball-security in regards to making yards after the catch?

BB: Well, there's nothing more important than ball-security. So we don't want to sacrifice trying to make a couple of extra yards for getting it knocked out of our hands. So there's definitely a balance there between open-field running and trying to be creative in the open-field and making people miss and gaining extra yards and all of that combined with not taking care of the ball. Ball-security is number one, but you know, our skill players do a good job of running with the ball. We've statistically been pretty high in that category the entire season and every once in a while you get a long catch-and-run play like the one we had yesterday. I'm sure every team has a couple of those along the way. It's really all of the other little – I won't say little – but a few yards 'here', a few yards 'there', a five-yard play goes for 10, a six-yard play that goes for 11, whatever it is.

Those yards pile up and I think our skill players do a good job of running with the ball. In the end they all have pretty much found a way to be productive with the ball in their hands and that's really what the job of the skill players is, is to get the yards that are there on the play through proper spacing, or following the blocking, or whatever the play happens to be. A certain amount of yardage that should be there if the play is executed properly and then the extra yardage comes from what the player can do with the ball when he gets it in his hands after he has first contact in a running play, or catches a pass and then is able to avoid or break tackles to create extra yardage. But ball-security trumps all of that. There's nothing more important than taking care of the ball.

Q: Does a win over another playoff contender and a top defense tell you more about your team than some of the other wins?

BB: Every game is tough to win in this league. Each week we kind of go through the same process. Build through preparation, go out and play as hard as we can and then empty the tank out there and leave it all on the field then come back and start it all over again. We'll do the same thing this week. The Ravens are a good team. They're tough. They do a lot of things well. We just did a few things a little bit better tonight but we'll take it.

Q: How important was it to stick to the running game against a stout defense like the Ravens and what did you think of the performance of that unit overall?

BB: Well, the Ravens are a good - they're a good run defense, as we've seen all year. They have good schemes. They get their safeties involved so they're hard to block sometimes with an extra guy and so sometimes its hard for the receivers to get in there and block them because of their alignment or because they drop down late or they show like they're coming down from one side and then they spin it and come down from the other side. You just can't get them. And then they have some very good players out there that are hard to block. [Timmy] Jernigan's hard to block. Obviously [Terrell] Suggs is hard to block. Brandon Williams is hard to block. [Michael] Pierce gives them some good snaps in the running game. So you know, it's a battle in there to make some yards and there's some tough yards in there that some of those three and four-yard runs, I mean they don't look like highlight plays but second-and-six looks a lot better than second-and-nine and those are important plays in the drive. The bottom line is they're a hard team to run against. They do a good job. I thought we hung in there. We tried to grind it out and stay with the running game just to keep chipping away and for the most part we went forward. [We had] a holding penalty that set us back, but again, generally speaking - two of them I think - but generally we went forward and that's good. Again, some of those runs the accumulation of them can pay off later on in the game and it also helped our play-action. We were able to create some big plays with our play-action passes to our receivers and tight ends and some of the check-downs to the backs. Even if you run it in there and aren't making a ton of yardage sometimes the yardage on the plays that go with that, some of the play-action passes or misdirection plays or flea flickers, a play like that, the opportunity with those plays comes from the running plays that have set them up or they complement them. I think that's kind of how we have to look at it, how those plays in the offense tie together relative to overall production. Not just if a team wants to stop the run, they can stop the run, but they give up plays on the play-action passes then that kind of offsets it or vice versa. When you throw it for 400 yards or whatever it was, some of the passing game is set up by the running game. Again, it's just trying to play complementary football when we can.

Q: How do you block out the distractions that come with the expectations surrounding the team?

BB: Yeah, we're focused on one day at a time. Like I said, I guess I missed some of the big reading you guys have had. Honestly, I don't really pay any attention to it. Sorry.

Q: How do you evaluate players who excel in a game but struggle in practice or vice versa?

BB: Yeah, well, it's all part of it. You know, it's a big mosaic. It's not just one polaroid snapshot. This is it. This is the player. It's a lot of things put together. Sometimes things happen in games that are circumstantial. It could be a good play that's not really a good play. It's more of our opponent making a bad play than us making a good play. Sometimes we might have a bad play that's really done pretty well, but it was just an exceptional play by our opponent. Normally, it might be good enough, but it wasn't good enough in that particular instance because they were just a little bit better than we were on that, but it wasn't like it was just totally misplayed. Again, it's, I'd say, a closer evaluation, a closer scrutiny looking at the competition, who are we competing against. In some cases, some guys we're playing against in preseason probably aren't going to be playing a lot of football in a month. Some of the guys we're playing against in preseason are going to be solid or very good or elite NFL players, and there's a difference in competition between that. So, it's not all the same. We try to look at all of it, and the more consistency a player has, the better. Guys that only stand out every once in a while, regardless of whether it's in practice or a game or a play here or a play there, we're all looking for more consistency than that. The more they can do it, the better, [and] the more they can help themselves. Honestly, every player in this league has enough ability to go out there and flash a play here or there. If they can't do that, then they're probably not in the league for very long, but all the guys that are in the league have enough ability to do that. We all respect that. It's the good ones to the great ones that can do it down after down, series after series, week after week, which includes on the practice field because those are competitive situations, too. So, we try to look at all of it.

Q: You mentioned the other day that your staff has put a lot of effort into trying to prevent soft tissue injuries. When did that begin to become a priority for teams in the NFL?

BB: Well, I'm a coach. I'm not a physical therapist. I'm not really as familiar with that as hundreds of other people you could talk to about that subject. I just know from a coaching standpoint that all I see is what's on the field. I don't examine a guy in a doctor's office or I don't look at an MRI scan or a bone scan, whatever it is. That doesn't mean anything to me. I just know what I see as a coach on the field and I've tried to learn more about injuries, preventing injuries, training and so forth. I feel like our staff has done a good job of that and we've made some modifications based on their suggestions, but I still try to go on what I see and what I feel on the team. I'd say the other coaches that I've worked under adopted maybe similar philosophies. Whether that's right or wrong I don't know. I know there's a lot of different ways to do things and we've certainly been progressive in trying to take some measurements and things like that to be more definitive with what an injury actually is or isn't as opposed to just eye balling it or 'How do you feel,' - that kind of feedback - but actually trying to measure it, so we've done a number of things like that. In the end you kind of put it all together and do what you think is best but I don't have any set formula for how all of that works.

Q: If a player has a repeated soft tissue injury or something like that, are you consistently changing what the approach is in terms of training, diet and all those things?

BB: Well, we're always looking to improve, so I mean that never stops. Certainly, if a player has a condition that there's a history of or there's a concern with, whatever that is, then we try to address it on the preventive end rather than sit in the training room and wait for somebody to come in with a this or a that or a something else - a tight back or a soft tissue injury or foot issues or whatever. If we know that there's something that we're concerned about - either they've had it or we think that because of the way they perform or their build or whatever that there's a risk. And our testing will sometimes tell us that, too, relative to like leg length - lower leg strength versus upper leg strength, or right leg strength versus left leg strength, or right leg flexibility versus left leg flexibility and things like that. We do that type of testing. If we see that there's an imbalance, then we would try to straighten that out rather than sit in the training room until the guy comes in, and then OK, here's the problem, now we'll try to fix it. We try to get those things taken care of before they become a problem. So that's really the idea. The idea is for the wellness to be on the front end of as much of these things as we possibly can. So, guys that are involved in more contact, like a lineman, for example, there's certain things we do to train and I would say prepare them and try to keep them out of potential injuries and situations that we've identified. We try to stay in front of everything as much as we can. If something comes up, then we address the problem to try to get the player back to being a full participant. But, we try to stay ahead of those things so that they don't occur. I think a lot of the players feel good about that, that something that was maybe a little bit of an irritant - maybe it didn't keep them off the field, but it was something that they noticed - has now been addressed, hopefully eliminated or minimized and they're able to perform at a higher level and the issue hasn't reoccurred. So, that's our goal, but when you have a lot of new players on your team like we do, then that process of finding out what it is - again, doing the testing, seeing where the potential problems or imbalances may be - and I think our strength and training staff do a good job of that and try to address them, make the players aware of them so they're working on them and then, for the most part, we've been able to avoid things in that area.

Q: What's the biggest indicator to you that a player coming off of an injury is ready to return to game action?

BB: Yeah, I think you just have to go by what you see. I mean the fact that he's been cleared medically tells you that he is to a certain point. Then it's a question of how he looks on the football field. Some of that is relative to what you remember from him in the past.

Some of it is relative to what is out there that he's competing against.

Q: Can you explain the thinking behind taking a game-by-game approach, especially as injuries pile up?

BB: Each week we really do the same thing. We take a look at what our resources are, what our options are, and try to match them up with the opponent that we're playing and what we feel like gives us the best chance to win. Every week is really the same as far as that process goes, and this week won't be any different.

Q: Is it safe to say that seeing snaps from him in a game mean a lot more than just observing a player in practice?

BB: Yeah, that's probably true. Although I think it depends on how many snaps we're talking about. We see a lot more snaps in practice than possibly we would see in the game. So just picking out numbers, I have no idea, but you might have 15 game snaps. You might have 75 practice snaps. Do you ignore those 75 plays that you've seen for a handful in a game or vice versa? I don't know.

Q: When a player misses time is it beneficial for them to get a larger workload in practice or is there a sort of cap to the amount of work they can get in?

BB: Yeah, that's a great question. I mean that is the question. How much is too much? How do you get ready for the speed of the game when you haven't been at the speed of the game? And anytime you bring an injured player back, sometimes the injury is part of that whole conversation. How much can he do? It could be other, again, situations. What kind of condition is the player in based on the time that he has been away? Whether that's a suspension, or a contract holdout, not that we have a lot of contract holdouts, but there was a point in time in this league when we did and it's the same thing. So yeah, it's trying to find that sweet spot for getting the player the best preparation you can. In all honesty, my experience with all of those players has been as time goes on they play better. Maybe their first game will be the best game, but most likely the third, fourth, fifth, sixth games will probably be better than the first. But again, that's just based on experience. I don't know what will happen with a new player who comes back. We have a couple of them. I have no idea. I think those guys are preparing well, they're competing hard, but again, if that was the best way to prepare then I think you'd see more people doing that. I don't really think that's the way to go.

Q: In what ways can an organization help a very injury-prone player improve in that area?

BB: Obviously, every player has his own specific personal situation in terms of his particular personal health, body composition, playing style and everything else, so that's all pretty individualized. It would depend on the player, what type of injury, what his role is, his age, relative to training and rehabilitation. There are a lot of medical questions there that I'm not involved with that would be way over my head. I'm not a doctor, so some of that is obviously done on the medical side of it. From a coaching standpoint, you just try to get the best care and help to every player you can in your organization in whatever way that is, which could be in a lot of different ways. But certainly the medical side of any organization, it's their job to care for the players and there's nothing more important than the health of the players on your team. There are important components for all of us, but again, each player is different. Even if it's the same injury, they're different players and athletes, and we're all made differently, so it's very individualized.

Q: What was the biggest challenge for you when arrived and wanted to establish a culture here?

BB: Well, I'd say, that's probably a question for another day. It's a good question, and I followed two great coaches in here with Bill [Parcells] and Pete [Carroll]. So, a lot of things that were established or in play, in one way or another - two great coaches, one of which I was a part of, so I had a lot of familiarity with what we did in '96. So, it was a lot of things involved. I mean, in the end, it comes down to winning. Once you establish that you can win, then that changes your program from not being a winning program to being a winning program, and that's all the difference in the world.

Q: How much does confidence play a role in various players' performances? Can their overall performance suffer if they have a bad play and it forces them to lose some confidence?

BB: Well, I think it goes a long way. We all do things in our normal lives. Things that we're confident in we do more aggressively, we do quicker, we do with probably better overall execution than things we're not confident in, that we maybe have to wait and have that little bit of hesitation to make sure that something's right or make sure you're doing the right things. It's a fine line there between confidence and overconfidence and taking it for granted, as opposed to just being right in that sweet spot of having an edge, having confidence, being alert and aggressive, but not too far that way that if something happens a little bit differently that you're caught off-guard. We just try to find that sweet spot in there for it.

Q: What kinds of things are you looking for when a player comes back to practice after some time off?

BB: It depends on the player. It depends on his position, what his situation is, but I mean we try to progress him into the things he can do, whatever limitations he has, then we do something else while we're doing those things. Sometimes it's walkthrough, sometimes it's individual drills, sometimes it's group drills, sometimes it's team drills, sometimes it isn't. I mean it could be some combination of whatever he's cleared to do. Then if he's not cleared to do it, then we do something else.

Q: What goes into process of filling the vacancy from a coach or coordinator leaving the organization?

BB: Well, in any decision that involves personnel on the team I always try to do what's best for the football team. That's what goes into it. There could be a thousand things, so if you're signing a player, drafting a player, however you acquire a player, or coach, or a scout, or an administrative positon then I always try to think of what's the best thing for the football team. You look at what the team needs. You look at what that area requires or one thing might be more important than another in that particular time or situation. Based on that, then sometimes you have one or two players to pick from, or three players to pick from, or three people at some other positon that all kind of fit the basic requirement of what the needs of the team and the organization are and try to take the best one. Sometimes you can't. Maybe none of them really do it, but you either go light at that position and wait until you can find a better option or you take the best option that's available. Every situation is different. All people are different. Everybody has their own personality, strengths, weaknesses and so forth. There's no two players that are the same. There's no two people that are the same. I mean, we have identical twins on the team and they're not the same. It just depends on each individual situation and what the circumstances are on the team and who the people are that are available. In the end, what I always try to do is what I think is best for the football team.

Q: Is familiarity with your system a big factor as you try to pick a coordinator?

BB: It's part of the same answer I just gave. Each person has their own – every player – look, every person, every coach, everybody has their own individual characteristics. Call them whatever you want; strengths, weaknesses, areas they can improve in, areas of leadership, areas of experience, so forth. Everybody's different. We're all different. To me, there's no right or wrong answer. There's no set model. The only thing that's consistent for me is doing what's best for the football team. I mean, I know that's hard for some people to understand why I would think like that, but that's the only way I can really put it into any kind of context. What other agenda is there? What other reason is there really for making any personnel decision? I don't know.

Q: After a fumble by one of your players, on the sideline, some of the first people to come over and encourage him were defensive staffers and the special teams coach. How much of that is a byproduct here where it's preached that the game is three phases, 63 players and one team?

BB: Yeah, that's a great question. It's an interesting dynamic because when you start in training camp everybody's on the team but everybody's not on the team. You have very competitive situations between especially the offense and defense, guys trying to make the team, guys trying to compete for playing time and you earn that by competing against your teammates, against each other. There becomes kind of a competitive rivalry that I wouldn't say brings the team together necessarily because that's the nature of the competition. At some point once your team gets settled, there's still a competitive aspect to it but then it separates to coming together at those moments in the game or in other team moments that the team goes through. I think that just speaks to the maturity of the team, not just the players, but the coaches and the other support people, the entire organization of finding the right time to do the right thing. There's time to go out on the field, which we'll have those this week. We had them last week where those guys will battle each other and they'll go back and forth.

There will be some emotional competition on the field and then there will be other moments, maybe like the one you described where it comes together a little bit differently, and so some of that is timing, some of that is judgement and certainly a lot of it is character and leadership by the individuals involved. But it's a balance and it changes. It's not always the same. Sometimes the competitive side takes over. Sometimes the passionate side takes over. Sometimes you're in the middle and it's a long season and there's a time and a place for all of them, and there's also a wrong time and a wrong place for all of them, too. It's an interesting dynamic that changes with every player, with every team, with every situation, but hopefully it can be more on the positive side at the right time. It's a great question, though. It really is.

Q: How much pride do you take in developing young coaches here?

BB: Well, I take the most pride in winning. The things that we do to help us win, the people that help us win and their contributions – those are all of the things that are important. Other things come with that. But, really this program is geared towards winning, so if it's about winning then it's important. There are other things that are subsidiaries of that, but that's the most important thing. That's what we're here for.

Q: Can you describe Matt Patricia's coaching style and in particular how he relates to his players?

BB: Good, yeah, good. Matt's really smart. He's had a lot of different experiences. He's coached in college, he's coached on the offensive side of the ball, coached on the defensive side of the ball, has been in this situation, this program for a long time so he has a pretty good understanding historically of things like the Vrabels and the Bruschis and the Troy Browns and all things like that that can have some relationship to sometimes current situations. He's really smart. This guy could probably build a plane and fly it – like this guy is smart-smart. He's got great recall and a really high IQ level in terms of just processing a lot of information. He's the kind of guy that he's got 10 projects going at once and then you're like, 'Hey Matt can you do this and do that – oh yeah, no problem.' He's got 12 going at once. Some of us can only handle barely one thing at a time. He's the type of guy that can keep a lot of balls in the air. But again, he's a blue-collar guy, certainly wasn't born with a silver spoon like most players, so they're just working for everything, working his way up through, I think he has an appreciation for that and I think he relates well to other guys who are doing the same thing.

Q: Do you guide him because of your defensive background?

BB: Matt and I have worked together for a long time so he's definitely a huge asset to me in a number of areas – again both historically, like, 'Hey this is what we did in this situation, think about that or should we do that again or the timing of it and so forth.' And again over a period of years, Josh is the same way, over a period of years, things that you did five, 10 years ago, I'm not saying they come up every day, but it might be, 'Hey remember when we did this against so-and-so back in '07 or '05 or whatever?' It's kind of the same thing here. For somebody that just got here last year or somebody that's been here for a year or two, there's no way that that's coming up – here's what we did in this situation back when we had this player. So there is some value to that. I'm not saying it happens every day, but guys like that – Brian Daboll, Matt Patricia, Josh McDaniels, guys that have been here for a really long time – they have some of those perspectives that are really good, so it's very helpful.

Q: They understand your thinking?

BB: Yeah, and again they can take a situation that happened, whenever it happened, and maybe it applies to something we're doing now and it's a good idea. If it was a good idea then, it might a good idea now, but maybe you're not really thinking about it or I'm not thinking about it. And again, a big part of the whole staff is just working together – offense working with the defense and particularly the defense working with the special teams because most of the players in the kicking game are defensive players so working their roles together and who's active and who's doing what and how to make it all work together as efficiently as possible, it's not the easiest thing to do in the world, I can tell you from experience. So I wouldn't say that's as much of a thing on offense. Again there are usually only a handful of offensive players in the kicking game. The majority of players are on defense, but that affects your defensive game plan and the roles that those guys play and the way that plays off each other. Again, there's a lot of staff chemistry things or staff relationship things that work like that that are maybe not as obvious, but they're really important and when they don't work well eventually it causes you problems and you're not efficient or just don't get the most out of what you have.

Q: As a defensive coach do you marvel at the things Tampa's defense could do?

BB: They have a certain style of play and it has been pretty effective for them. I think their style of play defensively compliments their style offensively too. It is a well-coordinated system. The players that they have fit what they are trying to do. I think when you look at a football team, people talk about being predictable, when you look at a football team I think it is good when you can say this team is predictable because they have a philosophy and you know what they are about and that's what it is. When you look at Tampa Bay's defense you see quickness out there, you see a lot of speed on the front seven, so you know when they draft a player or sign a player on defense that is the kind of player that they are going to get.

It's not like 'what are they going to do?' You know what they are going to do and they do it well and I think that is the mark of a good organization, good drafting, good coaching, a good plan in place. I mean you look at certain teams, you look at the 1970 Steelers or the 1980 Cowboys, they had a certain style of play. You knew what the Cowboys were going to do and the way they were going to play the game. I'm not saying you could call every play, but you knew the way that they were going to play, but defending, that was a different story. Stopping the flex defense, stopping all of the shifting, and all of that stuff that Tom Landry did down there. Joe Gibbs at Washington he knew what he was going to do, but stopping it was another story. You knew they were going to have big physical offensive lineman and big physical linebackers. Buddy Ryan's defenses you knew what they were going to do, but stopping them was a different story. So I think the idea of having a philosophy and developing it and being able to sit here and say, 'that's what they are and that's what they are going to be and they are pretty good at it,' is about a big a compliment you can give to a professional football team.

Q: How have the Steelers been able to maintain such success over the years much like your own franchise has?

BB: Well they have great continuity. I mean they've had three coaches since what - the late '60's? Coach

[Bill] Cowher, Coach [Mike] Tomlin, that goes what - 25 years? Two general managers, two coaches; they've had a lot of continuity. When you have continuity like they have in their organization - they haven't really changed defenses much over that same quarter of a century - so as a scout, I mean I could scout for the Steelers. I mean I've seen them, they do the same thing, they stay with it, so you know what kind of players they're looking for at each positon. They build up, they have a very extensive scheme through their continuity so they do quite a bit in terms of the volume of their plays that you have to defend but they can do them because they've been doing them over and over again and they have a lot of the same guys doing them. I mean offensively it's really all of the same guys here for the last couple of years. They've lost a couple of guys, you know, like Heath Miller's not there but the guys that are there have pretty much been there. Or guys like [Jesse] James who have come up through the system over a couple of years. Maybe he's gotten more playing time now but it isn't like he's new to their system. Same thing on defense, so a lot of continuity, and again they've built their team on explosive playmakers and guys on defense that can turn the ball over with speed. So that's [Lawrence] Timmons, that's [Ryan] Shazier, you know, that's [Vince] Williams. They've drafted guys like [Artie] Burns and [Sean] Davis who are fast. They can turn the ball over, so they've got some great size and athleticism up front; [Stephon] Tuitt, [Cameron] Heyward, guys like that that are very big and athletic.

They've got good players, they're well coached and they have a good program. It's all good.

Q: What are your recollections of dealing with Al Davis or just working them as an organization in general?

BB: I mean, it's a great franchise. Al Davis did a tremendous job with the franchise when he took over. I think it was in 1972 or whatever year it was he took over the ownership. I think he was there almost 40 years as the owner, had other roles with the team before that. I think that with [Reggie] McKenzie as the general manager, who came up through the Raiders system, he's certainly maintained some of the, I'd say, axioms that the Raiders were built on from a personnel standpoint. Al Davis is in the Hall of Fame, as he should be.

His contributions and his success in professional football, both in the AFL and NFL, are very highly regarded, the great Super Bowl teams that they had, his development of players and uncovering of players, especially in the '70s and early '80s with some of the smaller schools. They became great players, Hall of Fame players, a lot of people had never heard of until they started playing for the Raiders. They have a great tradition, a great fan base and intensity. Those guys play hard. They play with a lot of passion. They're always a tough, physical team, which they are again this year. Al Davis - I've always had a ton of respect for him. I had an opportunity to talk with him on many occasions. He was always very insightful and [it was] a pleasure to be around the guy with his passion and love for football, the coaching part of it, the scouting part of it. He was very special.

Q: How would you describe what it's like working for the Kraft Family and what they do for the Patriots that have enabled the success the organization has had?

BB: Robert [Kraft] and his family have been very supportive of me, gave up a lot to get me here, and have been supportive for the years that I've been here. Our facilities are good. Robert gives me the latitude to do what I think is best for the football team and I appreciate that. I appreciate the opportunity to do the things that I feel are best, make the decisions that I feel are best for the team. There's not a lot of interference, so I think that smooths it out on the football end. We have a lot of good people working for us in the organization. We seem to through the years have been able to be productive together.

Q: Do you have any connection to the Rooney Family at all from your time in the league?

BB: Well, they're pretty close to the Mara Family. When I was with the Giants we played them every year in preseason. Of course Coach [Bill] Cowher, I mean Coach [Chuck] Noll and Coach Cowher when I was in Cleveland, but that was in competition with them, not in the organization. But I have great respect for what they've done through the years. Coach Noll was a tremendous coach. [He] did a great job of I'd say developing a certain style of play on that team, both offensively and defensively. Really he's kind of the founder of Cover-2 with Bud Carson and the stunt 4-3 defense that they ran, which is a 4-3 - it's similar to what we did in Cleveland. It has some principles to it. Spacing is different, but it has a lot of the same principles that I've used in coaching 3-4 and those types of defenses throughout my career, as well as the Cover-2 foundation that Coach Noll laid. And then Coach Cowher came in there and had tremendous success with their blitz-zone scheme and a lot of two-back running with a couple of different quarterbacks - [Neil] O'Donnell and [Kordell] Stewart - guys that played the position differently but were very good. Coach [Mike] Tomlin has come in and played a similar version but has adapted it to his own style. Offensively they're a lot different than they were under Coach Cowher. Defensively [they're] different but some similarities, but he and Kevin Colbert have kind of changed the makeup of the team a little bit in the last decade or so, I would say, to the speed that they have at inside linebacker and the explosive speed that they have at the receiver position has I think kind of been a trademark for their teams. They seem to have built them that way through their acquisition of players and the development of their team.

It's been a very consistent organization in terms of coaching, scouting, ownership with some modifications over the years, as you would expect over a 40-year period. But I mean a lot less than some other organizations. They've been tough to deal with for going all the way back to Coach Noll in the 70's. They were pretty consistently tough to deal with through that entire period of time, which has been all of my years in the league. There might have been a year here or there, but for the most part they've been at a championship level or competing for a championship level for a long period of time. That's certainly a huge credit to that entire organization.

Q: What your background and thoughts are on Coach Landry?

BB: I didn't really have a lot of interaction with Coach Landry. I'd say most of it is kind of through [Roger] Staubach, stories that he would share, that type of thing. But I really haven't had a lot of interaction with Coach Landry.

Q: What were your thoughts on him as a coach?

BB: Well, he brought in, I would say, both offensively and defensively had two unique systems. I spent quite a bit of time in Detroit with Ed Hughes who was in the Dallas System for a long time. When he came to the Lions in 1977 I basically learned the Dallas system, so the protections, the passing game, the running game, the philosophy, the shifting and motioning, so forth. Offensively, they had quite an extensive volume of offense. They were predicated on a lot of complementary-type plays, plays that fed off of each other, that looked the same but weren't the same.

Defensively, they ran the flex defense, which they were really the only team in the league that did that when I came into the league and that was very difficult to prepare for because it involved - first of all, even practicing against it was hard because practice players weren't familiar with it, weren't used to doing it, so it was hard to get a good look at it. The things that they did with the flex and the package they had off of it was pretty challenging, especially if you weren't playing them twice a year and you weren't really familiar with it in their division, and they had great players on offense. They had great players on defense.

Looking at Gil Brandt and the job that he did with the personnel, he certainly should be in the Hall of Fame based on his contributions to this game and contributions to the personnel and scouting side of it.

He'd probably be the first guy I would put in there. The combination of the personnel that they had, and the coaching, and their system and their I would say, development of it, development of younger players through the system, which at that time without free agency they had the ability to take a little bit extra time to get those players to fit into their system. But it was very well thought out, very disciplined, and then when I coached [Everson] Walls at the Giants he talked a lot about the Dallas system defensively, so that was kind of where I learned about the defensive side of it and learned about the offensive side of it from Coach Hughes.

Q: Do you have any memories of coaching against longtime special teams coach Bruce DeHaven who passed away just recently?

BB: Did he pass away? Yeah, Bruce [DeHaven] is a great guy. He's one of the real good guys. I never worked with him, but yeah, he was always one of the - I mean when I came in there were no special teams coaches really to speak of and then he was one of the, I'd say, first wave of lifers kind of at that position. I mean guys like [Dick] Vermeil and those guys, but they didn't really last very long as special teams coaches. They moved to somewhere else or they coached special teams and another position; [Jerry] Glanville or guys like that. Yeah, Bruce was - that's sad. I always enjoyed seeing him. Fortunately we didn't play against him, well we played against him, but more recently not so much so it was a better relationship to compete against him.

Q: Coach DeHaven was involved in some memorable special team's plays as a coach, one being the onside kick recovery in Buffalo's

comeback versus the Houston Oilers in the Wild Card round of the 1992 season.

BB: Yeah, I mean it was a signature play; no doubt about it. I think those plays always, when you see those plays, whether it was the [Dontari] Poe pass or the special teams player in some kind of unusual onside kick or whatever it is, fake field goal that works. I mean those plays always kind of stick out. It's nice to have one of those in your resume if you can pull it off. But I think the more important thing is just the week-in and week-out consistency and performance of the unit.

Q: His teams were always great on special teams no matter which stop he was at. What's the secret to that?

BB: Probably good coaching. I mean obviously good players, too. I mean you could say the same thing about Wade [Phillips]. Everywhere that Wade's been - Buffalo, Dallas, Denver a couple of times - he plays the same system and they play good. It's obviously having a good system and getting the right players for it and getting them to believe in it and understand it.

Q: Would you put Doug Flutie's drop kick as a Patriot in the 2005 season up there amongst memorable plays on special teams?

BB: Yeah, it didn't really mean anything.

Q: It was a signature play.

BB: Definitely a signature; yeah. Two plays - the drop kick and the Hail Mary, right? See if you can work that into the epitaph somewhere.

Q: Who is the fastest player you've ever coached?

BB: It would depend on - how far are you talking about?

Q: However far.

BB: I mean, there's 60, 80 yards. That's not the most common thing in football. But yeah, [Matthew] Slater at that distance, Moss, Perry Williams. I mean, there's guys that run 30 to 40 yards and guys zero to ten. Guys that really don't have that long, top-end speed, but they have the first 20 speed. In some ways they're tougher to defend. That speed is more effective in football than 40 to 60 or 60 to 80 speed. If you're covering kicks, then you need 60-yard speed. Twenty is not really enough. They catch up to you after 20. Being able to get to top speed and I'd say being able to hold top speed, that's what a strong runner could do. He could hold it, not just get there, but actually hold it and sustain it for another 20, 30, 40 yards.

Q: What were your production meetings like with Jim Nantz and Phil Simms, and how much do you

miss the connection with Phil given your history with him?

BB: Well, I think Phil did a great job and I always enjoyed Phil. Even though I never really coached Phil, Phil was the quarterback and I was the defensive coordinator. We talked a lot. We had, I thought, a real good relationship with the Giants. We talked a lot about coverages and schemes and what do you see and how can I help you, how can you help me type of thing. Phil was great that way, and he's very knowledgeable. Phil was a very knowledgeable player that even things like the kicking game - which as a quarterback, you're not really a part of - Phil was always interested in. I actually involved him in it in different things, facets of that when I was with the Giants. Even though Phil throws the ball right-handed, everything else he does in his life is left-handed, including punt. So, when we had the great right-footed punters at the Giants, Dave Jennings and Sean Landeta, when we went up against a left-footed punter, Phil was my go-to guy there. So, things like that that he was always very accommodating and helpful, but he always had an interest in it, too. So, I thought he - honestly, I didn't hear a lot of the games that he did for us, but I heard other games that he did and I always thought he gave a lot of great insight into the game, not just from a quarterback's perspective but from a team standpoint.

So, yeah, I do miss seeing him multiple times during the season when he would have our games. Tony, I'd say, is similar - a very inquisitive guy with a good history of the game. He's asked a lot of questions about when I was with the Giants or the '70s or the '80s or Tom Landry or so forth. He's pretty knowledgeable for a player that wasn't in that era that he knows a lot about it and has obviously read and studied it. He sees a lot of things - a lot of fine points of a defensive scheme or a play that, I'd say, a lot of guys that I talk to don't - and asks about those and, 'What was this guy reading on this and why did this guy do that and was this guy's job on this play to do something that is kind of subtle?' He picks up on those things and, I'd say, asks a lot of very detailed, coaching, technical-type questions that you don't get in a lot of those meetings. But, he's good. I've enjoyed working with him.

Q: When it was Nantz and Simms calling the games, did it get to a point where it was like, 'Oh, you guys again?' Did it almost feel like a routine?

BB: Almost like doing the radio show with [Scott] Zolak, the weekly radio show. Well, yeah, I'd say when we had those meetings, sometimes when you do say like a Fox crew who only does our one game a year - 'How are you using your tight ends? How's this guy rotating in? What's this guy's role? Where does he play?' It wasn't like that with those guys. They saw enough games that they knew kind of what everybody's role was, what this guy played because somebody else was hurt, this guy played because you used a different package that week, and so forth. So, that part of it I'd say they were very on top of, probably as much as any TV crew we've had. It would be more specific to, 'Alright, what are you going to do this week? How are you going to handle this? How are you going to handle that? What do you think of this part of their game or how are you going to attack that part?' So, it was much more specific, not that I don't get those from other crews, but I would say there wasn't the, 'Who's your backup slot receiver?' They knew who that was.

Q: In addition to identifying some of the plays Atlanta ran that your defense had never seen before, how important was it for the players to also understand the concept behind what they're doing?

BB: That's the most important thing is to recognize the concept. I mean look, they're not going to come in here and run 60 new plays. They're going to run the plays they've been running all year but dress them up differently, put a different look or a motion or combination and try to make it look a little bit different than anything we've seen or maybe something that they think will give us a problem to adjust to, and then do the things that they've been doing. I'm not saying there won't be a handful of new plays in there, but I mean, look, the way they move the ball and score points, they're not going to come in here and put in a new offense this week. They've had so much success with what they're doing, they're going to keep doing it but make it hard for the defense to recognize this is the play, and by the time you recognize it, the play is over.

You know, they're spotting the ball and it's like, 'Aw, that's what that was.' You have a second-late reaction to that, so they do a great job of that. They do what they do, they do it well. They really know what they're doing, but defensively it takes you that extra split second to recognize it and sometimes you're just a step too late and they got you. Then the next play it's the same thing or another version of the same thing. I addition to that they have very good players, guys like [Devonta] Freeman, [Tevin] Coleman, [Mohamed] Sanu, [Julio] Jones, all of them. They've got the ball in their hands and what looks like a seven-yard gain could be 47. Their ability to make yards with the ball in their hands, break tackles, in Coleman's case, out-run people. I don't know how many times we've seen guys have a good angle on him and it looks like, 'Ok, they're going to intersect here,' and they don't. [Coleman] just out-runs him and now they're chasing him and now 15 now looks like 35, so they get a lot of yards on the ability of their skill players to gain yards after they get in the space.

Q: Coach you have said you don't care about playoff experience because you've seen young guys perform well and older guys perform not so well. Why does

the relative experience not really carryover into the
playoffs?

BB: I wouldn't say it doesn't. I would say there's no
guarantee that it does. I mean how'd you think [Tom]
Brady played in his first playoff games? How'd you
think [Julian] Edelman played in his? How'd you
think Lawrence Taylor played in his? If experience
was all there was to it than those games wouldn't
have been won by those players or those teams that
those guys played on.

**Q: Do teams ever change tendencies heading into
the playoffs?**

BB: Yeah, sure. I think, look, I think teams do it on a
regular basis anyway. We see it every week. Here's
something they're doing and then in the game you see
something and the first thing you think of is 'OK,
they're trying to break that tendency. They're trying
to offset that.' Now they might not be able to do all of
them. You might have, I don't know, ten tendencies.
You might see three or four of them that it's obvious
to you 'OK, they're trying to get in this formation, or
run a different play, or give you this look and not
blitz out of it because they've been blitzing out of it,
or put this player in the game and instead of doing
what they normally do with him, do something else,'
but I think that's pretty common. Normally, those
tendencies don't necessarily hold up for a long time.
The team does a certain thing and that's their

tendency and then you put in a couple of key-breakers, especially if it's early in the game. A lot of times you'll sit there and say 'OK, they were trying to break that tendency, but I don't think that's what they really want to do. I think they're probably going to go back to what their tendency is.' They just wanted to kind of try to scare you out of overplaying what they really want by showing you something that was a complement to it. But, you know, that's a little bit of the cat and mouse game that you play. But yeah, I think that's part of the playoffs, but it's really everything's part of every game. I don't think there's too many weeks that there isn't some element of that that comes up.

Q: How did you and Jon Bon Jovi initially become friends and meet in the first place?

BB: Well, Jon [Bon Jovi] is a big Giants fan. He grew up in New Jersey, so when I was coaching the Giants. We had a lot in common. We both liked the Giants.

Q: Was he just a frequent visitor at practice? Would Bill Parcells be the one to invite him over?

BB: Yeah, you know, I don't think Bill [Parcells] was a big Bon Jovi fan or Bruce Springsteen fan or anything like that. It wasn't exactly his musical style at that point in time. Some of the younger coaches on the staff, one in particular connected to him. [Sean] Landeta, you know Sean was another one. Sean and

Jon [Bon Jovi] and I - we've done a few things together. Yeah, back to the Jersey-Giants days.

2

PRACTICE PLANNING &
FUNDAMENTAL FOOTBALL

Q: How do you balance week-to-week adjustments with the foundation and system you install before the season begins?

BB: Well, I'll just say that when you start the season, you have, let's call it 20 practices, not including the spring. So let's call it 20 practices and some preseason games, and during that time you're trying to evaluate your team, work on a lot of basic and fundamental things and I'll say basically get your team ready to play not only on the opening day, but for getting conditioned and build your fundamentals and all that so that you can compete in the 16-game regular season. In those 20 practices and however many preseason games certain players play in - two, three, four, whatever it is - against other teams that are doing the same thing, so you're not getting schemed, you're not getting game planned, you're not getting some of the more sophisticated and the higher degree of difficulty things in any phase of the game. You're in more of an evaluation mode and a fundamental mode. That's where you're at, and then as you get into the season, you build on that and you have things that attack certain schemes or you have to use to address certain issues that your opponent is trying to pressure you with.

Maybe you just sit in your base, whatever it is, to handle it. Maybe your basics handle it, but maybe you need to go a little bit beyond that or maybe you see opportunities to create a play that you might install on a weekly game plan basis, and then all that accumulates. So, when you go from 20 practices to, let's call it 60 practices over halfway through the season, maybe 80 practices at the end of the season, you're going to have a lot more in with 80 practices and you could probably triple the number of meetings on that and everything else then where you're going to have after a relatively short period in training camp. So, along those same lines, I mean, if we keep running the same play all year, the same ones that you put in in training camp and keep running those same plays all year, it's not that difficult in this league to figure out what those few things are and game plan accordingly. So, if you don't increase the volume of your scheme on offense, defense and special teams, then every week, your opponent's just looking at a handful of things and probably most of them they've seen before. So, I don't know how much problem, how much stress you're really putting on your opponent if that's the way that you do it.

I'm not saying that's a bad thing because you can play your basic stuff, and if it's working well and if you're doing well with it and people can't handle it, then there's no reason to change it. But I don't know how many teams in the league fall into that category. I wouldn't say it's an exceedingly high number and it never really has been, based on my experience in the league. Although, I'm not saying that can't happen, but I would certainly say that's not the most common way that teams evolve throughout the course of the year. So, you do what you need to do each week to try to win. You put in the plays, make the adjustments, you don't want to overload things - I mean, nobody's talking about putting in a new offense every week.

That's not it at all, but are there some modifications you can make? Sure, and as you rep those and you use them and if those situations come up again, then maybe you can fall back to that same type of scheme. But to think realistically, which it's incomprehensible to me, but, I mean, I don't know. Maybe I just can't figure it out, but it's incomprehensible to me how anybody could think that a team that's practiced for six months and played 19 regular season and postseason games and had triple-digit practices, five months later, after not playing a game, after having a fraction of that type of experience, could be anywhere close to the level of execution that they were five months before that after all of the things that I just listed.

I mean, it's impossible in my view. So, each year, you start all over again. You start that process all over again. You build your team over the course of the year though practice repetitions, through preseason to regular season games, through the evolving of your scheme, and that's why each year is different and unique. But, I understand I'm in the minority and most other people don't see it that way, which is OK, but that's the way I see it.

Q: How important is it to evolve your scheme over time? Is that something that you can be proactive about in seeking out the tools to make that scheme work, or is it more reactionary in the mold of you need to work with what you have?

BB: Well, I think you always have to be ready to go with what you've got. I mean, you can't ever count on you're going to get somebody who's not here, get them off the street or get them from another team. They may not be available. If that option comes up then I think you look at the player and say, "OK, how would we use him? How would he fit in? What would his role be? What's the cost?" And so forth, and you make that decision on an individual basis based on that player, his situation and your team needs, whether it be short or long term, whatever you happen to be looking at. The scheme thing is, look, one thing you don't want to do if you can help it is to spend a lot of time on a scheme that you don't use. We're going to spend all of our time running this play, or this group of plays or these coverages and then you never use them. For example, defensively, if you were to put in a certain couple of coverages or a certain type of defense but you never face the offense that used it, like some two-back defenses, and the teams that you play are one-back teams, then when are you going to use them? It's a waste of time.

On the flip side of it, if you know you're going to use something like, "OK, here are our first four opponents. Three of them do this and we would want to do this against three of these four teams," then to not put it in in training camp, to not address it in training camp and wait until the first game when it comes up like "Alright fellas, here is what we're going to do," and now you're kind of starting all over again on this scheme, like well we haven't really done this before so on 'this' we're going to do 'that,' and we haven't practiced it. We're putting this in, a new thing, and now you're trying to get it ready during the week of practice - I mean, that's a hard thing to do, especially if it's somewhat extensive. If you just don't get enough practice plays and it comes up in the game a little bit differently than how you practiced it and then you get beat, then that's usually what's going to happen.

Q: Is it important to evolve with some type of foresight and try to do things that you may have never done before?

BB: Sure, yeah, but again, if you put time into it, you can put three days into a reverse and run it one time. I mean, that's a lot of time on not very much. Now if that play wins the game for you, then great, but you only have so much time. So how much of it do you want to put it into a sliver of what you're going to be using. But that's kind of the trick, to figure that out. When you commit to something and then at some later point you de-commit to it and you change, then that's a lot that's being washed down the drain. If you have a fairly broad package that you know you're going to use all of it at some point, and when it comes up you're not going to be repaving the road, you're going to be saying "OK, well this is what we did a couple of weeks ago. This is what we did in training camp.

Now here is the application for it against this team. Here, they do a lot of this. Here's a situation where they use a lot of bunch receivers. Here is our coverage and these bunch sets that we worked on back in training camp." OK, now there is some recall. There is some fundamental background that you can fall back on versus having never talked about it and like "Alright, well here's how we're going to handle this this week." Well, that's a lot to take on if you haven't taken it on in the first place. Fundamentally, what you want to try to do is have a system that covers the things that you're going to have to cover and be able to go to the different areas when you need to go to them. If you know you're going to be heavy in one area, then you're probably having to go 60-40 or 65-35 in your time allocation to be able to address it rather than 35-65, the other way around. You're spending all of your time on something that isn't going to come up or it isn't going to come up very much, then yeah, you're great at that but it only comes up ten percent of the time.

It's just not worth it. Sometimes you get things that come up that you haven't covered before, you've got to cover them. That's football. That's going to happen. You try to, I'd say, keep those to a minimum and when that does happen you just have to be careful about how much you try to do with it like "Alright, we haven't covered this before," so trying to do six different things against it is probably going to be hard. You're probably going to be limited to one or two and hope you can do those well. Yeah, those are the hard decisions in coaching, is trying to anticipate what you're going to need and trying to make sure you have it, and not only have it, but can actually do it. If you can't execute it, then it doesn't make any difference what you have. You've got to be able to do it. To get to that point, that's the hard part.

Q: When you bounce around to different position groups at practice, how do you determine where to go and when?

BB: Well, based on the practice schedule, there's certain drills that I'll plan on being at or maybe a certain group of players, but I try to look at everybody, see what we're doing, make sure that we're overall - you know, it's kind of my job to bring the whole team together from a lot of levels. Just, I think, being familiar with all the players, what everybody's doing, trying to see how we're doing and how we're on schedule or how the groups are looking. The coaches are obviously a lot more detailed and go into a lot more depth in their respective positions, but I have an opportunity to kind of see everything. They don't. I've been in that position before where you're so focused on your group or your side of the ball that you really are not that in touch with what else is going on. That's something that's really part of my job.

Q: Have you found that one-on-one drills are helpful to the coaching staff to notice something about a player you might not know much about? Is it easier to see something in those drills, as opposed to the team periods?

BB: Some players are better players in one-on-one, isolated situations, and some players are better in team situations. They don't necessarily correlate directly. Some guys, when you put the other 21 guys out there, just have an instinct and a feel and better anticipate and maybe react quicker than what they would if it's just a one-on-one matchup. Some guys, in a one-on-one matchup, do better. And then when you put everybody else out there, certainly when you start to change the situations a little bit - change the formation, change the plays, change the down-and-distances - then it slows down and you don't see that same level of performance that you see in one-on-ones. Now, sometimes that changes as the player gets more experienced and gets more comfortable and can transfer his individual skills into team skills and apply - because, again, not every play is the same play- so applying certain skills in certain situations.

Yeah, I mean, we definitely learn those things. It's not all equal. Each guy is different, but I think you try to take the positives and show a player, 'Look, here you are in one-on-one situations. You've got to be able to transfer that to team,' or, 'Here's how you can individually have more success by doing this technique better or that technique a little better because you're just isolated on that.' There's no I was reading this, or I got that call or something else happened. You can eliminate all of that. And the players learn from each other. You watch the other guys do it and you see another guy do something or you see him make a mistake and you understand why you can't do that or maybe you can do something that he can do. That also is a good time to experiment with a different pass rush technique or a different route technique or a different coverage technique or something that maybe you personally don't feel as confident about. Now, in a one-on-one situation, you might be more apt or we would tell the player, 'Look, here's a good time for you to use this so you can came some confidence in it,' so we would use it in a team or eventually in a game setting that he might not do if he didn't gain the confidence in a more isolated drill.

Q: Do you find that those drills simulate pretty well what a player sees once you get the whole team out in 11-on-11?

BB: Again, it's that fundamental. I mean, again, there are a lot of other things that could happen, and there are other players that are involved in a play that it's not just isolated. There are times when it's just isolated, but the majority of the time, it really isn't. But your fundamentals need to be good, and if they're good in the individual one-on-one part of it, then usually those fundamentals will transfer to stunts and combination routes and so forth and so on. Again, it's just the teaching progression. I mean, if fundamentals are wrong in a basic one-on-one situation, then it's just going to go downhill from there. It's not going to get any better. So, then when other things start happening, when you start getting games or combination routes or pick routes or whatever, whatever the next part of the sequence is, then it's just going to get worse. So, you try to start with a good fundamental. You try to start doing it right, and then, if you have to make adjustments during the play or as the play extends, then those are further coaching points, which we go from one-on-one to two-on-two, and pass rush and pass protection one-on-one to two-on-two, to eventually five-on-four, to team, sometimes half-line - not half-line, but just the interior line, like seven-on-six, six-on-six in pass protection - and then we go to full team. So that's just the logical progression to put it all together.

Q: What's your role in those game-like practice situations? Do you play a hands-off role in and let the coordinators make the quick decisions?

BB: I'd say it's to create the situations, and being on the field gives me a good opportunity to also see the players in the huddle and their communication, their overall posture and attitude in playing the game, and their line of scrimmage communication. Those things are hard to see from the sideline. In a game, certainly you get a sense of it, but it's nothing like standing out there a few yards away from the play to see the command that certain callers have or that other communicators have as part of the play. Those things, I kind of focus on those, and trying to set up the situations that I want our team to experience so we can coach from them, learn from them, and put it together. I don't want to go out there and have nine short-yardage plays in practice. I don't want to have nine third-and-17s in practice, so if that's what the situation is, then I'll modify it so that we're third-and-short, third-and-medium, third-and-long, second-and-long, second-and-short, red area plays, backed up plays, whatever it is. I try to create different situations so we can react to them, learn from them and coach them off film so they'll be playing better the next time they come out.

Q: What kind of evaluations do you make during scrimmages and what kind of evaluation are you

able to make from that as opposed to just individual team drills?

BB: Well, that's football. The big part of football is being able to change. The situation changes every play. It goes from first-down, to second-down, to third-down, the ball moves, you go from offense to defense, to special teams. You don't go out there and punt six punts in a row like you do in practice. You punt it once and then maybe the next thing you do is a kickoff return, so I don't know. It's doing things like that. It's getting players to understand the situation and then apply the call and the technique for that given situation. So, we do things in a lot of one-on-one drills. When those situations come up in the game you want to carry those techniques into the game situation and do it.

A lot of times that doesn't happen because players don't remember to use the techniques that they've worked on. They don't know when to apply it or they forget to apply it and they kind of lose track of it and that type of thing. This is football. It's as close as we can get to it. The drill work is good. The repetition is good. That's how you build your fundamentals. That's how you build your execution, but at some point you've got to play like we're playing and that's good, too. It's good for the coaches; handling all the substitutions, making adjustments on the sideline, seeing the game on the down and distance basis, seeing it live as opposed to making corrections on film. Not that we don't coach on the field, but when you don't know when it's coming, when the down and distance changes, we need work on that, too, so it's good for all of us.

Q: How much do you get back to the fundamentals of things while also working on scheme?

BB: That's a great question. It's a fine line. You try to ... There's nothing more important than fundamentals, so no play is good with bad fundamentals. It's just impossible. That being said, there are a lot of scheme things that come up over the course of the season that teams keep building. We build and our opponents build, and so each week, there's more to get ready for because they're further along. It's a lot different than the first game of the season when you only have so much time to work on stuff. We've had over 100 practices, and it keeps building and building. So you've got to deal with the scheme issues, and you've got to deal with the fundamentals. So it's trying to find that balance, but they're both critical. I mean, if you're out-schemed, you're out positioned, then you're in bad shape. And like I said, no play is a good play with bad fundamentals. Just, it won't happen, so that's the balance.

Q: What is the biggest factor in the improvement of defense throughout the course of the year?

BB: Preparation, practice, execution. There's no magic wand. You've just got to go out there and, look, there are five eligible receivers. Usually we get at least four of them out. In man-to-man coverage you've got to cover them. We've got to rush the passer, contain the quarterback, stop the run. Zone coverage; it's a short throw. You've got to be on the receivers tight or a good quarterback can get the ball into those windows. Again, good execution of zone coverage, getting to the receivers, filling up those spaces so it's hard to throw the ball in there. It really just comes down to playing good team defense in both the running game and the passing game and on the goal line, which gets into a whole new set of defensive calls and techniques. We've had a couple of big stops down there, too, over the course of the year.

Q: When you're taking a look at your defense and want improvements to be made, what's the first step?

BB: Identifying the problem and addressing the problem. Something's got to be one, something's got to be two, something's got to be, whatever, 18. I don't know. So, start with the most important things first, always. It's always the case. We're not going to start at 19 and work our way up to 18 and work our way up to 17. I mean, that would be a ridiculous way to approach it. I can't imagine doing that. So, if we have a problem, you take the thing that's most important and try to solve that first.

Q: How important is tackling to a defense?

BB: For me, I mean, I learned a long time ago, my dad told me this and coach [Bill] Parcells told me this, that the most important thing on defense is to get 11 guys out there that can tackle. Look, defensively, your job is to get the guy with the ball on the ground. In the end, that's your job. All the other stuff is great, but if you can't do that, then what do you really have? That doesn't minimize coverage skill, don't get me wrong. But in the end, somebody's gotta get the guy on the ground. I think that's a critical component for me, for us, for any player on the defensive side of the ball, regardless of what position they play.

But part in the secondary where you're right, you can be higher on coverage skills but, if you're willing to give up poor tackling for coverage skills, eventually there's going to be a problem there. Might be able to live with it, but eventually there's going to be a problem. I put a high priority on it, we put a high priority on it in the organization, in our defense. We practice it every single day. I don't think there's been a day that we haven't worked on tackling this year or any other year. It's the most fundamental, important thing for a defensive player to do well. That and defeat blocks -- everybody's going to get blocked at some point. Defeating blocks and tackling, those are the two most critical fundamentals that any defensive player needs. There's not really much that goes above tackling for me.

Q: How often do you focus on tackling fundamentals?

BB: Every day. It's like anything else. You're never going to make me fast, but we can all improve. Whatever the skills are they are. You can certainly improve technique, you can improve leverage, you can improve the fundamentals of tackling, just like you can improve the fundamentals of running. Those are the most fundamental skills in the game. To not work on those on a daily basis, to not work on them, and try to improve on them continuously, I think would be irresponsible for me as a coach to not teach blocking, tackling, running on a daily basis.

Q: Who is the best tackler you have coached or coached against?

BB: They come in different shapes and sizes. But not many guys got away from [Lawrence] Taylor. I'd say that. But probably one of the best tackles that I've ever been a part of was by a guy who had a reputation of not being a great tackler and that was [safety] Everson Walls when he brought down Thurman Thomas in the open field to keep it from getting closer in Super Bowl XXV. That was a huge, huge play. If you had ever said Everson Walls tackled Thurman Thomas, I don't know which of those you would've bet on, depends on maybe who you're pulling for. But that was a great tackle.

Q: How do you get a team to improve their tackling and how difficult is that now due to the practice restrictions?

BB: It's hard to practice it, there's no doubt about that. It's hard to practice it. Whatever the restrictions are, they are. There's nothing we can do about those. You just try and do the best you can to coach everything, whatever the techniques or coaching points are that you need to get across – blocking, tackling, running, catching, throwing, kicking, and so forth. I think it's something that is a skill that's probably practiced less at lower levels – high school, college – than it was in previous years or decades maybe. Therefore, that's kind of rolled into the next level. And again, the amount of time we have and the amount of opportunities really to do that, sometimes the risk of doing live tackling, there's definitely a risk to that. You've got to try and balance all that out. I'm sure every team in the league is having the same conversations. How do we improve our tackling, how do we practice it without taking too much risk? I know we've had a lot of those conversations, and like I said, I'm sure every team in the league has had them.

Q: Do you think coaches have found a way to replace that physical element in practice? You've said that practice is different now than it was years ago. Do you think players and coaches have found a way to replace that competitive fire in practice?

BB: Practice is just preparation. It's a necessary part of getting ready for the game. It's part of preparation. It's not punishment. It's preparation. Whatever you can do to get your team prepared, whatever a player can do to prepare to play, you know. Now full speed contact on every single play, every day of the week, at some point it is diminishing returns. It's counterproductive. I don't think anybody is in favor of that. But it's preparation, so you do the best you can as a coach to prepare your team. You do the best you can as a player to prepare yourself or prepare your teammates if you're working with them and you're giving them a look at what they're doing. You're the scout team, then you're helping them prepare, just like they help you prepare. That's the way I see all of that. It's not about - it's about preparation. That's what practice is.

Q: Do you take any particular enjoyment in the practice drill where you throw pads at the quarterback?

BB: Yeah, that's good. I mean, look, if they can't handle it from us, they're in a lot of trouble. They're going to get a lot bigger, stronger, faster, more explosive guys than what we have on the coaching staff. You know, we hit the receivers with bags and try to knock the ball away from them and make them catch through contact and make the quarterbacks avoid a rush and stuff like that. Look, if they can't handle us, it's going to be a long year.

Q: The fully padded practices seem to be coming a day later in the week than they normally do. What kind of benefit is there to the team in doing that?

BB: Yeah, each week we just try to do what we feel like is best for the team, and we move some periods around at practice. We don't always do everything the same as we did it the week before or whatever. It depends on what the needs of that week are, the emphasis points for the preparation and so forth, and pads or no pads is part of that discussion. So, it's really week-by-week.

Q: Since you've put the pads on, we've some of the one-on-one drills between the offensive and defensive lineman. What can you learn from players in those one-on-one periods?

BB: Well, you know, all those one-on-one periods are good periods because they give the players an opportunity to just focus on the technique. There's no play, there's no down-and-distance, there' none of all the other things that come and there's no adjustments. It's just focus on individual fundamental techniques, and every play has a lot of those in them. So, various drills - long ball drills, one-on-one drills, so forth - it isolates just the technique - footwork, hand placement, leverage, so forth - and all the things that are involved without all the other components of a play that factor into a play where players don't have to think about that. You can just focus on his technique. We just coach his technique so it's part of the overall process of the good play.

Q: Does putting the pads on change the tenor of practice to maximize those competitive situations?

BB: Yeah, absolutely. Yeah, that's what those are for. But there is a lead-up process to get to those and I'd say we're in an accelerated process, but that's what it is. We're not in pads. We're not tackling guys. We're not jamming the receivers. We're not blocking each other in the running game, or very infrequently. We're not defeating run blocks. We're not doing any of those things, so we don't evaluate them.

Q: How much does the mood of practice change when you finally put on the full pads?

BB: Again, whatever we can do we'll try and make the most out of it. It's no different than in the season when we have padded opportunities and we have non-padded opportunities. Whatever we have, we have and we just try and make the most out of whatever those opportunities are. It's really as simple as that. If we have 10 days of practice then we spread it out over 10 days. If we have 20, we look at 20. If we have five, we do it over five. It is what it is.

Q: How much is your preparation throughout the offseason altered by the limited number of practices you are allowed these days as opposed to years ago?

BB: Well, the way we look at it is we have a certain amount of time, whatever that is, and we try and make the most of that time. So, whether that's in the spring, in the fall, in training camp, meeting time, practice time, whatever it is, we try to make the most of it. A lot of things are considered. We have players at different experience levels. We have priorities of getting individuals ready, getting units ready, getting the team ready. There are certain things that we need to do, there are certain things that we have to prepare for in terms of our opponents. We just try and balance all of those things out and make the best use of the time that we have.

Q: How does where the fatigue, conditioning and health of players' impact how the coaches structure practices?

BB: That's a great question, and part of that answer is it's not the same for everybody. Where one guy is or sometimes even a group is … Sometimes you have another group that's in the exact opposite place. One group maybe needs a little more recovery. Another group maybe needs a little more work. I'd say we go through that throughout the year. It happens in training camp sometimes because of numbers and experience levels and so forth, but bottom line is you try to do what you feel like is best for the team. You have to take individuals into consideration, but you have to take the team into consideration, too. We just can't structure everything for one or two guys and be negligent of the other 61, including practice squad players.

We try to balance that the best we can. It's not always the same for everybody. Sometimes guys who need more work we try to get them more work, but we have to try to get the team ready and that encompasses all those things. I don't feel like there is any right or wrong answer. I've been on teams and with coaches that ... Well when I was younger, a lot of times, my job several years was to write up the practice schedule. So when we would meet and go through the schedule, then I'd write it up, put in what everyone is doing and hand copies of that to all the coaches.

We have coaches on our staff now that do that, and I can remember I could have written the practice schedule for December, a Wednesday in December, in July easily and there wouldn't be one thing that was different. A lot of times it's, "Alright what did we do last Thursday,' and it was the exact same thing. And that's not the way we do it. And I'm not saying it was wrong to do it that way, but there were some times, certain programs I've been in, coaches, it's just their routine and you do the same thing every Wednesday, every Thursday, every Friday, every Saturday, so you always know where you are. We would do blitz pickup and the other team hadn't blitzed in two years or vice versa. So, we kind of do it differently. We kind of talk each day about what the team needs, we have a basic structure of this is what we do, but we change that depending on what we feel like our needs are, and that is definitely a big part of it is the health and I'd say the overall readiness of the team. And that's very subjective, obviously, but we do the best we can in consultation with the training staff, the strength and conditioning staff, position coaches, a lot of times they have a good tempo of where their individual group or particular players are and sometimes that affects the rest of the preparation.

Q: What is your view of dropped passes from both an offensive and defensive perspective?

BB: I don't know. That's a tough question, it's pretty involved. Just like anything else, I think you have guys that have really good hands, really good catch skills and there will be an occasional drop from them and that's usually a concentration thing. Then you have other guys who maybe don't have quite the same hand-eye coordination skill, so catching the ball is a little bit tougher for them. A number of those players that I've coached in the past have had exceptional concentration, so there was kind of technique drops and there is I would say concentration drops. Then sometimes it's related …

As you mentioned some degrees of difficulty are harder than others, so it's related to timing and the ball location from the quarterback and so forth. In the end, if the player is not a dependable catcher, I don't think he's going to be involved much in the passing game, but again a lot of those catches are somewhat a function of the degree of difficulty of the ball that is being thrown to them or in some cases the coverage. That's another thing, too, where a player's got really good separation skills, it looks like he's always open and the catches are relatively easier. If a player isn't able to separate, then every catch looks like a great catch because there is somebody right there on him. I would say that there are certain players that without exceptional hands wouldn't be targeted very much because they don't have the ability to create a lot of separation but because of their catching skills they can be productive because they don't need as much separation. I don't know if that answers your question or not, but I'd say there are a lot of components that go into that. And honestly some players are better, just like anything else, like any other skill – golf or whatever – some players are better at some type of catches than others, just like some guys are better off the tee and some are better around the green. Some players track the deep ball better than others. Some players catch moving routes and routes where the ball radius that they have to catch in is larger than other guys. I'd say not everybody's catching skills are the same on every ball either. Bottom line is you want somebody that's dependable. That's the bottom line – you want to throw to somebody that's dependable.

Q: Defensively if a player is open but drops the pass, do you still view that as a completion when you review it on film?

BB: There are going to be plays defensively that when you go back and look at – like you said go back and grade the film – when you look at that you're going to get off the hook occasionally on a dropped pass, maybe a quarterback doesn't see a guy who is wide open and isn't covered properly. Maybe it's a penalty of illegal formation or something that calls back a play that you really don't have defended. Those are still concerns. They still need to be fixed. The next team that you play is going to sit there and say, 'Well if we don't drop the ball or if the quarterback reads it properly or if we don't align in the improper formation, those are good plays for us.' So you're still going to have to stop them. Yeah, the players are accountable.

Just because a guy dropped a pass it doesn't mean the defense was played well. That's not necessarily the case. That's why we talk about that after the game – just because the score of the game is what it is, it doesn't mean if you win everything is great or if you lose everything is bad. There are a lot of things regardless of whether you win or lose that are bad and good that happen in the game that you really have to address so those problems don't continue to occur. Of course at the same time there are a number of plays that will happen defensively where you feel like that's about as good as we can be, but the quarterback makes a great throw and the receiver makes a great catch and it's just a great play. And sometimes that happens, too, where you really want to tell the player, 'You did the job well. You did what you were supposed to do. You were in perfect position and the quarterback got the ball to a place that was a couple inches away from you and they made the play.' There are some of those, too.

Q: How much of a factor is conditioning in the opening regular season game due to the fact that a lot of players may not play a whole game during the preseason?

BB: Yeah, I think it's a really good point. It's something that we've been talking to our players about for several weeks now and just being exactly how you described it. Look, you're not going to play every play of a preseason game but in September you might be playing every play of the regular season game, so here are your preseason plays in preseason but we've got to work your condition level to a much higher point than that because the commands are going to be higher, and I'd say they're even going to be higher this week when we go to a 1:00 p.m. game on Sunday. Last night's game was indoors, and I mean if we had played that game outside yesterday that would've been even more challenging. I don't know what we're going to get here this weekend but I'm saying potentially a warmer day at 1:00 p.m. tests your conditioning a lot more than a cooler evening does in preseason.

All of those things are part of the buildup and we can't get them in preseason but we have to get them in our training camp and the practices to try to prepare for that. I thought that our levels were pretty good there and we executed some plays well at the end of the game that we really needed. I'd say one of the plays that kind of stood out to me was the screen pass on that last drive where you can see our defensive line and linebackers running to the ball with a lot of effort to close that space down very quickly. I think we tackled them for a loss on that but the energy and the speed that the players were moving with at that point of the game I thought was pretty good, so that's the type of conditioning we feel like we're going to need to win a 60 minute game.

Q: Do you taper practices to make sure you're at full strength at the end of the season?

BB: Well, there could be. It depends on the situation and it depends on the player, absolutely. You have some players that need more, some players that need less. And again, I think that's not just each player, it's the team. Even some guys that maybe are OK at where they're at, they need to work with their teammates. We can't just put 11 guys out there that have never worked together. In the end, we try to do what's best for the team, whatever that is. If it's work more, if it's work less, if it's taper down, if it's however we set the practice schedule. We can't do everything. We try to pick out the things that are most important, that have the most impact and do what we think is best. And sometimes doing what's best for one guy isn't what's best for another guy, but I don't know how else you can run a team. It's not like we've got a tennis team with nine guys playing their own singles match. We've got to work together.

Q: Does pushing the full-pad practice back to make it a day further from the previous game help the players rest their bodies a bit or is that reading too much into it?

BB: No, I mean there are advantages to Wednesday. There are advantages to Thursday, right? Thursday gives them an extra day. It gives you a day to kind of get everything in and work on it to a degree and then execute it on Thursday a second time, if you will, maybe at a little bit better tempo or level of execution. Wednesday puts it a day further away from the game, a day closer to the previous game and a day further away from the upcoming game. If it's one or the other - when it's one or the other, which it is now obviously, I think you just try to get the most out of whichever one of those days it is. If it's do something in pads or not in pads and its more beneficial to do it in pads, then you try to find a way to schedule it there.

Q: When a player doesn't have a ton of experience at a certain position, can you mold that player a little bit more? Have you found that there are not as many mistakes he's learned that you have to correct?

BB: Yeah, possibly - don't have a lot of bad habits. They can just build good ones, but the lack of experience is the flip side of that. But, some players gain that experience quickly. Some don't. So, it could go both ways on that, but sure. I mean, rookies in general, there's a little bit more - in some cases, they're more moldable than a guy that's played in the league eight years that's already doing things a certain way that's gotten him to that point. It's kind of hard to change, and sometimes it's not worth changing, that they can just keep doing what they're doing and it still works with the responsibilities that you give them.

Q: Is that a main thing you are looking for when seeing a player make that transition or what are some of the other factors that you're looking for?

BB: I mean, everything. A player has to be prepared to do all of the jobs that he's responsible for, whether that's in the primary position or a backup position. Again, we all know that situation can change very quickly in this game, so that's what a professional player does, is he's prepared for all situations if he's the backup or maybe even the third guy. Sometimes that's what it comes to, just being ready to go, whether it's offense or defense to special teams or whether its special teams to offense or defense or maybe some situational grouping - dime or goal line or a sub grouping - whatever it happens to be. That's a player's job every week, is to be prepared for all of the groupings and situations that he can be involved in.

Q: Is speed a factor as well in assisting in the evaluation process out there on the field?

BB: Sure. Look, we all know that younger players have less experience and are going to make some mistakes and hopefully they correct them, and learn from them, and improve quickly at a faster rate and show us that they're capable of handling the volume. Guys that have more experience will probably make fewer mistakes, generally speaking. They physically may be in a little different spot than some of the younger players so we'll just have to see how all that weighs out.

Q: For smaller guys, how important is their technique in making sure that they're effective blockers?

BB: Technique is important, willingness is important, but again there are a lot of things that go on in the blocking. Number one is doing the right thing, knowing who you have to block. A lot of times blocking secondary players you have to make decisions as to which player to block. We always want to block the most dangerous guy, the guy that can get there first, most of the time – not all the time, but most of the time. And so that decision of as I'm going to get this guy, is the guy that's on me going to get there before I get to that guy or do I turn back on him, do I go get that guy, who's lined up closer, those kind of decisions, taking the right angle, blocking from in front, not from behind because there are a lot of moving targets that they're blocking – those guys aren't always just standing there – playing with good pad level and good leverage, not going in there and getting blown up obviously by sometimes bigger guys they're blocking.

A lot of it is desire, a lot of it is leverage, a lot of it is technique – playing with a good base and getting your pad level down on contact and having your head in the proper location, things like that. Those guys have blocked really well for us all year – runs, passes, slip screens or scramble plays, things like that, they've really competed well, they've helped us get a lot of extra yards, and they block for each other. Like on Gronkowski's touchdown pass, a block from the receiver helped spring him and vice versa, Rob has blocked well for them. Those guys, I think that's really an underappreciated part of their jobs – tight ends and receivers – again it's all about the stat sheet and fantasy catches or whatever, however that stuff works. But those guys go out there and compete every play and that helps a lot of other guys. That means a lot to our football team.

Q: Is there any example of something that you can't teach a guy who comes in during the season as you don't have the time with him that you had with the other players during the offseason?

BB: There is a degree of difficulty on different things. There are some relatively low levels of a degree of difficulty, and then there are some that get higher and more complicated. Communication that involves multiple people in a very quick recognition, you might try to avoid that. Maybe a receiver that motions into a bunched look where you have three receivers together, maybe in training camp you've practiced this with your guys and you have a couple different ways to play it, and then when the pattern unfolds then we match it this way if we're in this call. Then we match it that way if we're in a different call. You don't have the time to rep all those looks. You don't have the time to go through all the problems, like it's good if they do this but it's not good if they do that, and then how do we handle all of those variations and so forth. Rather than deal with a situation like that, maybe you just say, 'Ok, here's what we're going to do. You two guys are going to combo these two guys and that's it. Or we're going to lock it. We're not combo-ing anybody, like you have your guy and we can't get picked.' But that's how we're going to play it. Rather than having multiple, maybe two ways of playing something that if you had an experienced team and guys that have been doing that all year, you might not think twice about making that adjustment.

Or blitz pick-up instead of - we're three-for-four but it could be this guy could have two or that guy could have two depending on what gap the defender is in or how it unfolds. Maybe if we're three-for-four, maybe we just go three-for-three and we throw hot off the fourth guy. Normally, we could pick up three-for-four but it's just too many looks, too many things, too much communication. If it's just hard, then we'll just go three-for-three, and if the fourth guy blitzes then we'll run a route that the quarterback can throw into before he gets there and we don't have him picked up. So things like that I would say you try to figure out what you can do, what you can't do. Sometimes I'd say, a lot of times where the problems come is you're playing a team that you think, 'Well this is what we're going to get and we can handle,' but then unexpectedly in the game, you get something a little bit different than that and then you haven't really gone over it or you haven't prepared them. It's not really the player's fault because you haven't covered it. It's not really your fault because you don't want to sit there and cover 50 things that aren't going to happen, in case they happen. That's really just confusing. Sometimes they just get you on it and then you pay the consequence of that play. Those are the things you deal with, making those kinds of decisions and those kinds of adjustments.

You can make it ultra-simple and everybody knows what to do. Can you handle it when they start calling plays that make that style of defense or offense tough? Then you run into other problems. That's the decision you've got to make.

Q: With the addition of new players, how do you develop player roles?

BB: Every year has its own individual characteristics and players on the team and the roles that they develop for themselves and that the team needs to place them in for us to be in the most competitive position possible. We have some players back there that weren't with us last year. We have quite a few players that were. There is definitely a mixture there. We've always been a team that's tried to do what we feel is best to play the specific opponent that we have, and that includes different personnel groupings, sometimes different positions, sometimes different schemes. But that's a part of what we do in varying degrees.

I think that's always been a component of it. Some games may look a little more different to the fans or the media or even ourselves than others. Some may look kind of the same. Some may look a little more different. I think they're all different, but as I said, the appearance sometimes can be a little more or less than others. Again, it's all an attempt to try to put ourselves in the most competitive position we can.

We ask a lot of those guys and everybody on the team to do that. They do a good job of it. They have versatility. They've all played multiple roles – inside, outside, man, zone, flipping over, not flipping over, matching up, not matching up – a lot of different combinations. We do that in training camp and in the spring to try to give ourselves some versatility and flexibility.

Sometimes we end up using more of it or less of it than others, but eventually it seems like we always need it, so we work on those things and how they come up from game to game just really depends on that individual game and the game plan. What we do this week doesn't necessarily have a great correlation to next week, but that includes all three phases of the game – not just defense and not just the secondary. You'll probably see that on offense and even in the kicking game too. Bottom line is we ask them to do quite a bit so we have some versatility back there and then we try to do the things that we feel are best.

Q: When you bring new players in, do you have to change the way you run the hurry-up offense? How important is the conditioning factor when you're doing that?

BB: Conditioning is definitely important, and it's important for everybody. It's important for the big guys obviously because it's the big guys, but it's important for the skill players because they're the ones who are doing a lot of running – run 40 yards come back to the line of scrimmage, run 30 yards come back to the line of scrimmage. The conditioning part of it is important and of course it's not just the conditioning but it's also the thinking part of it. It's being able to think quickly, make decisions, if Tom [Brady] changes a route or we call a play and then they run to their look and then we need to change it there is some quick thinking, quick decision making that needs to go on. That's really part of the conditioning process, too. It's definitely challenging to do that with new players. There are a lot of things that can happen when you're trying to go fast and you don't have a lot of time to think or communicate. You kind of got to know what to do, so terminology and communication and anticipation of all three of us, four of us, whatever it is, we all kind of see the same picture, but we all need to see it the same way. We don't have time to talk about it because the ball is being snapped and we're going to go. That part of it is challenging. You also get some defensive looks that obviously aren't the way you're going to practice them. They're struggling to get lined up, they're kind of scrambling, they're moving late because they're communicating on their end of it, too, so normally when you huddle up and run a play, you're going to be where you want to be and they're going to be where they want to be, and then you execute it from there.

When you're going fast, that's not always the case. Sometimes they're kind of where you think they're going to be and sometimes they're kind of scrambling at the last second – a linebacker or a safety or someone will get to where he needs to be on that call and it happens late. Sometimes it works to your advantage, sometimes it doesn't, but it's still being able to identify it and see it and all be on the same page in a short amount of time. It's challenging for guys who have done it multiple times, and it's even more challenging for guys who have less experience in that. There's no doubt. And you hear one word or two words or whatever it is, only a couple words, instead of calling out the whole play – the formation, the protection, the play, the blocking, the route. Now you're just sometimes saying a couple words and that tells everybody what the formation is, what the blocking is, what the route is. Sometimes it's two plays.

The terminology, it's cut down to make you go faster, but you have to remember a lot more things where if you just hear a normal play normally that will tell everybody what to do. You use three of four words to call a formation and you use words to call out the backfield action, the run blocking, the protection, the strong side route, the weak side route, maybe what the back's route is or what some auxiliary route is just to tie that in. Now it all just becomes one thing.

Q: How does having new players impact your decisions on what you watch at practice?

BB: Yeah, that's definitely part of it. Seeing the new players, how they're doing and also how they're doing relevant to the rest of the other players that I'm a little more familiar with. Again, each year is a new year, so even though we've seen some of these guys multiple years, it's still starting all over again, seeing where they are, how they're progressing in their training and preparation for the season.

Q: What is the process like of getting new players up to speed on the playbook and game plan for the coming week?

BB: That's challenging. We do it on a number of different levels. There is just the component of just getting the guy into our organization – here's how we do things. Forget about the X's and O's, there's that aspect to it. Then there is kind of learning what some of the basics are in terms of terminology and formations or alignments or whatever it happens to be, and then it's pretty much game plan-specific. What do you have to learn to play this week and then whatever you can get beyond that in terms of general fundamental foundation building, you do the best you can, but you're usually pretty consumed with trying to get in what we're doing this week. Here's how we adjusted against the different things our opponents do and then next week is next week.

In some of those windows where you have possibly extra opportunities, you try to build a better foundation, a better base, so even though this doesn't apply this week here's what this means because at some point you're going to want to build on that. It's a tough catch-up process, it really is. For a player like Keshawn Martin, who at least from an X's and O's standpoint and probably a program standpoint, too, had some familiarity with protections and adjustments and basic concepts, probably the learning curve for him would have been easier than say a player that comes in with very little in common. Maybe their routes are numbered and ours are named or vice versa. Or the protections were names and ours are numbers – that kind of thing where you're trying to put together a whole different language, trying to learn a different language as well as what to do but also trying to learn what different words or concepts mean, I think that's probably the hardest part of a new player.

As you go through that process with a player, there are some things you'll talk to him about where he'll say, 'Oh I got that. That's what we did here. That's this, this is that; OK good.' Then there are other things that are going to be different that are foreign that are new and those are going to take more time, and you don't really know what those are until you actually go through the process with the player, start talking to the player, get questions, get feedback, quiz him on the information you've given him to try to understand what he's getting, what he isn't. Some guys learn better by walking through it, some guys learn better by seeing it on film, some guys can look at it on a piece of paper and understand, some guys need to see it on the field. There's that whole process of getting to know the player and his best learning techniques. A lot of different components to it, but obviously you're fighting a losing battle in terms of a race against time that you're just already too far behind in to get all the way caught up. You just have to catch up enough so he can be functional for that particular game and then worry about next week next week.

Q: When you've talked in the past about acclimating new players to the team, you've mentioned how different players learn at different paces and in different ways. Is tailoring your system to different players always been part of your philosophy or is that something you've picked up over the years?

BB: No, I think I learned that pretty early and even going back to before I started coaching just being around my dad and other coaches and being around different players that I played with, you've just got to learn that everybody is different. Each of us is different as individuals and we learn at different rates, and some things come easier to some people and some things come harder to some people. There are some things I feel like personally I can pick up pretty quickly and there are other things that are very difficult for me to put together. When you teach somebody, trying to teach anybody, there are different methods you can use. You can read it, you can hear it, you can write it down, you can show pictures, you can stand and have kind of a spatial instruction as opposed to a picture or a diagram, and again, some players, some people learn in one way, some people learn in another way. I've done different studies or part of our testing on players includes information like that – how does a certain player learn best, what's the best way for him to process information – and again it comes in a variety of methods when you look at your entire roster. We probably do a little bit of everything and then with certain players if they want or need one more than another then the position coaches adapt to that and we give them more of that particular method that is most helpful to them. I think that's just fundamental teaching, which is really what coaching is – it's teaching.

Q: Do you measure your steps with a player who is learning a new system in terms of not putting him in positions to not succeed whereas maybe earlier in the year you would be able to do that?

BB: I think each guy is different. It's really hard to predict how it's going to go with any player. I think you just take it as it comes. You give them the information and then you move them along and see how quickly he adapts to the new assignments, the new techniques, and just the way he's able to handle the assignments that he's given. Again, each player is different – it depends on the positon and the guy. I don't think there's any set mind frame or you try to go fast, you try to hold back. I think you just kind of take it as it comes.

Q: In your experience, can the growth of a player be limited if he doesn't receive the game experience and game repetitions that a starter otherwise would?

BB: Well, I think in football we only play once a week, so if the only time a player improved was on the day that he played then I don't know how much better the player would get in what his skills are, period. We're in a sport where we practice a lot more than we play and so most of the gains that players make are on the practice field because that's where they spend most of their time. So, if you're saying that a player can only improve in a game, I would strongly disagree with that. I don't think that's even close to being true in this sport.

Q: I'm saying more from the actual pressure of a game. In practice you can simulate conditions and scenarios, but a game is a game.

BB: Yeah, they're different. I'm not saying they're not different but I thought you were saying you couldn't improve and I don't agree with that. But games are games. That's right. Games are games. Game experience is game experience and that's another way, another part of the process that is part of a player's development.

Q: How do you balance a player getting accustomed to a new system against keeping a practice moving and having productive reps?

BB: You see what the player can do. You put him in there based on the things you think he can do – if he can do those then you give him more, if he can't then sometimes you have to go back and spend a little bit of time to build the foundation and get it right before you move ahead.

You just kind of take it day by day. We meet with the players, the coaches get some feedback and get kind of a feeling for how they're picking things up – what they are comfortable with, what things they maybe have questions on or don't seem to have as a good of a grasp on. They substitute them or call plays based on what we feel they are able to handle and what's going on on the other side of the ball – how complex that is or what the degree of difficulty is there. You're right – we don't want somebody in there that doesn't know what to do and then that fouls up practice, but at the same time you want to try to evaluate them on what they do know how to do and see how that looks and then move forward at as fast a pace as you can go at, but it has to be one that the player can keep up with. Each situation is different – you just have to read each one independently.

Q: Are you ever surprised by a player's ability to pick things up that quickly?

BB: Yeah, all the time – to varying degrees. Some guys, if you haven't been with them – until you've really been with them you don't know exactly what they can do and how they process, how they can adapt to your system. Some guys can move very quickly, other guys move at a different pace. Sometimes guys are kind of in a little bit of a fog and then all of a sudden it just sort of comes together, and sometimes it doesn't, so it's hard to tell until you've really spent enough time with a player to know exactly what you have. Some guys, when they learn stuff they have it – they won't make a mistake on that, but you throw something new or have to make a quick adjustment in a practice or in a game, then sometimes that's hard for some people to deal with. Other people, they just get it, roll with it, understand it and move on, but until you've gone through that experience it's hard to know. That's part of what training camp and these preseason games and all that's for, is to try and get a feeling for what your team can do, what it can't do, with certain individuals, how they handle things. We put them in different situations, and a lot of times they don't get it right the first time, but if we keep working at it and build on it, then sometimes it changes, sometimes it doesn't.

Q: Does that take some work off the coaching staff when you do have older guys who are experienced and able to help some younger guys?

BB: I think the bottom line is just everybody being on the same page. Just, everybody has to be on the same page. I think as you work longer with a certain player and you develop a rapport and a communication pattern and a respect for each other, that we all understand that it's a little bit different. Some guys see things one way; some guys see them a little bit differently. I'm not saying one is right or one's wrong. The bottom line is for us to all see it the same way together. I've coached hundreds of players and they're not all the same. Some guys can do one thing and they have a hard time with something else.

The next guy, the other thing comes very easily to him and the thing that came easily to another player comes very hard to that guy. So as you're coaching that guy and he tells you, 'Look, I know what you're saying, I just don't see that. I just have a hard time with that.' Well, OK, then let's try to work it this way, or maybe we don't call that play or we don't run that type of a pattern because the way I'm seeing it as a coach isn't the way you're seeing it as a player and we have enough other plays, let's run something else. Or the player might say, 'I really like this concept. I can see this and anticipate it better.' Maybe that's not something that is a big part of your offense, but OK, that's a concept that's very comfortable to him.

Maybe you run that concept a couple different ways so the defense can't see that it's coming, but you have a couple different ways to get to it and it's something that he's comfortable with and he executes well. There's always that kind of modification with players and particularly quarterbacks or on defense, it's the same thing. Once you kind of get the guys and there are some things, like I said, there are some things they can handle and there are some things, sometimes they have a hard time with. I've coached linebackers, you could be three-on-three like, 'Us three got those three and however it goes, we can sort it out.' and they could get it, it was never a problem with all the different things those three receivers could do, whoever those three guys were.

Then I've coached other teams, you run 10 of them, we probably would get two out of 10 right. Somebody would come free or would be late going to a guy [and] he would be open. We just couldn't do it so you don't do it. You lock one guy and then you go two-on-two. But sometimes you have to find that out, what one team could do or what one group of players could do. Sometimes it's experience, but sometimes it's not. Sometimes it's just the way that a guy, what he sees and what he's able to process. It's a good question and it's something that's not, I don't think there's any textbook answer to it, at least it's not in my experience. It's just something you have to learn as you go. I think the communication between players and players, coaches and players, but the bottom line is however we do it, we all see it the same way, we all understand it, we all know what we're going to do if they give us a problem, we all know what we're trying to beat. What's our answer when they take it away? Make sure that we don't turn the ball over, we don't have a bad play, we turn somebody loose. How do we make the best out of not a great situation? What do we want to call it against? It's a good play, but it's not a good play against something we don't want to run it against. Maybe there's a way to just run it on terms that we want to run it on. I think all that plays into it. Long answer to a short question.

Q: At the end of the season, do you sit down with players and ask them to get down to a certain weight?

BB: No, look, we do that on a regular basis. So like wherever you want to start, let's say we start the season in April, not every player is here in April, but let's just say it starts in April. Ok, we sit down with that player in April and say, 'OK, here's what we want you to do in the offseason program – weight, conditioning, technique, position, whatever it is, here's what we want you to concentrate on.' We get to the end of that, we say, 'OK, here was your offseason, you did this well, you need to do a better job of this. OK, now we're heading into training camp, here's what we want you to do – this, this, this and that.' We get to the end of training camp, 'OK, you did a good job of this, you still need to work on that, this is better or this still needs to be improved – conditioning, weight, strength, flexibility, etc.'

We get to somewhere in the midpoint of the season and we sit down and have the same conversation. 'Look, this is what we told you at the beginning of the year, you've done a great job with this, you still need to do better at this, this, this and that, here's what you need to do – strength, flexibility, conditioning, weight, etc.' Injuries may play a part of some of those discussions. We get to the end of the year, somewhere close to the end of the year, 'Alright we have X number of weeks to go, here's what we need from you the last three weeks, four weeks, whatever it is, here's what you need to concentrate on. You did a great job of this, that and the other thing, but now we're into a different, here's what you need to do.' So we do it on a regular basis. We're not going to sit around here and waste a whole year and then say, 'OK, let's have a meeting and like alright we think you ought to do this.'

We're not going to have a meeting every day, but there are certainly different points in the year were you can … And we do it for the entire team, too. It's each individual player, it's each coach, each position, each unit, offense, defense, special teams, running game, passing game, kickoff return, punt coverage, whatever it is, that we evaluate those at various points and, 'OK how are we doing? Alright we're alright on this, we're not so good on this, we need to make this change – whatever.' We're our own R-and-D team. We can't hire some consultant to come in here like a company can do and, 'Alright let's take a look at this and you guys do a study on that and tell us this, tell us that.' Who's going to do that?

Q: Especially for younger players, is there a benefit to playing in close games? Does it help the team overall, too?

BB: There probably is. You learn something from every game. Every game is an opportunity and every game is a learning experience, so whatever that game brings, it brings. Over the course of the season you're probably going to touch all bases somewhere along the line, whether it be weather conditions or close games or playing from ahead, playing from behind, playing on the road, playing at home – all different combinations of those things that all mix together. That's why each game is unique and different and has its own characteristics. Part of your development as a football team is learning to play competitively in those situations. You practice all of them, but when you actually get to play in them you probably learn a little bit more from that. Not that we want to be playing from behind or not that we want to be playing from behind of the road or not that we want to be ... But whatever comes up, comes up, and you've got to learn from it.

Q: There were a few stories written this offseason about technology and things that can be used by teams to track workload of players while out at practice. Have you found that there are new systems or devices you guys can use to help in that regard?

BB: Yeah, well I think in that world, there's like 20 new products every day. We've looked at some things. We've used the things we feel are beneficial to us. There's probably a thousand things out there. We've probably used two of them. If we feel it's beneficial, we'll use it. A lot of it generates a lot of time, energy, a lot of numbers. I mean, there's a lot of great coaches - Chuck Noll, [Tom] Landry, I mean, you can go right down the line, [George] Halas. They won a lot of games. They seemed to coach pretty well without logarithms, exponential equations and everything else under the sun. In the end, it's about blocking, tackling, fundamentals. We'll emphasize those.

Q: On a forced fumble how much of that is a result of coaching versus just pure instinct and reacting to the play?

BB: Well, we work on turnovers every day. We work on getting the ball off of runners or receivers and different angles and so forth, so they have basic fundamentals that we coach. Each play is different. Each situation is different; which hand the runner has the ball in and where we're positioned and so forth.

We talk about it. We emphasize it. We have drills to work on but each situation is different. It's awareness and it's the player's judgment and ability to create pressure on the ball.

Q: With the quarterback position, is there ever a case of not wanting to tinker with a guy's mechanics too much because each quarterback has their own individual throwing motion?

BB: Right. Well, I think that's a good question. I think anytime that you look at an individual skill such as passing, kicking, punting, a golf swing, something like that, that each person – their physically ability is a little bit different. Their mechanics may have some variation and so there are a lot of different I would say styles. You look at the golf tour – not every swing is exactly the same but all of those guys are pretty good. I think what you try to teach in that situation, and I've talked to people who coach those specific skills like that, and when I was the special teams coach and coached punters and kickers, that there are certain fundamentals that are inherent and good in good passes, good kicks, good punts, the way that the ball is released and the angle and the spin on the ball and the delivery and so forth.

The same thing is true, as I said, in golf or punting or place kicking. I think you try to teach the players the basic fundamentals and if they can adjust their mechanics in a way to improve and still feel

comfortable with it, then we try to do that. And if it's
an adjustment that they're really not comfortable
making for whatever the reasons, then I think you just
have to decide if you can live with what the
deficiencies are in the mechanics and look at if the
punts are good but they're done in a little bit of an
unorthodox way and they've satisfied what you want
the punter to do, then you're probably going to be
happy with it. If they don't and you can't change it
because that's just not the makeup of the player, then
you're probably not going to be happy with it. I'm
sure that extends to other players, too.

There are players that use techniques and do certain
things that you wouldn't coach a player to do if you
were starting him off or if you were talking to a group
of players and you'd say "OK, this is fundamentally
the way we want to do something." It's the exact
opposite of the way that another player is doing it,
but the player is very successful doing it that way and
so you don't change the guy who has his own way of
doing it if he is successful and he's productive. But at
the same time you wouldn't necessarily start from
scratch and teach a player who has kind of a blank
slate to do it that way because fundamentally you see
some flaws in it. I'd say the biggest lesson or
experience I learned on that was with Everson Walls
when I had him with the Giants. He came from Dallas
and he had a very unorthodox way of covering in
man-to-man coverage and his footwork was

unorthodox, his eye control was, again, not something that you would teach.

That's probably because not a lot of guys could do it. But he had his way of doing it and he could do it pretty well and one of the first things I told Everson was "I'm not going to try to change your style but you have to understand what your responsibilities are on the defense and you have to perform those responsibilities, but I'll give you some latitude in the technique and the style as long as you can get the job done." He said "OK, I fully understand that. I want to meet the requirements of the position on the defense on a particular call, but let me do it my way and I'll get it done. I don't know if I can do it your way because I've been doing it this other way for so long. I said "That's fine," and the guy had – whatever he had, 60 interceptions – or however many it was. It was a lot. He played very well for us and, as I said, I learned a lot from Everson because he just did things differently than any other defensive back on the team, or in all honesty, really any other defensive back I've coached.

But he knew what he was doing. He knew where he had to compensate, and generally speaking, he got the job done on a very high percentage basis. I learned to accept that, but at the same time I had to coach the other players. "Look, this player has a lot of experience doing it a different way. I'm going to let him do that. I'm not going to coach you to do it. I'm not going to really allow you to do it. I want you to follow a fundamental sequence that I think is more of the right way to progress it." All of the players in the room understand that – Mark Collins and Perry Williams and [Myron] Guyton and [Greg] Jackson. They all understood that, that it was different, but they knew they couldn't do it that way, and again, Everson had a lot of experience doing it. It's a long answer to a short question, but that's kind of how I look at that. Those individual skills – there is certainly a guideline and a way that I think and I believe in that they should be coached, but if it screws the player up more than it helps them, then that's not really good coaching. Then I think you're better off letting them do it how he's most comfortable doing it. There's definitely a give and take on an individual skill like that.

Q: In your time coaching, what in your view makes a quarterback a good backup at the position, keeping in mind that he is always just one play away from being thrown into the game?

BB: Right. Well, that could be true of a lot of positions. Guys that don't play in the kicking game, like offensive lineman as an example, same kind of thing. It's like being a relief pitcher in baseball. You go to the stadium; you don't know if you're going to be pitching or not. It depends how it goes. That's part of the job. Each position, each player, each situation has its own challenges. If a player is in that situation, then those are the challenges to him.

Q: When it comes to the quarterback position, how do you balance encouraging a guy to take a chance he might not take in a game situation versus wanting to be as clean as possible in practice?

BB: Well, I mean, practice is the time to do it, and that's the only way - again, if you don't execute it in practice, it's hard to execute it in the game. I'm not saying never, but not very often. Yeah, you need to find that out in practice at quarterback - I mean, at other positions, as well, but specifically at quarterback - what windows you can get it into, what windows you can't, whether you can make this throw to that player or as you could do to another player. I mean, is it different? Can you do it the same? And that's finding that out, gaining confidence or understanding, 'No, I'm not comfortable doing that. I don't want to do that in a game situation.' It's a lot better to find that out in practice than it is in the game. Of course, we don't want to go out there and make a lot of mistakes, but there's definitely an element of aggressively executing a play in practice to find out what limit you can take it to in a more competitive situation. So that's what this is for. I wouldn't say all bad plays that happen are bad plays.

A lot of times those plays become good plays or good learning plays for situations going forward. The bad plays really come in the games. Look, nobody wants to go out there and - the same thing with a receiver. I mean, you might run a route to try to experiment or try something a little bit different. Not a good route, didn't work - alright, we're not going to do that again the next time, or if we do it, we're going to do it differently to do it right. Yeah, I mean, there's definitely an element of that.

That's not, again, to say we want to go out there and make 22 mistakes on every play because we're just winging it around and trying to experiment and find out and all that. I mean, that's not really what we're trying to do, but there is an element of that, especially at this time of year. But, you know, sometimes that happens in the regular season, too. You put in a play and, 'Alright, here's the play,' and you throw it in practice and, 'Can I get this in there? Yeah, you can,' or maybe, 'No, I can't. OK, if I get this look in the game, then I've got to go to my secondary receiver.' That kind of thing.

Q: Do you find that there's more of that aggressiveness when there are more new players involved, specifically receivers or pass-catching options?

BB: Well, again, there's always an element of that. I thought he was going to go behind, he thought he was going to go in front, and sometimes that's - I mean, we have rules on that. We coach things a certain way, but I mean, look, it's a fluid game. Once a player gets out there and he's in the play, he's going to make the best decision he can in that particular situation. Sometimes the guidelines are just guidelines and the player's going to do what he thinks is best in that situation. It's not always maybe the same as what his teammate thought it was going to be, whether it was a quarterback throwing to a receiver, whether it's two offensive lineman passing off a pass-rush game, whether it's a couple of defenders on a certain blocking scheme. 'I thought this was the way you were going to play it. I was going to play it this way. No, you're going to play it that way.

Alright, then I'll make the adjustment.' I mean, there's a lot of that. There's a lot of that in our meetings when we go through the practice film of each other understanding - I mean, there's that silent communication - but each of us understanding what our teammates are going to do. So, eventually, we get to the point where we're not thinking about it. It's not an, 'I wasn't sure. I was waiting to see,' type of thing. We can just go out there and play aggressively because I know where you're going to be, you know where I'm going to be and we've done it enough times that we're confident in it. Yeah, that comes up a lot every night.

Q: What signs do you look for when you are developing a quarterback to make sure he is going in the right direction?

BB: Well, I think that's a question that, you know, the coach has to answer because only you as a coach, the quarterback coach, the offensive coordinator, the head coach, whoever it is, knows what you're telling the guy to do and what his reads are on certain plays, what he should check to, if he should change a play, if he should stay with it, what his read progression is and so forth. Sometimes there are things that happen on film that if you're just not part of those meetings you don't know if there was a mistake in protection or if a receiver ran the wrong route or if he ran the right route and the quarterback made the wrong read. You just don't know those things unless you're part of it.

We try to give the players a plan or system to work in, let them do it, watch them improve, evaluate their performance, but there are a lot of things within that that if you're not really a part of it then it's hard to tell exactly, particularly at that position, how much the quarterback is right, how much somebody else is right, what are some things that are happening that he can't control and what can he control. There's a subjective evaluation there that's really only the person that's working with them have a good opportunity to make.

Q: Is it difficult to give a third quarterback the same number of reps to allow him to develop in an ideal way?

BB: Well, we have a lot of people out here so I think the reps have been split pretty equally across all positions. I think across all players, everybody's working. It's that time of year. Not sure that any of our players are ready to take the work load they would have in call it August or September. I don't think that's where we are right now anyway.

Q: How important would you say the quick release is to your offense? Would you say it's something that's been talked about more in years because of the advanced metric websites, or has it always been there?

BB: The, what now?

Q: The quick release, quarterback release.

BB: What metric are you talking about?

Q: The advanced metric websites that put emphasis on quick releases by quarterbacks.

BB: What is that? I mean, you could take those advanced websites and metric them - whatever you want. I don't know. I have no idea. I've never looked at one. I don't even care to look at one. I don't care what they say. As far as a quarterback goes, read the coverage, throw the ball to the open receiver and take the best matchup. That's what it is in a nutshell. The quicker we're open, the clearer the picture, the sooner the ball is going to come out. If we don't have anybody open, who is the quarterback going to throw it to? It's timing, decision making, execution by the entire offensive team. That's what the passing game is. The receivers have got to get open and catch the ball. The quarterback's got to read the coverage, make the right decision and make an accurate throw. All the metric pages and all of that, I mean I have no idea. You'd need to ask that to a smarter coach than me.

3

GAME PREPARATION

Q: Is there anything specific that you and the coaching staff do on a long week when you have more time to prepare?

BB: We try to use whatever time we have - long week, short week. We try to use the time as productively as we can. That varies from game-to-game, week-to-week, situation-to-situation, year-to-year. But, we look at the week - here's what we have to work with. How do we get the most out of it? That's what we do every week, whether that's four days, eight days, twelve days, seven days, whatever it is.

Q: During the bye week how much of a balance is there in reflecting and thinking 'OK, we've got to scrap this because it's not working' and saying 'If we can improve this we'll be alright.'

BB: Look, you have to answer that question every week, not just the bye week, and you do something that doesn't work out well so what are your options, get rid of it or continue to do it and see if you can improve it. That's the judgment you make. If you really feel convicted that you can do it well then you put more resources into it and try to improve it. At some point if it doesn't go well then you might decide that 'We've tried, we've invested a lot of time. We've invested in this and it's still not working. Maybe it's time to move on to something else.' And then you make that decision. I can't sit there and tell you what the book on that is. I think you evaluate each one individually but that's what coaches do. That's what we do.

We evaluate it, we look at it and maybe it's a difference of opinion in the room on the staff like 'Look, I still think we can do it if we just work harder on it,' versus 'We've put a lot into it. Let's do something else. We seem to be on a dead end here,' for whatever the reasons are and there could be a multitude of reasons. That's a whole other conversation but in the end you have to make that decision. It's a bye week decision but it's a weekly decision, too. You just have to decide what direction you want to go. I think in a lot of cases you can improve things. [For] some teams that's just not their thing. You have to find something else but that's true in every season.

Each year I think you have to find a little bit of a different way to win. You can't do everything exactly the same way you did it a previous year. Your team has changed and the teams that you're playing may have changed or you may be playing different teams and maybe that dictates that you do something a little differently than you did it in the past against a different set of opponents. Those are the judgements that the head coach, the coordinators and the position coaches make whether it's an overall scheme thing or whether it's an individual technique thing. It can be a technique thing, too, like 'Look, here's the way we're doing this technique but it's not as affective for us as we want it to be.' Do we keep working on it or do we modify the technique and do something a little bit different for whatever the reasons are; our players, their players, their scheme, whatever it happens to be.

Q: When breaking down film with the team do you view the opposing offense dropping balls as their ineffectiveness or do you get on your guys to show them that it could've been a breakdown on your defense that just wasn't taken advantage of by the opponent?

BB: Well, we try to coach and correct every play; good plays and plays that aren't so good regardless of what happened. Sometimes the offense misses an assignment or they make a mistake or whatever the case might be. We want to be aggressive and take advantage of it but at the same time we can't always count on those things happening, so we have to make sure we play our responsibilities properly so if that doesn't happen we're not out of position. So we try to coach and correct every play.

Q: Historically in tight games your team compares favorably to teams like the '70s Steelers and '70s Dolphins. Everyone else seems to be .500 in those games and you have a good record. What is it about

this team and what is it about Tom Brady that has you taking these close games and winning them so often?

BB: I'm not sure about all that. I think looking at the Jets game that the statistics on that were – the odds of us winning that game statistically were very much stacked against us. So, I'd say of all the games, that was pretty much an aberration there. I'd say in the end it just comes down to the players: playing good, sound situation football and making the right decision at the right time under pressure. Whether that's recovering an onside kick or getting an onside kick that we do, like what happened against Cleveland last year, or being able to offensively manage the clock or defensively kind of in this case, again kind of similar to the Cleveland game, Cleveland had that, it was like a 58-yard field goal or something like that on the last play of the game. This one was about the same length. We kind of kept them just far enough out. I mean, I don't know, it got blocked. I don't know if he would have made it or not, but it would have been a really hard kick. Each game is different, each situation is different, but what I would say is common is the players making good decisions under pressure. Of course offensively that's Tom.

Q: Is that something you emphasize as a coaching staff?

BB: Yeah, I'm sure every team in the league does that. Of course, we definitely try to do it. I'd say if you want to look at the whole, go all the way back on it, we've had a good quarterback who is very good at that type of thing – decision making, clock management, game situations. We've had a good kicker, whether it be Adam [Vinatieri] or Steve [Gostkowski]. We've had good guys in those spots, although we won a bunch of games with [Matt] Cassel in 2008, but the quarterback play and the kicking are important. Defensively and special teams, we've had our share there, too. But I'm sure the quarterback and the kicker, if you had to pick two guys, those are two pretty important guys.

Q: You've done different things in the past though regarding travel situations for road games though, correct?

BB: Yeah, it was based on the schedule. It's based on where you're playing, when you're playing, what the other circumstances are. Sometimes the options are maybe not endless based on whether it be the hotel, or the airplane, getting a bigger plane for a longer trip. Maybe those aren't available 24/7. I mean, there are other factors that go into it. Again, each trip has kind of its own characteristics so I don't feel that there's just like one way to do things that we've got to do it this way if we're traveling here or traveling there. As much as we can we try to stay in a routine.

Q: Do you plan all of that months in advance or is that something that's determined the week of the game?

BB: [If] you try to change your travel plans in a week you're trying to ship, whatever it is, 200 people out to wherever you are; players, coaches, staff, marketing, equipment, everything else, what the FAA regulations and so forth [are]. I mean, you can't just throw whatever you want on an airplane now. You've got weight requirements, you've got packing requirements, things like that. There are things that we did years ago, even as little as a couple of years ago, that we can't do anymore. A lot of times we truck our equipment to the away sites. That's definitely not the plan this week, but again, there are issues with smaller planes, and weight, and cargo, and baggage, individual player baggage. Look, we're moving a lot of people here. Now that's something I think you can do - now look, every once in a while something comes up.

Like when we played Pittsburgh in the AFC Championship Game [in 2004] and we had the snowstorm we left a day early and went up there. You see what your options are and make the best of them. Sometimes there's availability and sometimes there isn't, and then you figure out what the next best thing to do is. But no, we're not in an environment where whatever we want to do, 'OK, let's do that.' There are a number of hoops to jump through.

Q: I've heard the phrase that availability can sometimes be as important as ability.

BB: Dependability is more important than ability.

Q: Yes, I believe that was the phrase.

BB: Yeah, I agree with that.

Q: When you're talking about player availability and you're making a long trip, is that going to affect the timetable of evaluating whether or not a player is going to be ready to go and make the trip, or does that have nothing to do with it?

BB: No, I think it could have a lot to do with it. It would depend on what the player's individual situation was. It's certainly a lot different than being at home where you could literally wait until an hour and a half before the game and make your decision on the player. I don't think there's a lot of downside. We've certainly had discussions in the past if the player has, whatever his particular condition is, if we think it's probably less than 50-50 that he would be able to play. Again, if we were playing at home it would be a bit of a different situation. If we feel like it's probably a long shot if you will, then do we really want to put him on the plane for five hours? Do we really think that after all that the swelling is going to down or that the 'whatever' is going to loosen up or whatever the case, whatever the nature of the condition is, is really going to improve? Is that the best thing to do, or the right thing to do?

And could it set us back, and now we come back after the game, let's say the player either does or doesn't play, and then here we are on Monday and we're further behind than we were on Friday. Yeah, I think that's a legitimate conversation. Again, it would depend on the individual player's situation and I think it would have a little more effect on a trip like, like a west coast trip than if we were going to Buffalo let's say. But it might affect that, too. A lot of cases, as you know in preseason, a lot of players that don't travel, they get a lot of work in here. We usually play night games, so we're gone for a solid two days and then we come back after the game and it's three or four in the morning or whatever, so then you're already kind of losing part of the next day. So if a player is recovering or is in a condition that needs constant maintenance, how productive really is that, right? We would be a lot better off just leaving the player here, letting him get a good day on Thursday, a good day on Friday when we play, and be ready to have a good day on Saturday rather than travel, do whatever on the road, come back, be tired, being here for 'X' number of hours. I mean, preseason is a good example of what we're talking about.

Q: How long does it take for you to be able to identify what it is a team wants to do from week to week and you can rule certain things out, as

opposed to the early season when there is an element of surprise?

BB: I don't know that you can ever rule them out but I'd say the term 'midseason form' is pretty accurate. What a team has done by that point, I mean it's pretty much who they are. They've seen a lot of different matchups, however they've evolved, they've evolved. There might be a few things that are a little bit off, a little bit out of the fairway, but they're pretty close or there's a reason for why they were a little off the mainline. But you know, you just need to get enough looks - five, six, seven games; whatever it is - to see that. It doesn't mean somebody couldn't throw in a new wrinkle. I think that's always part of football, but you know there's only so many of those you can get ready in practice in a normal week so you still have to be able to go out there and execute it. I don't think it ever goes away but there's a certain point where every team pretty much shows they're out there trying to win every week, they're not evaluating players, they show their hand, and you tell everybody what kind of team you are.

Q: Are some teams more fun to watch and breakdown on film as opposed to others?

BB: Well, it's not all the same. I'd say it's all different. Each team has kind of their own way of winning. They've got their own, obviously, personnel and their coaching staff. Even though the systems may be similar, they're different because the players are different and the actual people who are responsible for that system are different. I'd say each team is unique. Every game, even if you play the same team over again, it's different.

There are certain circumstances that are different. Each one has its own challenges and I think that's the intriguing part to me, is to try and figure out what it is about this team and how they play, how they win, what gives them trouble. You break it down from a team standpoint; offense, defense, special teams. And then individually and try and put it all together the best that you can. But yeah, each one is different. I mean I find that fascinating, to be honest with you. That's really what it's all about, to try and figure that out, who you're playing, what they do, how you're going to attack it. Some teams you know fairly well and it's a quicker process, especially if you've dealt with them more recently. But teams that you haven't or if they've made significant changes to their team since the last time that you played them then you've got to start - not start all over again - but you've got to figure out a lot more. I think that's the very interesting part of it. It's a lot of work. Its time consuming, and of course every team wants to be balanced. There are certain things that you want to do but you've got to have complements to them because you just can't keep doing the same thing in this league all of the time. It's just impossible. Trying to figure out how those are, what they are, when they come, how you're going to deal with them.

Q: Is there value in a new player just traveling with the team to be around and see how things operate?

BB: Sure, absolutely. Yeah, no question. It gives us time to help catch him up on assignments and procedures and things that relate to the team and for him to see the operation pregame, during the game, whether he's active or not active just to take some of the surprise element out of the next time that it happens. I'm sure there will be some new things that if any of us went to any new team that would be different from whatever team we're used to being with. Sometimes those things are an adjustment. Sometimes they're not. I think it's good just to get into that routine of the new team that you're on. I think there's always a little bit of hesitation until you know for sure exactly. The first day at work is always a little 'How is it? How does this go? How does that go?' And then once you get comfortable it's just different. It takes time so this will be part of it.

Q: Based on your experience are you more likely to stick with what you're doing midseason or switch it up?

BB: It depends. I mean we've done both. We've gotten to points, again, it's not even a midseason conversation. It is a midseason conversation but it could be anytime really and just say 'Look, I'm done with this.' I've said that before - 'I've seen enough. I'm done with it. We're going to do something else. We've tried and it just didn't work,' or 'I believe in it. We should be better at it than we are.' It's maybe circumstantial why we don't have production. Eight guys are good, one guy is bad. The next time its eight guys are good and a different guy that [isn't]. If we just get this right we'll be OK but we just haven't been able to do it. Well maybe you keep trying.

Q: In your time in New England, each time you've lost to Buffalo in the first matchup your team has responded with a victory in the second matchup. Do you take this as sort of a revenge game due to their victory earlier in the season?

BB: Every game is its own entity. I don't care about the games that have happened in the past. We've won them, we've lost them. I don't think it matters. What matters is what happens this week. I'm not just saying on Sunday. It matters what happens the week leading up to the week; the preparation. This game will be different than any other game, like it always is. I don't really care about those other games.

Q: What changes from a preparation standpoint when you play an opponent that you just recently played a few weeks ago?

BB: We start all over again. We've been focused on three other teams in the meantime. Now we turn our attention to Buffalo and obviously need to do a better job than we did in the last game if we're going to be competitive. We need to coach better, we need to execute better, we need to do a lot of things better. We need to start all over again. We emptied the tank against Pittsburgh. It's time to fill it up again.

Q: Will it be beneficial to be back on a more normal schedule here this week to maintain the routine you're used to?

BB: I think it will help us stay in a normal routine in preparation. I think our team has played with good energy the last few weeks; Baltimore, Denver, the Jets. I mean I thought our players were aggressive and played fast, played alert, taking advantage of turnover opportunities, taking advantage of some big-play opportunities, playing fast and playing physical. I think they've done a good job of that. I think from a practice routine standpoint, a normal Wednesday, normal Thursday, normal Friday, normal Saturday leading up to the game that we can be a little more routine this week.

Q: How do you balance practice versus getting enough rest on a week like this where you're traveling on a Friday but coming off of a game late Monday night?

BB: Yeah, sure, absolutely. I mean, we could practice for these guys for another week if we had it, but we don't. You try to take the time you have and use it as efficiently as possible. Could you use more time? Absolutely, but we have what we have. They have what they have, and we try to use it the best that we can. That's definitely a balance between preparation, practice reps, rest, travel in this case, whatever the components are that play into that week. You try to take them all into consideration. The ones you can control you can make a decision on. Travel - we can't control that. We've got to go to Denver. Now we can decide when we want to go, but I mean, again, you do all of the things that you do to try to make the situation the best that you can for not only the players - they're the number one thing - but you have to have coaching staff preparation as well. It doesn't do any good to not do a good job preparing the players from a coaching standpoint. Then whatever you've gained on one side you've lost on that end, so I think it's a combination of us being able to give the players a good plan in a timely fashion so that we're ready for them, they're ready for us, and we're able to go out there and prepare as best we can.

Q: Does the point in the season play a factor at all in those decisions?

BB: Yeah, sure, I think it factors. But again, your time is your time. So if we play on Thursday night, which we did earlier in the year, then you work in that timeframe. If you play on Monday night then we had a different timeframe last week. I think you take what you have to work with and you try to figure out how do you make the best of this time. Whatever it is, four days, five days, six days, seven days, eight days, bye week, whatever it is you just try to take the time and maximize it and all of that is important; player rest, player reps, film study, meeting time, travel, all of those things. What's the right mix? It changes from year to year, from like you said, early in the season to late in the season or maybe where your team is at a particular point in time relative to injuries or a variety of other things that can impact and affect the mental and physical condition of the team. You try to take all of those into consideration, look at your options and pick the best one.

Q: At this point of the season does player rest factor more into decisions like that?

BB: Yeah, absolutely. We've had a lot of snaps. I mean, we've taken a lot of snaps when you go all the way back to OTA's, and training camp, and all of the practices and all of the meetings. Do we need another snap at 'Ride 34 Bob?' I don't know. We could always use it but we've had a lot of them this year. Do we need another snap at a coverage? You try to balance that out; how many more plays versus how much rest, walkthroughs versus practice, pads versus no pads, all of those things. But the more snaps you have, the further along you are, I would say in particular if you're doing something well then the more confidence you'd have that you'd be able to execute it at a good level. But you can't just stop doing it. I mean, I don't think just sitting on a couch for a week is the way to get ready for a game. Even though you'd be well-rested you'd leave a lot of other preparation components behind. So there's some kind of balance in there.

Q: Over the years have you learned how much rest you need for yourself and do you advise your coaches that they need to get their rest in order to perform at their jobs?

BB: Yeah, I think we all learn that; sure. But again, it's the same thing. Maybe you want a certain amount of rest but you have a certain amount of preparation to do so where do you draw the line - 60/40, 55/45, 70/30, 30/70? You have to make that decision. One thing that comes with having a long a week that comes with a short week, to a certain degree you try to either get ahead or maybe get a little more rest in a long week knowing that you have a short week coming up, or get further ahead so you don't have as much, if you will, as much to do as you would normally have because you try to push some of it to where you have a little bit more time.

Time management and efficiency, combining rest with your work product - yeah, it's all part of it. We're all different. Some of us need more rest than others.

Some of us work faster in certain areas than others. We're all individuals yet we have to come together in a team concept and figure out some kind of schedule that we can all be on. Once you know what that schedule is then you as an individual try to maximize the time that you have and how you get the most out of it. All of those things are important but it's hard to maximize all of them. You have to pick and choose and figure out what the right mix is.

Q: How important is this next couple of days to reset for you?

BB: Well again, it's an opportunity to use the time that we have available as efficiently and productively as we can, so that's what we'll try to do individually and as a coaching staff. There are things that if we can get ahead on and that would help us then great; we'll try to do that.

Q: I mean more personally for you to reset yourself mentally.

BB: Yeah, of course. It's an opportunity for all of us to get a little rest. Again, get caught up on some things that we all need to get caught up on, whether it be in our personal lives or moving forward into the November/December second half of the season, whether it's Seattle - the next game on the schedule. There are a lot of different things that can be addressed that can be helpful moving forward.

Q: What would help you decompress more, sneaking off to your vacation home, playing in a mock lacrosse tournament or spending the weekend at Rob Gronkowski's house?

BB: That'd be a three way tie. Those are three good options. It's a really well thought out question. I appreciate it.

Q: How does it change your approach to watching a tape of a team when the quarterback has changed since your previous matchup with them?

BB: Well, it's no different than any other position. You look at the new player that's in there and you look at what things are different and acknowledge those, and you look at what things are the same and those things are the same. [C.J.] Fiedorowicz is out. Watson is in. [Julian] Edelman is out. I mean, you know, like every team goes through that. That's football, unfortunately. That happens in just about every team. We deal with it every week.

Q: How do you prepare for the uncertainty at quarterback?

BB: We always prepare for all the players that are on the active roster. Whoever we think the first player in the game may be, by the third play of the game that might all change anyways, so we have to be prepared for everybody. Really I think the Eagles are a team that has really two legitimate starting quarterbacks, and both of those guys have had a lot of production throughout their career. They've won a lot of games, been in a lot of big games. I think they have great depth at that position and there aren't a lot of teams in the league that can say that. We'll prepare for both of them, and again whoever starts the game, any week there is no guarantee that you won't be playing against somebody else anyhow, so we always have to prepare for all of them. We do that at every position, not just quarterback. They're both very good players. They can run their whole offense, do whatever they want to do with whichever guy is in there. It doesn't look like it matters.

Q: How difficult is it to come up with a game plan that fits well with all of the new pieces you have at the skill positions on offense?

BB: There's some element of that every week in the National Football League. Every team is dealing with something and some circumstances and some unique situations about the game. We have ours and everybody else has theirs. I've seen weeks a lot worse than this one to be honest with you. We'll work our way through it and we'll be ready to go on Sunday.

Q: Will dealing with crowd noise and silent snap counts be a big part of practice this week?

BB: We always are prepared for that on the road. Yeah, it's the home opener down there. I'm sure there will be a lot of energy in the stadium. It's a great crowd. The Saints do a great job and they play very well at home, so I'm sure that will be a big challenge for us.

Q: Does a player's injury history ever dictate when and how you will use him in a game?

BB: Well, if a player's cleared to play and he's healthy, then we would, for the most part, just operate normally like any other player. It might depend on the individual circumstance or situation, but I think if the player's healthy, then we treat him like he's healthy.

Q: How much more did you learn from a regular season game, as opposed to the time you spent with the team in the spring and summer? And how much might the extra days you had over this weekend benefit you to process what you learned?

BB: Well, the spring and training camp and all that is certainly beneficial. It's good for a lot of things. The regular season is different in terms of game planning, schemes and the way that an opponent will specifically play you, as opposed to just the generic fundamental and basic things. But, they're important, too. We learned a lot against Kansas City, certainly in the fourth quarter. Hopefully, we can improve on it and do a better job here the next time around. The extra time - I don't know. Every long week has a short week. Every short week has a long week. So, in the end, it all evens out. We just try to do the best we can with each day. But, I mean, obviously we have a lot of work to do.

Q: Is part of preparing for this final preseason game doing some work on all of the little situational aspects of football that could come up during the regular season?

BB: That's part of the 16-game preparation, right. We don't know if they're going to come up opening night or not. Some will, most won't, but we'll still have to be ready for them. It wouldn't matter who we play opening day. You want to be prepared for those situations. It's not about the specific opponent, although we'll get to that maybe if they run a certain play in a certain situation, obviously, we would prepare for that but, just in general, those hundreds of situations that can come up and rules and so forth, yeah, that's part of this week.

Q: How do you prioritize which situations to work on over others?

BB: Well, we cover all of the situations, some in more detail than others. When you go through each situation - last play of the game - there could be 20 situations for that one situation. Where is the ball?

Kickoff return, scrimmage play, scrimmage play backed up, scrimmage play midfield, scrimmage play on the plus-10 yard line, so there are a lot of situations just on, let's say, that one play and just keep going right down the line. So you pick out the ones that you think are most important. If you can get to all of them, you get to all of them. If you can't, you get the ones that cover the most specific situations or the most frequent situations and then do the best that you can on the other ones. I would say most of the time we can at least watch those plays on film based on our library. Maybe we don't get to practice every single one of them or get every one of them on the field, but we've at least talked about them, at least gone through the awareness part of what we're trying to do, what the situation really dictates regardless of what play we call. At least we understand what the situation is. We need to get out of bounds, or we need to stay in bounds, they don't have enough time for two plays, or they do have enough time for two plays or whatever it is.

Q: When OTAs wrap up and the team leaves for the summer, what's your message to them for their time off and what you expect from them when they return?

BB: Well, I think it's obvious we all have a lot of work to do - coaches, players, each individual, each unit. We need to, I'd say, make the gains that we can make in that timeframe and be ready to come together to put a good product on the field when we come back in July and through training camp and August. But we've got a long way to go. We all have a lot of work to do. There's some things we can do over the next month, there's some things we can't, and then when we regroup, then that will obviously be a key time for us. The better prepared we are for that, probably the better and the more production we'll have. If we're not prepared for it, then we'll miss another opportunity.

Q: How do you feel both the players and the coaching staff have done this year in dealing with some adverse situations and key guys missing from the lineup throughout the season?

BB: I thought the players and the coaching staff have both done a great job this year of being focused and looking just at what's in front of us, that next game, not getting caught up in other distractions or things that we really don't have any control over. They've happened in the past or they're too far down the road in the future to deal with. The players have been really good on that. The coaching staff has been good on it, too. There are always things from week to week from a coaching standpoint that you have to make adjustments on, personnel things, or it could be a number of issues. But whatever they are, that's part of coaching, is being able to adapt and improve and make adjustments and I think our coaching staff has done a very good job of that.

Q: What have you learned over the years about the process of coordinators on your staff being allowed the opportunity to pursue other coaching positions but still managing their time well and remaining focused on the upcoming opponent?

BB: Well, every situation is different so they're all unique. I'd say in the end the most important thing is for this team to do what's best for this team and balance that with some of the other things we have to balance. We'll comply with everything we have to comply with in the league rules. We'll take it case-by-case.

Q: What does it say about the reputation your coaching staff has built that they continue to draw interest each year for head coaching vacancies?

BB: I think I've said many times this year that I think our coaching staff does a good job. Collectively they work hard. They're well-prepared. They do a lot of extra things and they're very committed to what we ask them to do.

Q: Besides the normal game planning and practice, is there anything you do specifically on road week games that you feel gives your team an advantage?

BB: I think I would give the credit to our players. It's hard to win in this league, it's hard to win on the road and it takes a lot of mental toughness, focus, discipline and good execution - and sometimes a harder situation offensively and in the kicking game with crowd noise and the energy that fans in other stadiums bring. Certainly, last night, as usual, the Broncos crowd was full of energy. But, it takes a lot of concentration and focus and, as I said, mental toughness. You know, we had one penalty last night, so being able to play that type of a game where you don't give your opponents extra opportunities and played with good toughness and focus for 60 minutes, that each player is doing his job and staying at it for a whole night. So, we're very fortunate. We have a lot of good players, and they did a great job again last night, as they have for quite a while for us.

Q: How does mental toughness play into a game like last night? What did you think of the offensive line's play?

BB: Well, I don't think there's any way to understate the importance of mental toughness. It's a long season. Every game is competitive. Every team has got good players, good coaches, good schemes. There are always challenges to overcome every week. Every day is a competitive challenge to try to prepare harder and better and do more than your opponent is, even though you're not facing them on the other side of the field yet. We're in our separate locations, but there is still a competitive race to have everything done and be in the best possible place when the game starts from a preparation standpoint. So it's not easy and mental toughness is a big part of that, being able to sustain it, deal with whatever the ups and downs are, whatever the distractions are, all the things that could get in the way of your performance, some of which are out of our control, controlling the ones we can control but not getting distracted by the ones that are out of our control and doing a good job with all those things, too. I don't think that can be understated.

Offensively, in general there wasn't a very consistent performance in any area. We didn't throw the ball particularly well. We didn't run it particularly well. We've got to do a better job of all that. We've got to coach better. We've got to block better. We've got to get open. We've got to run better. We've got to do everything better. It just wasn't the kind of production or offensive performance we were looking for. That being said, we had enough production to win and certainly it was a good complementary game from the plays we got from the kicking game, from the defense, and we had the one turnover offensively but that didn't really hurt us as much as it could have because the field position they ended up with was not very good. It was kind of similar to a punt if you will, so it wasn't one of those devastating turnovers, so overall our ability to take care of the ball and take advantage of some of the opportunities that we had, although we were only one-for-three in the red area, we left some points on the field, weren't very good on third down, but we still had 350 yards of offense. So we moved the ball some, but again there were just too many inconsistent things, not enough production in some of the critical areas that we needed to be. We've got to do everything better on offense. I don't think it was one guy or one position. We had issues everywhere at one time or another.

Q: Is that where the resiliency comes in?

BB: Yeah, absolutely, we're not going to go out and score 50 points every week and shutout the opponent every week. We've got to battle through some bad plays, bad calls, bad coaching calls, whatever it is, and find a way to make it work and find a way to win. That's a big part of the mental toughness and resiliency, no question about it.

Q: It seems like your team has converted a lot of third-and-longs on offense. Is that something that is sustainable or is something you stress to the team that you don't want to be in often?

BB: Yeah, well it's never where you want to be. There's a lot of situations that you don't want to be in in the game, but you practice those situations and try to make the most out of them when they come up. Whether it's getting the ball back at the end of the game on defense because your behind or two-minute offense at the end of the game when you're behind. That's not the situation you strive for, but sometimes those situations come up and you've got the ball on your own 1-inch line. That's what it is. That's where it is. You've got to find a way to compete in that situation and make the best you can out of it. It's not where we want to be. I don't think any team wants to be in third-and-long. I don't think any team wants to be behind at the end of the game, but sometimes you're in those situations. You still practice for them and try to execute them to the best you can when they come up.

Q: What's the challenge for a reserve player to prepare each week as if he is a starter, especially when it comes to on-the-field reps?

BB: Well, the players that work on the scout teams get as high quality of work as anybody because they're working against - like our scout team defensive players are working against our offense, which is our best players doing the things that those players are best at, and we're asking the scout team players to cover them. When you're on the scout teams, and all of our players take reps on the scout teams for that very reason - to keep that sharpness - so that's a great opportunity on the scout team to work on your techniques. You don't have to work on calls and adjustments and things like that because those are usually on a card or they're pretty standard. So, that's not the challenging part for the scout team guys. The opportunity for those players is to work on their fundamentals and techniques without having to worry about a lot of calls and adjustments and things like that. I think that's an opportunity for every player - again, very few players would take, call it more than 50 percent of the reps in practice, maybe 55 at the most, but nobody's taking 100 percent of the reps. So, when they're on offense or scout team offense, either one of those are quality reps - either running our offense or running against our defense and vice versa. So, players get plenty of snaps in practice, and the ones they get they can take advantage of to work on the things that they can work on. And, the things that they aren't able to work on, then we have to find another way to be able to prepare the players for those, and that's meetings and walk-throughs and other things like that.

Q: There seemed to be frustration earlier in the season from the players about how they were performing given the fact it was not up to their standards. How have you harnessed some of that frustration to help the team and eventually turn things around like you've done the past few weeks?

BB: Well, look, we all work hard and anything you work hard at you want to do well at. If it doesn't go quite how you want it to go, then you want to try and improve and do better. I think that's pretty straight forward.

Q: I guess what I'm asking is if there is a way to make sure early in the season that the frustration doesn't become a negative mentality?

BB: I don't know that I quite see it the way you saw it, but regardless, I think in the end whatever problem you have, whatever degree it is, it's still the same process. You analyze it, figure out what you need to do to correct it and then work hard to make those changes. No matter what you're looking at you've got to figure out what's wrong. Then you have to figure out what you need to do to make it better. Then you have to work hard to improve the area that you've identified that you need to address. I think that's, honestly, what we try to do in every phase of the game every week on everything. Some things may not be as good as others or may be better than others, but it still gets back to the same process. If you want to improve it, you've got to identify it and work hard and dedicate yourself to making progress there.

Q: Throughout the week would you say you spend more time talking about the way your opponent can beat you guys, or the way you can beat the opponent?

BB: Yeah, both. We look at their strengths and figure out how we need to defend them or neutralize them, however you want to look at it, and then we look at areas that we think we can create an advantage on and try to figure out how we can take advantage of it, I think it's definitely a combination of both. Sometimes one overrides another, but there's components of both, I would say, every week in all three phases of the game. You've got to find a way to stop the things that they do well, and at the same time figure out ways that we feel like we can gain an advantage in our attack.

Q: How similar is Joe Judge's job to the other coordinators and coaches in terms of preparation, film study and game planning each week?

BB: Well, I mean it's similar in that he has a responsibility for the units that he has. It's different because each unit is comprised of different players and there's a lot of situational football that comes up in the kicking game. Not that there isn't on offense and defense, but there's an awful lot of situational football in the kicking game that, again, involves a lot of different people. Usually, on offense or defense you have about the same 12-13 guys you're dealing with.

On special teams you could have all of the linemen on the field goal team, all of the defensive linemen on the field goal rush team, and all of the linebackers, tight ends, running backs, defensive backs, receivers on coverage teams, and return teams and everything else, plus the specialists and all of that. So, there are a lot of moving parts, a lot of decisions, a lot of getting everybody on the same page and you start factoring in weather, like we had on Sunday, where the wind affects the kicking game a lot more than it affects the passing game, then that's another variable that has to be taken into consideration, too. Yeah, there's quite a bit there. Joe does a great job with it. Bubba

[Ventrone], they both do a great job. It's different, but it's similar in terms of the responsibility and all of the things that have to be handled one way or another.

Q: It seems like more and more frequently you are going up against a quarterback with some mobility. Do you envision devoting more time to that in practice?

BB: Well, I mean I don't know. We look at the guys that we play every week and those are the guys that we prepare for. What those players' skills are, the types of plays they run, those are the plays that we practice on. Those are the players that we prepare for every week, so next week is next week. Last week is last week. This week is Matt Ryan and Coach Sarkisian's Atlanta offense. That's what it is that we're preparing for. So, all of the elements that they bring, which are numerous, certainly not one thing you have to stop, you've got to stop - it's a long list. We work on all of those and they're all difficult. They make it hard on you. They do a good job and so it's a big challenge for us.

Q: How do you prevent your team from overlooking an opponent?

BB: We prepare for everybody. We prepare for everybody's best game.

Q: Are there any special precautions you're taking to keep the players safe during the cold this Sunday?

BB: There's nothing more important than the health and safety of our team, so we always take that into consideration. You can't play football without football players.

Q: What concepts do you try and implement in practice so that you are able to execute a play like you did at the end of the game with so much chaos going on?

BB: Well, it's just the awareness of those two plays - the spike and the fake spike. As a spike, we really can't do anything about that play but we can play the fake spike if they throw it. That's what we try to do, is defend what really can hurt us which is the fake spike play. If they spike it then that's really, I mean, not a play that we can affect too much.

Q: After a unique game like that, do you ever think back on similar games you have been a part of?

BB: Well, it was a similar ending to the Seattle game. But, again, the difference in that game was they had to score a touchdown. They were down by four, and so this one a field goal changed it, which again, highlights the importance of the two-point play. Had we not hit that two-point play, then they would have just kneeled on the ball and kicked a field goal at the end. Again, there were so many big plays in that game as you go back through the fourth quarter of the game and really every play is a huge play. The difference in any of those plays in the fourth quarter, maybe call it from the second half of the fourth quarter on - the last seven, eight minutes - a change in any one of those plays could have affected the outcome of the game. So, that just to me showed how competitive the game was and how critical every single little thing is - each play, each player, each call, each situation. But, it was a great football game. As I said, we were fortunate to make one play more than they did to win it, but it was a very highly competitive game against a good football team, and I think the message for us is just every play's important and every situation's important. You've just got to be prepared for all of them. You never know which ones are going to come up, but being able to execute under pressure when they do takes the other 59 minutes and 30 seconds or whatever - not saying it's meaningless - but it takes all those plays out of the game and now it just comes down to one play or one situation or one short period of time, a few seconds, and that determines the outcome of the game. Situational football is so critical at this time of year, and fortunately we were able to make the plays we needed to make yesterday.

Q: Over the years have you had to change or evolve the ways in which you motivate the team for big games?

BB: Every week is different, so we look at whatever the challenges are that week and do the best we can with those, so every week is different.

Q: How do you best balance turning the page from last night but also making sure you learn and correct the mistakes from that performance?

BB: Yeah, that's a good question. That's what we have to try and do when the players come in tomorrow. We have to spend a little bit of time on the things that we need to make sure that we correct and address or we'll see them again and they'll be a problem again and also, as you said, turn the page and move on to Pittsburgh. Pittsburgh is schematically quite a bit different than Miami, so we can't dwell on the Miami game. Pittsburgh is a great team. They have their way of doing things and their schemes that they run and we'll have to start preparing for those, but there could be, as always, some carryover if you show them that you're vulnerable to a certain type of play or problem that if you don't get that fixed you'll see again the following week. We'll have to move quickly on that Wednesday. If it's a situational play, that could come later in the week when we go over those specific situations. We'll have to try and balance that this week; particularly tomorrow.

Q: Will you ever encourage players to watch film on various players around the league to perhaps pickup

subtle nuances of their game and not just for the reason of needing to mimic their skill set in practice on the scout team?

BB: Sure. We do it all the time. Yeah, do it all the time. You could say to a corner, 'Hey, watch how so and so played this receiver. Make sure you watch this game or watch the way he played him in the red area,' or something like that. Or say to an offensive lineman, 'Hey, watch this game. Watch the way so and so blocked this guy - the way he set him or the way he did whatever it is he did.' So, yeah, there's plenty of that where you tell a player that the way we want to do it is the way that somebody else did it. There's usually an example of that. If you're trying to illustrate what we want to do, there's usually an example of somebody else doing something similar to that with some success, or conversely, 'This isn't the way we want to do it. Watch this player in this game and you see the trouble that he had doing it that way. We definitely don't want to do that against this particular matchup.' But, that's fairly common. Of course, we always try to tell our players how the other team is going to run their plays so that when they practice them - because our offensive players don't study the other team's offense and our defensive players don't study the other team's defense - but we do want them to understand how they need to simulate the plays that our opponent is running, and so we show them those plays and make sure that they understand the key points.

You can't tell them everything but, 'This type of runner likes to cut back, or this type of runner loves to go outside, or this type of player isn't going to go outside. He's going to always try to get downhill or this quarterback is going to scramble and run. This quarterback is going to scramble and try to look deep,' those kinds of things; whatever the coaching points are for that particular guy or that particular situation, because if you don't tell them that they're not going to be able to get it on their own. They're not even looking for it. Yeah, we try to do that. I think there are examples of it, as I just gave, on both of those, whether it's simulating what another player does or watching another player play a guy that you're going to play against and learning from his play against him.

Q: When you're preparing the team for situational football, how do you get proactive instead of reactive, making sure that players know specific rules? With the rulebook as expansive as it is, how do you make sure the players know things beforehand rather than after the mistakes or situations come up?

BB: You try to coach them before they happen.

Q: How is it different preparing for a team that you really haven't seen very recently?

BB: Well, I mean, we go through that with half the season. We play four NFC teams and we played a variety of teams in the AFC that we haven't played in a couple of years, like we did this year with Oakland - teams like that - [Los Angeles]. It is what it is. Some teams you are familiar with because you play them in your division or you play them kind of annually like we have with Denver and Pittsburgh and teams like that. Then there's other teams that you don't. Like I said, probably half of our season has been that way and half of our season hasn't.

Q: What makes preparing for a playoff game different than preparing for regular season games throughout the year?

BB: Well, it's a one-game season. This is what you work for, is to get to this position. Now we're in it. Now you put everything that you have into this one-game season. We have one game left against the Titans. We have to play better than they do to be able to continue playing. That's a huge challenge. Obviously, every team that's playing, I mean, there are eight teams left. All eight of them are good teams. Every team is good at this time of year. There's a reason why they're here. They've earned their way here. There's no other reason why you're playing this weekend unless you've earned it. We've earned it, the Titans have earned it and I'm sure it'll be a very competitive game. They got a great football team. I can see why they're here. They're good, as I said, in all three phases of the game. They're well coached. They're a solid team. They've played under pressure. They've won under pressure. They've won on the road. They've had a good year and they've got a good team, so we're going to have to be at our best. We know that.

Q: Do you talk to some of the players who don't have playoff experience about the added pressure now that you're in the postseason?

BB: Well, I don't know about pressure. It's a one-game season, so I don't know how much more pressure you can get than that. We're all living in it. Yeah, I mean, I talk to the team about the situation that we're in, what we expect going forward, what to expect, how to approach it. It's different. There's no other game on the schedule. It's a one-game season. It's not like that during the rest of the season. We're in a different season now. We've definitely talked about that, but it really applies to everybody. You can talk about players that have or haven't. I don't think that really means anything. It's more about how we individually and collectively perform and how we prepare to perform. We all need to do a good job of that regardless of whether we have or haven't experienced any of this before. I don't think it really matters.

Q: Is there anything you can take away from watching the playoff matchups live this weekend?

BB: Well, I mean, we watch some TV tape. Some; more coach's tape, but the actual real time that the TV covers it in is sometimes pretty relevant, situationally. Yeah, overall, I mean, TV scouting is limited. I wouldn't say it's zero. It certainly gives you the flow of the game and you don't get the flow of the game on the coaches copy, especially if its broken up to offense, defense, special teams, which is usually the way you watch it. Sometimes you watch just continuous plays, but usually, particularly at the beginning part of the week when you're trying to learn as much about the team as you can, it's easier to compartmentalize it and just look at certain sections, whether it's offense, defense or maybe it's first and second down, third down, red area, two minute and try to separate those out so you can get a little clearer picture of what they do in those situations. So, sometimes if you just watch it continuously – I don't want to say it runs together – but it can and you end up looking at things that, 'Well, yeah, they did this but it was because of the situation. It's not what they normally do. The situation kind of overrode it.' But, watching the game live certainly gives you the flow of the game. Again, there's some real time things that happen in a game that override, I'd say, the X's and O's part of it.

Q: When you send a scout to one of these playoff games...

BB: Well, every team in the league sends scouts to

every game of the next team that they play.

Q: What do you gain out of that?

BB: There are a lot of things that the scouts look for. They have a checklist of probably – I don't know – 100 things. Some have application. Some they can say, 'Well, it didn't come up in the game or you couldn't evaluate it. It didn't happen.' All of the things that they could see that would be helpful to any of the three coordinators, any operational things, any things that might be helpful to me. Again, there's a long checklist of things that they look for. The game itself can get broken down in a lot more detail by running plays back and forth and all that, but the live view gives you some things in-between plays or where the camera isn't focused, whether that's the live game camera or the coach's camera isn't focused, sometimes you can see things that are relevant that the person at the live game can see and can show you.

Q: How do you organize that or prioritize certain situations?

BB: I don't know. I mean, some things show up every week or frequently, let's say - two-point plays. There's other things that show up - kickoff return after a safety might show up once a year. You know, I don't know. But, they're still important when they show up. So, over the course of your teaching progression, you cover them and things that they change from week to week based on the situation, then you go over the changes of how you would play this differently or do it differently than you would normally do it because of whatever the reasons are. So, it's part of the weekly preparation is to go through those things.

Q: How much time at this time of year do you spend with the coaching staff going over particular situations that could pop up over the course of the playoffs?

BB: We do it on a regular basis.

Q: How do you go about that? Is it going over film from practice or is there a different way of going about it?

BB: Well, if it's a specific situation we go over it in practice, yes, but mostly we have to create those situations in practice. It's fourth-and-two, or there's five seconds left, or there's 10 seconds left. I mean we have to create the situation to react to them when those come. I mean we talk about them after the game. We talk about them prior to the game that we're going to play. What we anticipate happening in these situations, what we want to call, what we think they'll do, and then there's just the generic situations that come up. You can flip on any game in the National Football League and probably find five, half-a-dozen situations in any random game that are worth talking about.

And again, it doesn't really matter what they did. It's just 'OK, here's the situation. What would we do? Or what would we not do?' Every once in a while you see something that's a little bit different and that stimulates you again, like the San Francisco play where they tackled the receivers on the play before the half, took the holding penalty and forced a field goal, things like that that aren't - I won't say you've never seen them before - but maybe you haven't talked about them in a while or maybe you haven't seen them before. That comes up from time to time.

Yeah, there's a lot of film to look at here. I mean you take a team like Miami that's been in all of the close games that they've been in, all you've got to do is go through their film and there are a lot of situations that come up and we talk to the team about that. Again, you don't know which situations are going to hit but there's the basic ones you have to cover and then there's always a couple that are maybe a little off the main road, which is worth talking about for when it comes up. And then there's usually - I know Dean [Blandino] sends you guys or the league sends you guys a weekly rules update and sometimes there's things in there that are worth pointing out.

Again, especially if we get something from the league that's 'OK, here's what's happening on this type of play. This is the rule. Here's how we're going to call it.' You need to be timely on that because that's what they're sending their officials and that's how they're going to call it. So if it comes up again this is the way they're going to treat it. So I don't think you want to wait until next year on that because if that situation comes up again you want to be ready for what they've told you they're going to do.

If they come down and say 'Look, we're going to crack down on whatever, this or that, and here's why. Here's some of the plays that are coming up and this is going to be called,' well if that's something that's in your framework, in your boundaries, and you do it then you're probably going to get called so you might as well change it.

Q: What is the challenge in preparing for a defense like the Rams that does so many different things?

BB: Yeah, that's a big challenge. Coach [Gregg] Williams does a lot of things there. They play some zone and they mix in some man and they mix in some pressure, they mix in some blitz zone; they get into the five-down bear [defensive] look. Again, they have good team speed and then they're very active up front. They're hard to block. So a lot of different schemes with good players - if they just played one scheme it [would still] be hard because like I said, they're hard to block and they have good team speed. Trumaine Johnson is hard to throw on, period.

So a combination of good players and identifying and getting the right blocking and assignments, getting those right - because if you're just half a step late or you just hesitate a little bit or they just catch a little bit of an edge on you, [Robert] Quinn, [Aaron] Donald, [Mark] Barron, all those defensive linemen, or if you're a little sloppy out there with Johnson - I mean, if you turn the ball over, they're very athletic and long and fast. The multiple schemes that Coach Williams employs and explosiveness and quality of the athletes that they have on the field, those two combined make them a tough team to prepare for. It's tough for us to simulate that in practice. I mean, I don't know that many teams could do that no matter who they put out there because these guys have so many players like that. It's tough to simulate in practice, as I said, if you're just a little bit late on it, then you're looking at sacks, negative runs, strip sacks, turnovers, all of those things. As I said, it's going to be a challenge for us.

Q: Is giving a lot of playing time to the younger players in preseason a way to build depth going forward?

BB: I think it's a combination of building depth, but also evaluating players that we haven't seen as much of, particularly in practice. The majority of our practice reps, especially this week, went to players that have had more experience – the group that's a little bit ahead of some of the guys that played – and so to take a look of the guys who didn't get as many reps in practice, we tried to give them more reps in the game. That's how we try to balance it out. Part of it is depth; part of it is just straight up evaluation – trying to figure out the best way to put this team together.

Q: How important is the practice squad to your weekly preparation?

BB: They do a great job. Yeah, they help the team prepare for the game. They improve their individual skills, and at some point those players may be needed, but in any case they develop their own skills.

Q: What do you look for when you're signing a practice squad player in regards to physical make up or personality?

BB: Yeah, it's like everything else - try to put people on your team that you want on your team for whatever combination of reasons are.

Q: When you evaluate players in regards to the practice squad, how do you balance having a reserve at a position and also having enough guys to carry a scout team to prepare your team on a weekly basis?

BB: That's a good question. In a way, the players that are on the practice squad are in the same positon as the players who are on the roster but not active. Obviously, you can protect the players that are not active that are on the roster and you don't have as much protection [for practice squad players], but either way they don't play in the game. They practice, but they don't play in the game, so in that way, it's similar.

So your depth really is those inactive players and the players who are on the practice squad who are also inactive, even though they're on a little different list, if you will. Sometimes that's a team management thing. Sometimes there are other reasons for it, but in the end, that's where it is. Then there are some players who are your depth who are not on your roster – they're not on anybody's roster. They're available now. Whether they'll be available in a week, two weeks, a month, two months – that's another story. So, it's a combination of all those places, and honestly there are other players on other practice squads that are potentially available to you on your roster.

They're not available to you on your practice squad because you can't go practice squad to practice squad, but you can go from another practice squad to your roster, just like somebody else can go from our practice squad to their roster. That's all in play. How do you find the right guys, what's the right mix and all that, some of it is the individual player, some of it is the circumstances that are surrounding him. Some of it is maybe your overall read of what the league perception is of that player or your position or whatever it happens to be, and you just try to do what you think is best.

The exception rules on that for the two practice squad players add a little bit of a twist there because there are practice squad players and then there are practice squad exception players, so you're limited to how many exception players you can have, so they're there to a point but only a couple of them and then the rest of them have to come from the other pool. That's another thing for consideration. If you have three exception guys you really want, but you can only have two of them, then which two is it, and so forth and so on.

Q: When do you start seriously considering a player for the practice squad? Is it this week? Is it earlier in camp?

BB: It could be the draft. It could be a guy that you want to work with that you feel like probably has got too far to go to realistically be ready. You never know. Like we don't try to cut the team in April – I'm not saying that. But realistically, you take players or you bring them on to your team, whether it's draft choices or sometimes it's college free agents – guys that aren't drafted – with the kind of thought that it'd be hard for this guy to make our team, but a year from now, with a year of development and so forth, it might be a different story, and so that's a player you want to work with. Yeah, it goes back as far as that. It's certainly a lot easier to get one of your players on to your practice squad than it is to get another player on to your practice squad.

The fact that a team has a player, a team has been working with that player, they release the player at the 53-man cut, unless another team claims him and then they have to carry him, which obviously frees up somebody else, unless they do that, it's a pretty high likelihood that you would be able to put that player on your practice squad – not 100 percent, but pretty high. Guys that we see get released that we would like to have on our practice squad, the question is, how are you going to get them there? You could claim him, put him on your roster and then maybe move him later or maybe you have to carry the guy as a roster player. But ideally that isn't maybe what you want to do, whereas it's easier to get our players from our team to our practice squad, just like it is for everybody else. If you really feel strongly about a guy and you want to put him on your roster then that's another story, then he's going on a roster.

But in the pool of 320 practice squad players throughout the league, those guys are an important part of your team's depth or every team's depth, and so you want the best ones you can get there, but sometimes it's hard to get them if they're not on your team, or harder to get them.

Q: When you build a practice squad do you try to have five positions represented or does it matter?

BB: I think the practice squad in part reflects what's on the 53-man roster. First of all you want as much quality as possible on the practice squad. You would like to have guys on the practice squad that you really want on the team, but you just can't carry them with a 53 man cut. You would like to have players, but if you could keep 58 you would really want 58. The next thing would be to create some depth for your team. So if you are heavy at a position on your regular roster then it probably would be harder for you to carry a practice squad player at that position because that just creates more weight there. You may want to balance it off by carrying practice squad players that would give you more depth at the position that you didn't have as many players at on your 53. Again it is a trade off there between having enough people to practice with and be balanced and be able to work against each other along with the overall quality of the group. You want guys to come off the practice squad that eventually you think will are going to be able to play for you.

Q: You are carrying three wide receivers on the practice squad currently. Why the need for depth at that position over another position?

BB: Most teams in the league are carrying six [wide receivers] on their roster. We're carrying five. One of those is obviously our core special teams player in [Matthew] Slater, so like most positions the more guys you have on the roster, the fewer guys you have on the practice squad. The fewer guys you have on the roster, the more guys you have on the practice squad. It's the same thing with the offensive line. The transaction we made last week, we were down to eight offensive linemen. That's probably the lowest in the league so we have more practice squad players on the offensive line because we have fewer players on the active roster.

Q: With many of the younger players still on the cusp of making the team, how much does the idea that other teams could claim those players and prevent you from keeping them on the practice squad factor into some of the roster decisions you're going to be making over the next week or so?

BB: It's something you take into consideration. It's a hard thing to predict. There's going to be, I don't know, certainly going to be a lot of players, probably over 1,000 players that will be exposed to waivers in the next eight calendar days or whatever it'll be. I think the average claim is somewhere in the high 20s there…so that's what the odds are. We've had years where we haven't had any of our players claimed and we've had years where we've had multiple players claimed. I think at the end you just have to do what you think is best for your team. It's pretty hard to predict what's going to happen when you put players on the wire because in all honesty, you don't know what the other [31] teams are going to do and who they're going to put on the wire.

Even though you put a player out there that you don't want to lose, if another team happens to put a player out there that may be a team that needs that position and would be better with your player, your player gets claimed. Sometimes we waive players that we didn't think would get claimed and they were, so that's really hard to predict. In the end, you've got to make the decision that you feel like is best for your football team, and if you really want that player and you just can't bear to live without them, then you shouldn't be exposing them to the wire. That's the reality of it. We keep an eye on them, but I don't think it's an overriding factor. If you're prepared to waive them, then you've got to be prepared to lose them. That's just the way it is.

Q: Is there a balance between players expecting a lot from themselves but also not beating themselves up if things don't go the way they expect them to go?

BB: Yeah, I think that's the sweet spot that every player wants to be in - expect a lot, expect a high level of performance. It's a very competitive league. It's hard in this league; you just don't go out there and win 53-0 every week. It's impossible. The other teams are too good. We go out there, we all make mistakes, we all have plays that we wish we could have over again, or do better on, or calls, whatever the case might be. You kind of regain your balance after those and do it again and try to do a little bit better the next time.

You don't lose your confidence, but the next time you go out there and have a high expectation, a high level of commitment to perform to the very best of your ability. Inevitably, you always come up a little bit short, nobody plays a perfect game. Then you live with those, whatever the level of disappointment is, whether it's one percent or maybe it's 50 percent, whatever it is, and then you don't lose your confidence. You go back, correct the mistakes and turn the page and move forward. I think that's where you want to be, yeah. But sometimes it's hard. When you're disappointed and you put a lot into it, those games that you lose, if you put a lot into a particular situation and it doesn't work out well, there's obviously a high level of disappointment, which there should be if you put a lot into something and it doesn't work out well.

You're not just going to walk away and say, 'I don't care.' When you say you don't care it's when you didn't put anything into it, because you really don't care. So whatever happens, you just live with it. But yeah, the ones you put a lot into and they don't work out, it's harder to get over those. But that's what we all have to do.

Q: How valuable has Tyler Gaffney been the past few weeks on the scout team in mimicking some of the really big backs you've faced and will face again this week?

BB: Yeah, he's done a good job for us. Again, he's another guy similar to Jacoby [Brissett]'s situation. Sometimes it's a ball-security thing we talk to him about like 'This back kind of swings the ball around a little bit,' and even though he shouldn't do that he'll do it to kind of help our defense prepare for it or 'This is the way he runs a certain type of route.' Again, there are a lot of little things and the players do a good job with him, too. The linebackers - they'll say 'Hey, he'll cheat on this,' or 'He'll cheat on that when he's got protection or a certain route. He lines up deeper on certain plays or closer to the line on certain plays,' just as we go through the week to sort of help each other there.

But yeah, he does a great job. Tyler [Gaffney] - he's a smart guy, very team-orientated. If you ask him to do something he's going to give you a great look. There's nobody that takes more punches than he does. He must get punched in the stomach 10 times a day. The defense is trying to take the ball out. That's his role. That's his job. But they're slapping at the ball, they're pulling at it, they're trying to punch it, half the time they miss. He does a great job.

Q: How far in advance does the scouting department begin to look at potential NFC opponents and in this case the Philadelphia Eagles?

BB: Well, first of all, we cover every team. There isn't a team in the league that isn't covered by the pro personnel department because in a fairly short amount of time in a couple of months, we'll be into free agency and there will be players form every team in free agency, so you can't neglect a team, their roster and their composition, which includes scheme and coaching staff and so forth, because there's a lot of ways that the team comes together. Every team is covered in the league and then as things narrow down we know who our opponents are for 16 games.

When we get into the playoffs then we can start to narrow that down at some point - Week 14, 15, 16 - whatever it is, and then our scouting department puts a little different focus on those teams and probably some of the people that have those teams during the regular season for eventual free agency or if a situation were to come up, say a player was released off another team, like **Kenny Britt** for example, when he was released from Cleveland. Even though we don't play Cleveland, we still do Cleveland somewhere in the organization. As it narrows down, then we start to look to the teams that potentially we could face. Again, we're not into the NFC for two games, so our first focus is the AFC and then at some point in that process as we already have gotten Jacksonville after they got to the AFC Championship Game, we got to the AFC Championship Game, then we started to turn to the two NFC teams. That's kind of progressional.

Q: What sort of things can you do at practice to prepare for the Jaguars physical defensive backs?

BB: You know, we do the best we can every week to prepare for the team that we're playing and the schemes that they play, the style that they play, the type of players that they have. We have players that try to simulate their style of play, whatever position that is. So, that's what we do every week at every position, not limited to one particular guy or one particular position. It's across the board. It's all 11 players on every play, whether it's their punt return team, their offense or their short-yardage defense or whatever it is. We try to do that every week. That's part of the preparation.

Q: How much discipline does it take from a defense to be prepared for what Tyrod Taylor can do as a runner?

BB: A lot. Yeah, a lot. We want to try to keep him out of those situations as much as possible. We don't want him extending the play. He's a lot better at extending the plays than we are. Inevitably, those are going to come up and we're going to have to defend them. The more that we can limit those loose plays, extended plays, I think the better off we'll be. I don't think you can eliminate them completely, but we certainly aren't looking to get into those situations. Go back, let him run around, let him extend the play and see if we can defend it. We're certainly not trying to do that and no team has been very successful with that with him. He's very good. If you don't let him run laterally and throw the ball, he can run up the middle and run the ball and he's hard to tackle. Tampa was a good example of that. It's a tough problem. There have been teams that have - I'll ask the questions before you guys ask it - 'Why don't we just put a mirror on him?' Oh yeah, great, that's fine. You've still got to tackle him and that's an issue. Plenty of teams have put a spy on him and then he beats the spy and there's nobody left, and so it's 20, 30 yards. To just throw a spy on him, that's not really the answer. You've got to do it right and he's got to be able to get him and he's got to get him.

Q: How much can the Steelers take advantage of putting you in a hole on early downs so it is tougher to put together a successful drive?

BB: Yeah, huge, and well that's what they do. They have a lot of pressure schemes and if they get you on a negative play and get you in long yardage then they're very good on third-and-long. One of the best defenses in the league on the longer yardage situations and offensively they have very few negative plays in the running game. They're one of the top teams in the league on that. They don't take a lot of sacks, they don't have a lot of negative runs so the ball's moving forward. It's first-down, either they get a first-down on first-down, which they do that a lot, or its second and they're not in a real bad situation. And then third-down they're not in a real bad situation there either. You get the first-and-10, second-and-13, now what do you do? Now its third-and-long and third-and-long in this league is a 20-percent conversion, maybe less. You start getting in third-and-10-plus, nobody's picking up many of those. That's just not where you want to be. Penalties, negative plays, sacks, negative runs, I mean those are drive stoppers.

Q: Is that even a bigger problem on the road?

BB: Well, I mean look, Pittsburgh's good regardless. But yeah, sure it's tougher there.

Q: Does their success over the past provide a better measuring stick for you when you play them in the regular season?

BB: I mean look, wherever the schedule is we actually have to play it. So this week we're in Heinz Field playing Pittsburgh. That's where we're going to be. It's a great team. It's a great challenge and we're going to do our best to be ready for it. But whoever's there then that's the one we've got to meet that week. That's where we are this week. I have tremendous respect for the Steelers, their program, their coaching staff, their players, the way they play, the way they compete, so hopefully we can match that and be competitive on Sunday but that'll be a huge challenge.

Q: What are some of the factors that have gone into the lack of turnovers forced by the defense this season and how important is it to turn that around Saturday?

BB: Just got to keep working to get the ball out. Sometimes you get opportunities and sometimes you don't. Sometimes you have to create your own and you always try to create as many of them as you can. You want to take advantage of the offense's mistakes if they make them. Sometimes you're fortunate and you get those plays, sometimes you're not. It's a combination of those two things. We've just got to keep working hard to get the ball out and take care of it.

Q: Is there a fine line between trying to create turnovers and sticking to the fundamentals of the defense?

BB: I don't think there's a fine line at all. I think you're coached to do things a certain way and you do them that way – no different than tackling, blocking, tackling, pulling the ball out, playing the ball. There are fundamental ways that you teach your players to do that and that's what you want them to do. It's pretty clear cut to me.

Q: Is there one specific part of your preparation for Jacksonville that keeps you up at night and concern you going into the game?

BB: Yeah, it's all of it. I don't know what the play is going to be. I don't know what the situation is going to be, so we have to be ready for all of them. We've seen a lot of situations come up in the last couple weekends that were one play, one situation type things that determine the outcome of the season for the teams involved. So, you tell me what those plays are and we'll make sure we work on those, but there's really no way of knowing. So, you have to be ready for all of them.

Q: How much does Jacksonville move their defensive linemen around to isolate specific matchups, like moving a guy inside on certain plays?

BB: Well, I mean, their base defense is an over-under defense. So, if they're over, then they're over the tight end. If you put the tight end on the right, then they're over to the right. If you put the tight end to the left, then they're over to the left. If they play an under defense, then if you put the tight end to the right, then they're under to the left. If you put the tight end to the left, they're under to the right. So, they flip-flop their defensive line, so depending on where you line up and depending on what they have called, then they're going to line up based on that.

So, they're either going to be on the right if they're in over or they're going to be on the left if they're in under if you're in right formation and vice versa. So, you tell me where the tight end is, you tell me what their call - over or under - and then you'll know where they're going to line up. Before that happens, then you don't really know. But, I mean, you know that's what it's going to be. Third down is a little bit different. They have some third-down variations.

Campbell is more of an inside rusher on third down when Fowler comes in the game, so that is what it is. But, on their base defense, they're an over-under defense that flips sides based on your tight end location and their call. So, I don't know if that answers your question of not, but I mean, yeah, they're going to flip their defensive ends on every play. If they stay in the same defense and you flip your tight end, then they're going to flip.

Q: What are some of the nuances for a young player when it comes to preparing for an opponent the second time around in one season?

BB: I think learning from what happened in the first matchup, things that if, I'm a player, things that I had trouble with that they would try to do against me, and things that worked well for me that either I want to try and do more of or have a counter or complement to go with those thinking that they might try to take that away, then what would my adjustment to that be. So, yeah, it's definitely different. All of the college players talk about that. You don't see the guy until the following year and this is different where you see him within a few weeks, or in this case a couple of months but, still, it's the same season and it's a rematch of the same matchup. Now there's always things that are different, which there are this year on their offensive line. There's some moving parts there that are different from what it was in our first game. We have some differences. It's not the same, but there's certainly carryover.

Q: After an emotional win like last Sunday, a team sometimes needs to refill the tank in order to play their best following such a big win. Where does that characteristic rank in importance among some of the great teams that you've coached and had success with over the years?

BB: Yeah, well, each team has its own chemistry and its own personality that the players on that team form every year. Really, every game is different. There's constant change in the emotions and in the makeup of the team. We'll see how we respond each week with this team. I know that the other teams were what they were. Some were great, some weren't quite as good. But, this team will write their own story and none of us know how it'll come out. We'll see, but it's one of the weekly challenges that we face, one of the many challenges and it's certainly present this week.

Q: How do you feel that this particular team has done turning the page on a weekly basis?

BB: Some weeks better than others. I don't think it's perfect. It's certainly not all bad, but really it doesn't matter. This week is about this week, so we'll have to do a great job this week against a good Buffalo team that's in the postseason picture, has had two big wins the last two weeks. Really, pretty much controlled the Miami game. Certainly something we couldn't come close to doing. As I said, we know that'll be a big challenge for us.

Q: How much of a factor in the passing game on Sunday is Tom Brady being at practice versus not being at practice some weeks?

BB: Well, it's always good to have everybody practice to get their preparation and to get it with their teammates. So that's how you build team execution is from team practice. The more of that we can do the better. It's not always possible. We do the best we can. Every team in the league deals with the same thing. It's not a unique problem here or anywhere eels, so we just do the best that we can with it.

Q: How difficult is it to identify a tip that could help you be ready for gadget plays?

BB: Right. Look, you could draw up any gadget play you want. In the end it comes down to the basic fundamentals of your defense, so every defense is designed to defend the perimeter, to defend the deep balls, whether that's man to man, or zone, or four-man line, three-man line, whatever it is. It doesn't matter. You can't defend an offensive formation without defending the perimeter of the formation, without defending the vertical element that the formation could bring, defend the outside, defend deep, everything is in front of you - every defense has to have those elements to it. Who knows what you're going to be in? Who knows what play that they're going to run that you haven't seen before? You just have to count on the sound fundamentals of the defense to handle all of those things. Every time we put in a defense that's the first thing we do, is run strong, run weak, reverse, half back pass, passing game, four verticals, three verticals, double moves, deep crossing routes. Make sure that those plays are handled by the assignments in the defense. If you're going to be light on something you don't want to be light on those. You want to be light on something else. You don't want to be light on a seam route or on a post pattern or not have a run-force guy if they run a reverse. I mean it doesn't mean you have it done right every single time, but there's somebody that's responsible for it and it's their job to make sure that they handle that responsibility based on however the play is designed.

Q: Will you relax at all this weekend with their being no game or do you just keep preparing as best you can despite not knowing your opponent?

BB: I mean we're in the home stretch right here. I don't think this is the time for the coaches to back off, or anybody for that matter. This is what it's all about. This is the highest level of competition that you can have. It's the best teams. We're going to have to play and coach our best, and we don't know who it is so there are right now three teams that we could potentially play that we have to be ready for. Regardless of who we play, there are things that we need to do but then we also need to know as much as we can and be prepared for the players when they come back in to give them the best information and the best scouting report and the best game plan we can to give them the best chance to win. That job isn't done yet. We've still got a lot of work to do.

Q: How important is it for the scout team quarterback to approach practice with a competitive mindset in terms of helping the defense get ready for your opponent?

BB: Yeah, I mean that's an important part of that person's job. That extends to all of the other people who are doing the same thing. So the player who's playing [Jarvis] Landry, the player who's playing [Kenny] Stills, the player who's playing [DeVante] Parker, the player who's playing [Dion] Sims, [Jay] Ajayi, right down the line, all of them, the guy that's playing [Branden] Albert, [Laremy] Tunsil, all of them. The same thing on defense - [Tony] Lippett, [Michael] Thomas, and [Xavien] Howard and so forth. We spend time talking to those players about how that individual plays or maybe how they play a particular play like 'On this coverage here is what they're going to do. Here is how they're going to handle a vertical route, handle a cross route, handle a whatever it is,' and try to get the best look we can at those plays.

That certainly helps our players prepare the best they can to see what they're going to see in the game during the week as opposed to seeing something else that's a facsimile but not really what it's going to be. It doesn't help the timing. So I think our players do a really good job of that. They understand how important it is for the people who are showing them what they need to see, and then they know it's incumbent on them to return that same look. And our practice squad players, that's probably their main role, which is a very important role that we recognize every week and they take that very seriously and professionally. That's their role, is to get somebody else ready. Someday that'll change, or might change like it does for a lot of our practice squad players where they're the one that's getting ready and somebody else is doing it for them.

Q: You went into last night with only really three full-time receivers active on the roster. Have you been in a situation like that before with numbers that low and can that affect your game plan at all?

BB: Well again, I think that's pretty common in the National Football League every week, that there will be a position somewhere along the line that you don't have the type of depth that you'd like to have for that game or within that game. You have to have alternative ways to - well you have to find a way to deal with it - how you're going to back it up or use a different grouping or whatever it happens to be. It happened on defense last night when we had two players at corner who were out for a period of time and you have to make those adjustments. Fortunately they came back, like Chris [Hogan] did. When you have a 46-man roster you're going to have to deal with it somewhere. So wherever it is then you find a way to deal with it. Is it challenging? I mean, I don't know. It's like that every week at some position, or positions I should say, and then it can happen during the game, too.

Training Camp

Q: Why is training camp so important?

BB: OK, this is just our grinding through camp period now. We need to keep stringing together good practices, good days, consistent improvement and there's really no shortcut to it. This is where we build our fundamentals, where our team comes together from a chemistry standpoint, also from a communications standpoint and there's just no shortcut to it. We just have to grind away here day after day. So, that's where we're at today. That's where we'll be tomorrow. That's where we'll be out here for a while.

Q: Even though you have been coaching a while, how much do you still enjoy starting over from scratch at this time of year?

BB: We've put a lot into the offseason program, put a lot into the spring. I think we're at a point now where we're ready to move into the next phase of it, and then there will be a later point in time we'll move into another phase of it. So, this is where we are. We'll hopefully make the most of the opportunities that we have going forward to put our team in the most competitive position. We have a lot of decisions to make and a lot of those will be made for us by the performance of the players and the team and so forth, but we'll still be involved in that. So, it's that phase of it, but yeah, it's part of the team-building phase. It's good to get going.

Q: When there's a fight at practice, the rule is that those guys involved are asked to leave. Is there anything positive that you can take from that sort of instance in terms of the competitiveness or intensity the players are showing?

BB: Well, I don't know what the rules are. I just try to coach the team the best I can.

Q: I was just referring to your rules.

BB: I don't know what rule that is. I do what I think is right in all situations, so that's what I do.

Q: What typically happens if there is a fight between players at training camp?

BB: I do what I think's best.

Q: What can you say about staff communication during a training camp?

BB: I don't think it's an issue. It's fine. It's easy now, there's no pressure. The tough part is when you have four or five seconds to make a decision on the field and the clock's running, play clock's running. You have to make a substitution, you have to make a call, you have to make a coaching decision, strategy decision, whatever it happens to be. That's where the rubber meets the road. Anybody can sit around a meeting and talk about it and probably come up with the right thing or justify what the right thing is, but it's making decisions on the run. That's why those blue/white-type [scrimmage] practices are just as good for the coaches as they are for the players. We have to make quick decisions, we aren't sitting there.

We don't know what the play is. We don't know what the defense is. It's not like you're looking at a script and you call a play offensively and you know what the coverage is going to be so you can kind of tell whether the players are doing the right thing or not. It's more of a game situation, it's on the fly. You don't know what the defense is in, so did the player make the right decision based on, whatever, the leverage of the defender? Did the defense make the proper reaction based on the pattern? You have to see all that and you have to recognize it, so when we switch sides and the other offense comes on, the other offense comes on. Then we talk about those things on the sidelines and try to correct them. That's what we do as coaches. It's good practice for us. It's something we haven't done in several months. We can, again, sit there and watch film in the offseason, but that's not the same as making in-game adjustments, seeing things happen quickly and having to react and coach them quickly.

Q: Is the idea then to get everybody working with everybody at some point over the course of camp?

BB: Yeah, definitely. Now, you know, again, there are some players – everybody can work with everybody, that's not a problem – I'd say the knowledge base, the overall level of execution of certain things is higher in one group than it is in another group. We have some players with less experience spending more times on the basics and the fundamentals, Not that they don't practice some of the little more sophisticated things, but that's not the point of emphasis for them. It's for them to work on their fundamentals and more of the basics first. But it's a balance, it's a tough thing in camp that you've got to balance, and at some point you've got to turn the corner and get your players that are going to be ready to play, whoever those are, ready to play. We're not there yet, but there comes a point in camp where you have to turn that corner.

Q: What are some of the unique challenges to preparing your team for Week 1 due to the uncertainty level? Are you ever 100 percent sure of what kind of team you have?

BB: No, I don't think you really know your team until the middle of October, especially now with limited training camp. It's different than what it was when I was with the Giants; 50 preseason practices and, you know, you had a lot better idea, but it is what it is. Every team has the same opportunities. I think you'll see a lot of movement, a lot of adjustments in the first third of the season like we've seen historically here in the last few years. So, there is uncertainty on your team and then there is uncertainty in the team that you're playing against, in this case Arizona. We've got – whatever it was – 18 games from last year. Obviously, they can't do everything that they did in those games but you've got to be aware of it. There are things that they did in the regular season and post season that they felt good enough about doing them in those situations. We've got to respect them; different combinations of personnel and so forth. There is no way they could run the 1,200 plays on either side of the ball that we have on them from last year – 1,100, whatever it is – so there is a lot to get ready for on their end, and then as you said the uncertainty with every new team at the start of the season in the first, I don't know, four, five, six, whatever games. That's normal.

Q: What do you learn about each individual's mental toughness as they progress through this?

BB: Well, I think everybody…it's something that's necessary for all of us – players, coaches. You just have to be able to grind through it because that's the way it's going to be during the season. Look, we've all done it before. Players have all, this isn't the first time they've ever played or been through a training camp. Just the process that I think is necessary to get you ready for the long haul. Each of us has to find a way to do it, be productive and again continue to improve and get better at what we're doing. That's our goal every day. We talk about that. We set different targets. There are different emphasis points, things that we work on. Eventually here toward the end of the week we'll start pulling more things together, more game type situations. Right now, a lot of things are a little bit segmented – third down, red area, short yardage, special teams phases and so forth. Then we shuffle those around from day to day but at some option down the road then it all comes together. But it's just, we've all got to do it. It's not any one person or one experience level of guy or anything else. It's all of us connected with the team.

Q: For guys like James Develin and Ryan Wendell to make an impression they needed an opportunity. Devin McCourty said that this was a good place to play to make an impression because you'll get a chance. Have you always structured your practices to give everybody in camp as many reps as possible? Is there a coach or experience that shaped that philosophy?

BB: Yeah, I think so. I think the key to it is not so much how people get here but what they do when they're here, whether that's a draft choice or a trade or a free agent or whatever it is. We've had successful and unsuccessful examples in all those different categories. The past isn't necessarily a predictor to the future. The future is now. Some guys have good years and then some guys have not so good years and that may fluctuate from year to year. I don't think there's any way to really predict that until you see it.

Our philosophy has always been to put them out there, let them compete and we can't control how the competition is going to go, nor do we want to, but the best players are going to get more opportunity than the ones that don't perform as well. That doesn't mean those guys are out of it but until their performance changes, then the guys that are ahead of them are going to get more opportunity. We've had a number of examples of guys that weren't drafted or guys that weren't on the radar come in and play football for us and make big contributions – the Steve Neals of the world. We've had guys line up in some of our biggest games that were either long shots or not even on the roster but ended up playing in championship games, making plays for us in championship games, things like that. You know, it's an open, competitive situation. It's not as much about what you've done as it is what you can do for this team this year. That's kind of our philosophy.

Q: When the weather is hot during camp how do you balance between pushing guys too hard but also getting their conditioning ready for the season?

BB: Well, that's what our medical and nutrition staff is for. We try to do a good job of educating the players and also making sure the players are prepared for practice, and then at the end of practice that they recover, which there are various tools that we employ for that. But I think as a team we spend a lot of time educating them on all of the things that they need to do. Whatever the conditions are, that's part of it, but then there's just a general high performance, recovery, rest, high performance, recovery, you know, that's training camp, that's football season. Part of that we do as just the normal procedure and then whatever the conditions are that may require a little specific adaptation. For example, full hydration in conditions like this then we try to make sure they're educated on that. We also make sure we give them an opportunity to do it.

Q: You've often embraced inclement weather because ultimately it is out of your control. Is that something you developed from coaches that you've worked under previously in your career?

BB: We didn't have much choice. In Detroit we had a dome, but Denver, Baltimore, the Giants; those had no options. I guess there are options now, but football is football to me.

Q: With the officials here for the next few days, would you ever go to them and ask about the legalities of certain formations?

BB: I think that's what the whole point of being with the officials is, is to understand their interpretation of the rules. And any questions we have about what we're doing, we ask them to watch what we're doing and tell us what we need to do to make it legal or make sure that we're doing something properly and at the same time we know what we have to defend. We've seen this team do this or we've seen other teams do this. We want to make sure we've got this right what we're telling our players – whatever it happens to be.

I think the communication between the officials and the teams at this time of year is good. It's beneficial for everybody. It's good for them to see us. It's good for us to see and talk to them. It's good to kind of have the communication and get on the same page as to how various rules are going to be interpreted or called, or kind of what the key thing they're looking for in making the call. All of that is helpful. I think [NFL VP of Officiating] Dean Blandino has done a good job of trying to have a good line of communication between the coaches, the teams and the individual officials or the officiating department. That just helps all of us understand better what we can do, what we can't do and how to make sure that we all understand the rules that we're playing under and the way they're interpreted and how the game is going to be called.

Q: It's different now because you don't get your free agents and rookies in pads in the spring so does that must add importance to training camp for rookie free agents and guys coming in to evaluate them?

BB: I think that's pretty much the way it's always been. I can't remember being able to pad up in spring practices. But certainly with the limited number of practices we have now, relative to, I think as I said when I was with the Giants in the '80s, we were in the 50's, number of practices before the first game. Now we're at half that, maybe a little less. If a player with no experience isn't able to participate and misses two weeks – five, six, eight, ten practices, whatever it is – that's like missing half of training camp and it's a lot of ground to make up. There's definitely a premium for durability.

There's definitely a premium for taking advantage of the opportunity by being out there. As we all know and we talk to the players all the time – they understand it better than anybody – you can't get better if you're not on the field. How can you improve really by standing there and watching? You can learn and you can hear it but you're not doing it. As a football player, you need to do it and you need to do it with your teammates. That's an important element to it. At the same time, you can't let – as a coach, sometimes you can't let one week of the frustration of not being able to see a player affect the year or even a career. You still have to do what's best for your team, try to make the right decisions. A lot of time it's on partial information and of course the less information you have, probably the more chance you'll make a mistake. But sometimes there's a guesstimate that definitely goes with that. You have to live with those decisions. It's based on partial information but you have to make them one way or the other.

Q: How important is it to have the rookies under contract before you get going as opposed to holding out?

BB: The sooner they're out there, the more chance they have to understand what they're doing and help us. All the rookies are faced a little bit with the same battle, learning a new system and in some cases gaining their confidence in the techniques that they have to do against the people they have to them against, and there's no substitute for gaining that confidence other than doing it.

Q: Could you talk in general terms, the position coaches obviously make recommendations to you, can you talk about the process, whether you stepped in and how it worked and how much debate went on between you and the coaches?

BB: I would say for the most part, of the players that we released they all had certain strengths that they brought to the table, but for the most part there wasn't a whole lot of discussion. You understand what one player can do, you understand what another player can do and it is pretty clear that one player is more valuable to you than another. There were a handful of cases where it really was a tough decision, not that they all weren't tough, but tougher in that it really looked like a pretty even match, one guy brought one thing one guy brought another thing and we need both. That's where it came to more of a trade off. If you get special teams from one player then maybe you get a little more defense from somebody else or vice versa. I think in the end it all fell together about the way everybody thought.

Q: How long did it take for the meeting, for you to sit with the assistants and decide who would be cut?

BB: We had several meetings. We have met every day for the last four days. You kind of do it the first time and rough it out. People throw out their opinions and you talk about it and then you come back and do it the next time and it starts to become a little bit clearer. Then you do it the next to last time and say, 'Okay this is it, we are going to sleep on it, we are going to digest it overnight, but for the next to last time right here does anybody have some final thoughts?' There may be one or two, but at that point everything is pretty well in focus you just want one more day to digest and to feel like this is really the right thing to do. Then we came in this morning and for the last time went through it again and just reviewed it, 'This is what we are going to do, this is where we see this player, this is where we see that player'. I think everybody walked away from there thinking that is where we are going to go. Everybody has their input and I think it was a collective decision.

Q: In general terms, do some players make the team because of the last game or did you and the staff change your opinion much based on what happened in the last game?

BB: I think it is a combination. You try to weigh in a players' total performance. I don't think you can evaluate just one play or even one game. Sometimes that is all you have, but the players that have been here a little bit longer you go on the total performance. What the player does with the opportunity that he has and some players have more opportunities than others in a preseason game. We can't totally control that.

How they look at practice against competition that we know the level the competition is at. We know who is playing against each other and how they perform off the field and also their rate of improvement. If it looks like a guy is really gaining ground, whatever two players performance, they may be equal one guy looks like he is really gaining ground the other guy looks like he is kind of leveling off and that is kind of what I have been talking about, seeing the player a month from now or trying to see him a year from now. 'Okay it is nip and tuck right now where are we going to be in November?' And you try to project that and it is not an exact science and I'm sure we will be wrong here somewhere, but right now we have just got to go with the information that we've got and do the best that we can and I feel that is what we have done and time will tell.

Q: I guess there's also situational benefit to first down on the five. It's preseason and you get situational work that might not come up again in the preseason. I thought maybe you figured you'd benefit either way with the situational work.

BB: Right, well – I think just what we've talked about as a staff is that it's preseason for us too, so we kind of want to get into the process of getting ourselves ready for these type of game situations where 'Do you challenge? Don't you challenge?' And we haven't done that in six-plus months or however long it's been, so now that's something that we have to get back and sharpen up on – all the things that have always been in place, you know, getting a good look at it, which plays to challenge, which ones not, how important is the play? Does that override how good of a look you have on it? We've talked a little bit about those things, again just for our – to be familiar with it as a coaching staff.

We've looked at some plays just kind of 'Would we challenge this?' or 'Would we challenge that one?' Just kind of 'Would we, wouldn't we' kind of thing to just kind of get our mind thinking about it because we haven't done it in a while. But that was actually a good situation that came up on our end as well, just from a staff standpoint. But without a good look at that play, I think it would be a hard one to challenge and we just didn't see the TV shot, which I still haven't seen, so I don't know if that would have shown enough or not, but certainly what we saw live wasn't enough. But I'd say again, even after looking at it this morning on the coaches tape, it's pretty close and both officials come in there pretty quickly and ruled it incomplete. There wasn't a lot of hesitation from either guy, so I don't know. But maybe the TV shows it differently, I'm not sure.

Q: In your experience, does looking good this time of year translate to looking good in September, or is that not always the case?

BB: Well, just on the practice schedule to get started, what we're mainly doing out there is working on the running game and some play action passes in the morning. Now yesterday afternoon was really a morning practice. What our normal schedule is, we saw it there this morning is the running game, play action passes, a little bit of one-on-one pass protection and the players in full pads. And then this afternoon, a little more emphasis on the passing game, we'll just be in shorts; shoulder pads and shorts. There will probably be a little bit less contact, so expect a little bit more contact in the morning, a little bit less in the afternoon. I think relative to last year, we've shortened practices up a little bit, you've probably noticed that, we're back in here sooner. But I think the intensity level and the tempo are a little bit better, at least that's what we're looking for. We've had two pretty good days, two good tempo days and we'd like to be able to stay at a good consistent level there. Hopefully we can do that.

It's a teaching camp. The most important thing for us is to get the information taught so the players have a chance to go out and execute it competitively in training camp.

Q: How much have you learned about rest and monitoring the number of reps for players starting at this time of the year?

BB: I mean, I don't know. I mean, we have 90 players. They're all in different situations. Some guys were here last year. Some guys weren't. Some guys played more than others. They're different ages, different levels of experience, so it's a little different for everybody.

Q: Have you been pleased with how the first-year players have picked up the system in a short amount of time?

BB: Yeah, this group has worked hard, similar to last year's group. Yep, they've been good. They've worked hard. They're trying. They've got a long way to go, but they're getting better every day and they're making progress. But they've got a long way to go, so we'll see. Just keep trudging along.

Q: How much of a balancing act is it to make sure you get enough reps for each guy in these final preseason games before cutting the roster size down?

BB: Well, the whole thing is really a balancing act between getting your team ready and evaluating players. Of course it's always good when you can evaluate – especially by this third preseason game, fourth preseason game – evaluate players against known players. It's one thing to play them in the fourth quarter against other players who don't really have much of a track record in the NFL, whereas if you put them in at other points of the game you'd be able to see them against a guy that you have a lot better idea of what their skills are and how a young player would matchup on that. But you have to get your team ready, so there's definitely a balance between that. We're just not looking at people; we're trying to get ready to play football.

Q: How much of a piece of the pie is looking at players outside of the organization?

BB: Well, there is a lot of player movement at this time of year. We all know that. There is going to be a ton, more than any other time during the calendar year, from Tuesday to Sunday, so within that five, six, seven day period and the days surrounding it I'm sure there will be a lot of activity. Let's call it in that 10-day period, that'll probably be 90 percent of the transactions the entire year other than the draft. So yeah, it is busy. We talk about it on a regular basis, try to keep up with it. Between the preseason game, this game, the Giants game, the Arizona game, even the Miami game – that's a new staff – roster decisions, other team's personnel, conversations, however you want to characterize that, the wheel is spinning pretty fast this time of year for the coaching staff and for the personnel department. It's just that time of year.

Q: How will having thousands at fans at training camp affect the overall energy of the team?

BB: We've had them out there before. Training camp is training camp. There will be a lot of people in the stands, there will be a lot of people watching on TV, there will be a lot of people at training camp. In the end, we all have a job to do. We all have something that we'll need to accomplish, whether it's in practice or during a game. Whatever our role happens to be, we'll have to go out there and do it for us to get better. That's the only way we can improve is to go out there and do our job and get better at it. I'm sure we'll have a lot of people telling us how we're doing, but that's the way it always is.

Q: Would you say that the foundation for a well-conditioned team begins in training camp?

BB: No.

Q: When does it begin?

BB: In the offseason.

Q: Typically how far into training camp do you get a feel for what kind of team you're going to have that season?

BB: Yeah, I don't know. Just keep grinding it out day-by-day and do the best we can every day. That's really the way I approach it.

Q: There were lines of fans waiting to enter training camp this morning. Do you ever stop and think about how this has become much bigger than it was when you started coaching?

BB: You know, when I was in Denver, we were up at Colorado State, Fort Collins. We used to have 10,000 fans at practice. You know, it varies from team to team. We were down in Atlanta, and [when] you were down there, it's different. So, yeah, it's a good experience for the fans. You know, you get to see the team under different conditions than game conditions, which is where most of it is. We get great support from our fans. If they can be here, great. I'd say Giants practices, I mean it didn't hold a lot at Pace [University] or Fairleigh Dickinson [University]. But people take their week or two weeks' vacation to come and watch us practice. I mean, I don't think I would be on that list, but yeah, there was a couple house. It was all it hold. There wasn't as much space as what we have, but like I said, at Denver in Fort Collins, there was a lot of space. I mean, there had to be 10,000 people.

Q: You mentioned the exchanges between units on the field. Is that any more challenging now because you have so many bodies with 90 guys on the roster?

BB: Yeah, of course. Yeah, we have 90 guys and we have basically three groups on each side of the ball, whereas in the regular season, however many players are doing most of the playing on offense and defense - I don't know, 15, 16, 17, however many guys it is - there's a lot fewer substitutions. It's a lot cleaner. Of course, if something happens during the game to somebody, then that affects a lot more, so you don't have a backup for every spot in the game in the regular season like we kind of do here. But, yeah, it's challenging.

Q: How have you felt about the cleanliness of those exchanges thus far in camp?

BB: I'd say it's probably much like everything else in training camp. I think we're improving at everything that we're working on. You always want to go at a little bit of a faster pace, but we're a lot better than where we were. But, we still have a long way to go. We've got a lot of work to do. It's really hard to measure those things until you actually compete against another team and see where you are relative to them. Where we are is we always are looking to get better. We're always trying to improve. We always want to be as efficient as we can. How does that compare to everybody else? Who knows. We won't find that out until we start competing against them.

Q: When it comes to planning joint practices, do you submit a plan of what you want to work on and then amend it based on what the opposing team wants to work on?

BB: Well, since this is the first time we've worked with Jacksonville - I'd say, for example, New Orleans is a team we've worked together. So, in that example, last year, we could go back to things we'd done previously and [say], 'This is the way we'd laid it out. Do we want to do it this way?' But in this case, Coach Marrone and I have talked about it. What are the things that we want to try to accomplish? How many days? What do we generally want to do each day? What are the points of emphasis? And then we put together something and kind of red penciled it. How about if we do it this way or adjust it this way? And so that is, I would say, relatively easy.

There are some things that a team - you know, we have a certain practice structure, a certain way of doing certain things. It's not right or wrong, it's just the way we do them. You have another team that they're playing the same game, but maybe they do things just a little bit differently. I'd say, when those don't coincide, then as coaches, we try to find what the common ground is. Either we're going to do it your way or you're going to do it our way or we're going to maybe split the difference depending on what the issue is. And so that's, I wouldn't say challenging, but I think that's one of the things that needs to be ironed out. And I think it's usually better if everybody can do it the same way, so there are certain periods of practice at the beginning of practice where both teams do their own thing separately, and then when we come together, then there's a certain standard or conformity that we want there to be so that everybody's on the same page. It's not one way for our defense and another way for their defense or vice versa, that kind of thing.

But Jacksonville's been great to work with. Their support staff, the people that are part of the operational side of it, that's been great. Our people on our side have done a great job, as they always do, in working with the team that's coming in. We've had great cooperation when it's gone the other way. We're expecting three days of very productive work against Jacksonville. That's just, I'd say, in general how it goes. Once you have the conversation with the coach and we kind of agree to, 'Well, this is conceptually the way we want to do it,' then it's kind of dotting the i's and crossing some t's and just working it out so that we can actually get to the point that we agree on.

Q: How much ability do the quarterbacks have to change plays in intra-squad scrimmages?

BB: Well, it would depend on the play. Some plays we have that flexibility built into it because we kind of know, "Well, this is a good play against this look. If we get it, we want to run it, but if we get something else, then this isn't really a play that we want in that situation." So then we try to have some type of companion play that goes with it. Same thing on defense, "This defense is good if we get this, but if we get something else, we really need to do something else." Then there are other all-purpose plays. We have plays that we feel we're pretty competitive with against everything. It doesn't really matter what they're in that we can handle it.

Defensively, it's the same thing. It's a basic call and whatever they do, we have to be able to defend. Plays like that, we wouldn't necessarily need or want to be checking in and out of. The players know what they are, so they can go out there and run them and be aggressive. They don't have to worry about, "Is it going to be this or is it going to be that?" Other plays, again, just to run a play that you know is going to be a bad play is not really what we want to do, so those types of plays would have some type of option that would hopefully get us out of a bad play and give us a chance to run a good play.

Q: How do you as a staff teach the quarterbacks group to balance risk versus reward in practice so that they get the most out of the reps without encouraging bad habits?

BB: That's a great question, and it's a tough answer. It's a balance, but certainly I encourage the quarterbacks to take more of a risk in practice than in the game. That's when a quarterback can really develop confidence in a player; throwing it into a tight spot or having the guy make a touch catch. Can he get it into a small window? You don't want the first time that happens to be in a game and then find out and have him say, "Well I shouldn't have thrown that." If that's going to happen, let's have it happen in practice if we're going to take that kind of risk. At the same time, we don't want to go out there and throw 12 interceptions every practice either, that's not the idea. But as far as taking a risk, doing something in practice that you wouldn't do in the game, if there's a reason for doing it, which I'd say there's a lot of reasons for doing that, and we talk about those, then I'd say there's definitely a place for that. It's a way for, in the passing game particularly, to have a better understanding of what to do, and sometimes what not to do; what you can do, where the risk is worth it and where it isn't.

Those are all good teaching situations. Again, bad plays are bad plays. There's a difference between a bad play and taking a chance in practice in preparation for a similar situation coming up in the game. Would you take that risk, again, how big of a risk is it? And so forth. Those are great points that come up in practice that we teach from and the quarterbacks need to understand that it is OK to do that in practice, provided it's done in the right situations and the right circumstances. It's OK to do that as long as we learn from it and then don't make it cause a mistake in the game.

Q: What kind of things can you learn about your players when they are practicing against a different opponent?

BB: Well, we'll see. It's definitely a different scheme, different matchups, different players. We've worked against each other, we kind of know each other, so we're in a whole different environment now. We'll see what happens.

Q: Is it beneficial that you can control the situations here when you are practicing against another team as opposed to not knowing what to expect in a game situation?

BB: It's no different than our regular practice. We control our practices and so the coaching staffs have agreed to "This is what we want to do, or there are a couple of things we don't want to do." So, that's what it is.

Q: Do practice preparations differ at all when you bring in another team for joint practices?

BB: Not too much. I'd say the biggest difference would be if we were not practicing against another team, we would continue to install things next week, so we'd continue to add things to our daily routine. When you practice against another team, I think you're better off just going out there and running what you know.

So, there won't be a lot of new installation next week for Jacksonville. We'll run what we've practiced through tomorrow and try to do it that way. I'd say that'd be the biggest change. If we weren't practicing against them, then we would continue to add things next week. But, we also would have to commit time to getting ready for the game next week, so running scout teams and running Jacksonville's plays against us, whereas when you practice against the team, that is the preparation. It kind of kills two birds with one stone there.

Q: Is there something specific you look for in an opposing team when you schedule joint practices or is it just a matter of having a relationship with the head coach?

BB: Yeah, somebody you can work with, that's the number one thing. That's above all else. We have a great relationship with the Saints, with Sean [Payton] and his staff, the organization. It's always worked out well the times we've done it with them, so if we have an opportunity to do it with them we try to take advantage of it. It's been really good. They're great to work with.

Q: How much does it complicate things when one specific position group gets pretty shallow with minor injuries in training camp?

BB: Yeah, that's part of training camp and part of just practice in general is managing your team, trying to keep everybody moving along. But sometimes, as you said, if a certain group is lower in numbers, that affects what either that side of the ball can do or maybe what the other side of the ball can do against it. Occasionally, we have to make some kind of modifications.

Hopefully the train doesn't come to a complete halt and we're able to maybe do a little more of something else in order to manage the reps of a particular player or a particular group, like when Joe Cardona wasn't here at the beginning of training camp. We modified our teaching schedule a little bit there to work on a couple phases of the kicking game when he wasn't here and changed that to work on the ones where we needed a snapper. It's not an uncommon thing. We talk about that every night when we go through our practice schedule. We go through the overall where our team is, where our individual position groups are, where the individual players are and put it all together. Occasionally, we have to make a team adjustment, but usually it's more within the group of how we're going to rep the plays with the players that are there. Not an uncommon thing.

Q: Are there certain positions you can evaluate better in a scrimmage setting than in a traditional practice setting?

BB: Well, again, this is putting it all together. So, instead of doing one thing for a sustained period of time, which isn't really the way football is played, this gives us a chance to simulate the moving game - first down, second down, third down, ball moves, field position moves, the kicking unit comes on the field, other offensive or defensive unit comes out on the exchange - and that's how you play. You don't run 10 first-down plays in a row. You don't run eight third-down plays in a row or eight sub-blitzes in a row or 10 punts in a row. That's just not football, but those are good teaching methods and it's a more efficient way to do it, so there's a place for that. But, at some point, there's a place for trying to simulate a game, so that's what we're going to do.

Q: What kind of stock do you put into what you see in preseason games?

BB: Well, a lot of stock. You're able to evaluate your basic fundamentals against another team's basic fundamentals. So, it's not an X-and-O game. It's just a basic fundamental game. There's a lot to be said for that. I mean, that's the foundation of every play is good fundamentals. So, we win some, they win some, but along the way, even if you're losing on a fundamental matchup on a particular play, hopefully you're improving, you're gaining experience and you're correcting mistakes and moving forward on it for the next player and the next game, that type of thing. I think it's very important, but obviously, it takes out a lot of the scheme part of the game. But, the fundamental part of the game, in the end, is more important than the scheme part of the game. So, without good fundamentals, the scheme play is - I mean, they're no good.

Q: You mentioned having to strike a balance in joint practices given that you play the Texans in Week 3. Where does that affect practice the most?

BB: You know, Bill [O'Brien] and I have talked about it. I mean, honestly, I don't think it's that big of a deal. I mean, I think this is another event that's hyped up by a lot more of the people who are watching it than the people who are involved with it. So, I mean, look, we played this team three times in the last two years. Half their coaching staff coached here. It's not a big secret how we run a certain play or how we coach a certain defense, and I'm sure they're coaching it the same way when we played against them. That's not really what this practice is about. It's not what the middle of August is about.

It's about building your team's conditioning, building your team's fundamentals, building your team's awareness, having them learn to play together with each other against good competition. That's what we're going to do this week. We're not going to show them our triple reverse and they're not going to show their triple safety blitz and a bunch of other garbage. That's not what this is about. It wouldn't be about that with any team, but it's certainly not about that with these guys. They're a tough, sound, fundamental football team. We've seen that and we know that from their coaching staff and the way they prepare and the way they coach and the way we've competed against them. This is about us trying to get better, them trying to get better, and when we play each other in the regular season, then we'll game plan and we'll strategize and we'll do everything we can do to try to win the game. They'll do the same thing. That's not really what this week is about. Honest to God, Bill and Mike [Vrabel] probably know our calls as well as we know them, and I'm sure we know a lot of the ones that they use because they're the same ones that we use, but I don't think that really is – I mean, that's so overrated in my opinion, not in everybody else's, but in mine. I'm just trying to get our team better this week. That's what we're going to go down there and do. The rest of it, I say, is like way less than 1 percent in my mind.

Q: How important is it for some of these guys that are trying to win roster spots to be able to adapt quickly to the special teams phase of the game, even if they're not familiar with it?

BB: It is important. Again, a lot of college players don't get a lot of experience on special teams. They maybe play their freshman year, and then a lot of coaches use their freshmen and sophomores to use those roles. And then as the players that we get, who are generally the better players, play less in some of those phases in their last two or three years in college. Sometimes it's no experience, or sometimes it's experience but three or four years ago. So, a lot of players improve there in the second, third, fourth year of college, so they're not really great comparisons of what a guy did his freshman year or redshirt freshman year or something like that. But, these guys have all adapted to it. They're trying to understand the speed of the game and the way the kicking game is executed at this level, but we'll see how it goes. Jacksonville - Joe [DeCamillis] does a great job and Coach [Doug] Marrone. They do a great job with their special teams units. They have good specialists, so we'll see how it goes. That's a hard - you can evaluate it in practice, but it's a little bit different in the game. So, we'll get a good look at it Thursday night and see what it looks like then. That will be a good evaluation and a good test for us.

Q: After two weeks of joint practices and one week on the road, what's been your impression of how the team has returned to its normal routine and tried to get back to the basics?

BB: Well, it's an adjustment for all of us. It's a process we've all got to go through. We're working our way through it. That's the way it's going to be all year. We're going to practice. We're going to have to get ourselves ready for the game. We're going to basically practice and train here. It's just getting back into the routine. I'd say we've got a ways to go before we're really maximizing everything that we do, but hopefully we'll get a little closer each day, fine-tune the process. We have new players on our team - veteran players, rookie players. It's certainly an adjustment for them, but we all need to get back into it. I haven't done it in six months and neither have any of our other veteran players, so it's an adjustment for all of us.

Q: Do practice preparations differ at all when you bring in another team for joint practices?

BB: Not too much. I'd say the biggest difference would be if we were not practicing against another team, we would continue to install things next week, so we'd continue to add things to our daily routine. When you practice against another team, I think you're better off just going out there and running what you know. So, there won't be a lot of new installation next week for Jacksonville. We'll run what we've practiced through tomorrow and try to do it that way. I'd say that'd be the biggest change. If we weren't practicing against them, then we would continue to add things next week. But, we also would have to commit time to getting ready for the game next week, so running scout teams and running Jacksonville's plays against us, whereas when you practice against the team, that is the preparation. It kind of kills two birds with one stone there.

Q: How do you balance the introduction of a player versus someone who can contribute with

experience? Does that thinking change at all around the cut down days?

BB: Well, I don't know if it changes, but it certainly gets highlighted because that's the point where you have to make the decision. Up until that point, you can have both, if you will, and you can work with a couple scenarios or three or four, really, depending on how your roster is comprised and what your options are. But, as of 4 o'clock tomorrow, everybody's going to have to play their cards on the table and show their hand and decide what choices you want to make. Now, there will still be some roster movement and roster manipulation over the next few days - I'm not saying that - but, certainly, tomorrow at 4 is a key time for every team to make those choices and to try the course, most of it anyway, that they want to be on. So, really every player, at this point, that's in a roster discussion - whether it's the 53-man roster, the practice squad - they all have strong points, they all have things that they can do, they all have roles that they can fill on the team. If we could have 60 players, we'd have 60. So would every other team. But, we have to reduce to 53, and so that's what the reduction will be to and we'll try to figure out how to maximize that number and all the positions that we need to cover and the 66 on special teams and the 11 on offense and defense, not to mention all the special situation substitutions and that's what we need. That's way more spots than we have players for. There has to be a lot of doubling up and guys have to do multiple things. So, we'll just have to figure out how to get all those covered, in addition to kind of the original part of your question is: do you go with a player with more experience and a little higher performance level now versus a younger player with more upside that has the chance or you expect will pass the experienced player that you're talking about? And each one of those is different. There's no book on it. Every situation's a little bit different. You just have to do the best you can with each one.

Q: When looking at who may become available after roster cut-downs, do you look at other teams and try to evaluate who you think will be left off of their 53-man roster?

BB: Yeah, that's probably part of it; yeah. Nick [Caserio] and the personnel staff do a lot of work on that. Obviously, we're going to have eleven-hundred players, or whatever it is, released here in a few days, so there are a lot of guys to keep track of. That's what they do - they keep track of each team and different situations that different players are in. Injuries - how that affects other teams and so forth.

Q: Is that period going to be a little more chaotic this year with all of the cuts essentially coming at the same time?

BB: I mean, I don't really think so. I don't think that the players that are released between 90 and 75 are going to have a huge impact on the final rosters. Now I could be way off on that, but my sense of it is those players who - I think we can identify most of those players on every team. So whether they're released last week, or this week or whenever it is, I think that's probably about the same group of players. I don't really see that as a big obstacle, personally.

Q: When you get down to the final few roster decisions, how much, if at all, do the first few weeks of the schedule have an impact on who makes the team?

BB: Well, realistically, I'd say probably not too much. The teams in this league, we're all going to keep a 53-man roster. We're going to activate 46 players on game day, so seven players will be inactive. I mean, I can't imagine that there are too many players at 51, 52 and 53 that are a key part of the game plan. Not saying they're not important, not saying they don't have a role, but I mean, realistically, I don't think the decision between the 53rd and 55th spots are going to impact too many teams' game plans this week when you can only have 46 players active. A lot of those players are developmental players that are younger players that you know are going to be inactive for a while, depending on the health of your team, but just on their development, how quickly they can develop and either earn a spot on the active roster or be needed on the active roster due to injury, or possibly game plan or scheme if there was something that they were that integral for. I think that's what a lot of those players are is just where you want to keep your depth and where you want to try to develop players, like James White three years ago or [Tom] Brady in 2000 or whoever it is - guys that aren't going to play that may eventually, hopefully, have a much bigger role on your team. I think there are a lot of players that fall into that category at the spots you're talking about.

Q: How important is it for the guys who have received limited opportunities and are trying to make the roster to not press or feel the pressure when they do get the chance to make a lasting impression as we get closer to roster cut downs?

BB: Right. I think that's a good question. It's a fair question, but this is the National Football League and there is pressure every week. There is pressure this week. There is going to be pressure in October. There is going to be pressure in November. We're going to be under stress all year every week. We're going to be under stress out on the field every week against every opponent. Playing in the National Football League, that's what you sign up for. If you're looking for vacation weeks and weeks off where we play some Division 4 team and all of that, that doesn't happen in this league. There is stress every week. So is there stress in training camp? Yeah, there is plenty of it. There is stress on the coaching staff to get the team ready, to pick the right players.

There is stress on each player to establish his role, or to make the team or play for playing time, whatever it is. There is stress on everybody and there is stress on every team. We're not in any different situation than any other team in the league is and every player on every one of those teams is having the same thoughts that our players are having, I'm sure. One way or the other, either the guys who think they're on the team are trying to get ready to have a good year, and there are a lot of guys who aren't sure whether they're on or they're not or what their role is, and there are a lot of coaches who don't know the answer to that question either. We're trying to figure it out, so there is no right answer. At this point it's still a process. But there is pressure every week in this league. If there's too much pressure in August, it's probably going to be too much pressure in November. This is the world we live in. You tell me a week in this National Football League when there is not pressure, I don't know when that is. Every week is a tough week. Every week is a good team, good players, good coaches, work hard that have a lot of things that you've got to deal with, and if you don't deal with them then you're not going to win that week. That's the NFL.

Q: How difficult is it this time of year when trying to decide whether or not to keep a guy you may want to work with in the future but is being blocked on the depth chart while also worrying that if you cut him he could be picked up somewhere else?

BB: That's the 64,000 dollar question. That's what it is. It's been like that since the day I got into this league. From all of the personnel meetings I've ever been in it's a [matter of] a player who's more experienced [and] more ready to help the team now, versus a player that's not as ready now but at some point you think the pendulum will swing in his favor. Will you do that? Can you do that? What are the consequences of making that move? What are the consequences of not making that move? How likely, as you said, is it that you could keep both players in some capacity? That's what it's about, trying to balance now with later. We're going to field a team in November, we're going to field a team next year, we're going to field a team in 2018.

Not that we're getting too far ahead of ourselves, but we're going to be in business in those years, so we have to sort of have an eye on those moving forward and a lot of the other factors that go into that. Those are all tough decisions. They're all things that you really have to think about. It's no different than acquiring – well it's different – but it's the same thing as acquiring a player. So, if you acquire a player who are you acquiring – a young player for an older player, an older player for a younger player, help now versus help later, development versus known performance – and so forth. They're all interrelated but it really gets back to the same key points. When its close it's tough. If it's not close then it's not really a tough decision. It's a relatively easy decision, but the ones that are close, some people in the room want to have one opinion, other people have another opinion. You kind of have a split camp there and both sides' arguments are good arguments. It's kind of your perspective. Is it today or is it tomorrow? I'm sure every team in the league is having a lot of those discussions about eight, 10 players; five and five, whatever it is, four and four, but that kind of thing.

Q: How much consideration do you put into releasing a guy early who may not earn a spot on your roster so that he can try to catch on with another team?

BB: Well, I mean, I don't know. [We do] what is best for the team. If you need somebody to play then that's good for the team but it's also good for the player. Even if he's not going to make the roster it gives him an opportunity to play and the other 31 teams to see him and it gives him exposure. That's probably better than him being released and not playing and nobody sees him play. It's tough. That's a tough one. Look, to me every player that is here is competing and they're competing for us, but in reality they may be competing for a spot on another team's roster, too. Everybody is being scouted, we're scouting everybody, I'm sure everybody is scouting us. It's the player's opportunity to play and I think that's really how the players try to look at it. Veteran players encourage younger players like 'Maybe you'll be on the team, maybe you'll be on the practice squad, but if you go out there and do well then somebody else will see you.' Rob Ninkovich is a great example of that. I know he has talked to the team about that. It's just about opportunity, making the most of the opportunity. We can't control what happens but if the opportunities are available then I think that's all really any of us can ask for. I think that's what a player can ask for and once he gets it he has to do the best that he can with it. That's the way I look at it.

Q: In years past, have you seen guys that are fighting for those roster spots respond differently to this shift when you move into more of a regular season schedule?

BB: I don't know. I mean, every day's an important day for us. I don't think there's any switch that flips. There's just different stages that we go through. Hopefully we've been working hard all the time.

Q: How important is it for players on the roster bubble to get an extra look now that there is only one roster cut down?

BB: Yeah, every day's important. Every opportunity is important. Hopefully everybody's taking advantage of all of them, no matter what their situation is - you know, for roster spots, for playing time, for preparation for the season. I mean, it's all important to me.

Q: Does having only one roster cut change your approach in terms of how you will do homework on the hundreds of players that will soon be available?

BB: Well, I mean, it's not that much different than what it was before. I mean, a lot of the guys that went at the 75 cut - I mean, the better players came from 75 to 53 than from 90 to 75. I don't think it's that big of a deal.

Q: As difficult as it is to release a guy, what's the experience like to tell a guy who is fighting for a roster spot that he has made the 53-man roster?

BB: Well, the reality of it is this is the National Football League and there are plenty of guys that are going to be on rosters today, tomorrow and Week 1 that won't be on them in Week 3 or Week 4. That's the National Football League. You keep your job by earning your job on a day-to-day basis. I think that's one of the things sometimes that players, younger players especially who don't have a lot of experience in the league, can make a poor judgment on. They work hard in training camp. They make the roster, make the practice squad, or earn playing time or whatever it is, and then feel like they don't have to do as much or that they've kind of arrived at a certain point, and a few weeks later other players pass them by and their situation changes. That's not uncommon at all. I think that's hard to sustain a high level of performance in this league, so you start at the end of

July and sustain it all the way through preseason games and training camp practices and all of that, but the season hasn't started yet. Mental toughness, consistency, resiliency, dependability, being able to do it day after day after day at high level - the competition level is moving up now, not down. The players that aren't NFL players are off rosters and the guys who are on them are theoretically better than the ones who are off them. The competitive level is higher weekly in practice. It's higher in games. Some players will rise with that, that competiveness. Competition will push them up. Some of them, it doesn't work that way. If that's the case, then they're going to be replaced. If they don't know that and they make that mistake, they're going to find out the hard way. Yeah, as much as you want to say "Nice job. You made the team," they're not a permanent fixture on the team. They're here until as long as they're doing their job and they're dependable, and reliable, and consistent and improving. Once that curve starts to head the other way, I would say it probably isn't going to last too long. If they can't figure that out then they're probably going to suffer the consequences. Look, that's the NFL. That's the way it is here and really that's the way it is on every team I've been on. I imagine it that way on every team in the league. I know what you're saying - it's a good moment, but it's a castle in the sand. It could be gone very, very quickly. I hope none of our players, young players, guys who this is the first time they've been on this team, take that attitude. I think that would be a big mistake on their part. Hopefully, they won't do that.

Game Planning for the Super Bowl

Q: Can you talk about your team being a team of destiny?

BB: Well, I don't know about all that. We just try to go out there each week and prepare as well as we can and play hard. We are playing some really good football teams this time of year. We are going to be just as well prepared as we can and play as hard as we can, and things have worked out for us well a few of these past few weeks, and I think it's due to the -- you have to give the players the credit. They are the ones that have gone out there and made the plays. We'll try to make it again on Sunday.

Q: Do you reflect on the number of Super Bowls you have coached in?

BB: There will certainly be a time to reflect on that at some point. Right now, I'm really just trying to put all my energy in preparing our team as well as I possibly can for the Falcons. The Falcons are a great football team and well coached. They have a great organization with great players and are very difficult to play against. At some point I'll take a look back. It's certainly an honor to be in this game. It's a privilege to represent the AFC in this championship game and to have done it that many times. It's special this year because (Tight Ends Coach) Brian (Daboll) and (Safeties Coach) Steven (Belichick) are on this staff as well. It's special to be here, there's no question about that. In terms of numbers and other games and all of that, we'll get to that at some other point.

Q: What are some of the things you've learned over the years that you need to get done before you leave for the Super Bowl site?

BB: Well again, I think whatever point you get to, you get to. If that's - not to put a percentage on it - but 60 percent, 70 percent, I don't know. Whatever the number is, whatever you have, you have. Where you never want to be in game planning is you work on something but you don't really have it, so then what do you have? You've worked on it, you've covered it, but you don't really have it, then well you might as well go back to square one and start all over again. I think the best thing to do is wherever we are, that we're actually there, legitimately on our preparation. Not just we checked off a box, but we really don't have it. It will be important for us this week to get the things done that we're trying to get done. If we don't get all the way through what we thought we might get through, I mean that's not nearly as big of a problem as making sure that what we do cover, we actually have it right.

Q: Has that schedule of preparation evolved over the years as you get more familiar with the process leading up to the Super Bowl?

BB: Yeah, we've done it a couple of different ways. We've traveled on different days. Now it's a little different schedule down there than what it was. We've had one week Super Bowls. I think each one is a little bit different and each team is a little bit different, so what's right for this team may or may not have been right for some other team. There's not like a set grid that we just match up to. We try to do what's best for the particular situation - the team we're playing, what areas we need to emphasize maybe more in this game than possibly another game like this where just the emphasis points are different.

Q: In your past Super Bowls your offense has never scored a point in the first quarter...

BB: Thanks. Yeah, all of the negative stuff in the Super Bowls we need to be aware of, too.

Q: How much do you look at that history this week and try to emphasize it to the team?

BB: Look, we try to score in every game. I know that's probably hard to understand, but we try to go out and score and keep the other team from scoring. That's our goal every game.

Q: What is it about these players on this team that allows them to make big plays at the opportune moments? How do you go about finding that out about these guys?

BB: I don't know. I mean, every game is different. Every situation is different. What we had to do this week, what we had to do some other weeks are probably not quite the same thing. It's everybody being prepared, everybody knowing what to do and when the time comes to be able to need to come through, have to come through. That's what makes a good football team. That's what a team is – everybody pulling their weight, everybody doing their job. When your number comes up, stepping out there and doing what's right for the team, making the plays that the team needs you to make.

Q: How do you prepare for unusual plays in the game?

BB: Those kind of plays come up sometimes once in a career. They are very unusual. First of all, you have to explain the situation so that everyone understands it. In some places, as a coaching staff, we may need further explanation from (Vice President of Officiating) Dean Blandino about particular nuances or that type of thing that could come up. In the end, you try and cover your bases on those. The closest that it really came for us at the Patriots was against Miami in 2002. At the end of the game, we had them backed up and there were just a few seconds to go in the game. They punted but we couldn't make the catch. If we caught the ball, we would've had a free kick opportunity with Adam (Vinatieri). It was a kick that was into the wind and we just couldn't quite get to it. It hit the ground but it would've been a free kick situation. Things like that are unusual. We saw a couple plays this year that were not the norm. For example, the San Francisco play against New Orleans at the end of the half. Things like that that you don't see or haven't seen in a long time. You have to refresh yourself and then remind the players and coaches as well. We do that on a regular basis. We go over situations weekly. A lot of those happen in other games. Sometimes that situation doesn't even lineup with something that happens in our game but it makes you think about things and other adjustments or plays. Some of the situations, if you just add or subtract a second from the situation or add or subtract a few yards and put a timeout into that equation, with or without it, you get a pretty dramatic shift on what the strategy would be, the type of play you would want or wouldn't want. It doesn't take much to tweak some of those situations to really change your thinking. That's where our communication, specifically between the signal callers comes in. That's Tom on offense or (LB) Don'ta (Hightower) and (S) Devin (McCourty) on defense. To know what we want in that situation is critical. It's an ongoing and moving target. It's not so much even the play, it's just knowing how to play the situation. Every team has a different play.

Q: Are you holding on to gadget plays, like the flea-flicker, to use in the playoffs because they haven't been seen yet? How do you decipher when to use a play like that and when not to? For example, like when Mike Vrabel caught a touchdown pass in 2003.

BB: Right, well I mean in Mike [Vrabel's] case, he was part of our goal line offense that was a standard formation. It was a standard play. We ran the ball just as much as we threw it and I mean, the play we threw to him was just a crossing pattern. I wouldn't call it a gadget play at all. Other plays, I mean again, I don't want to get into a whole game planning thing here, but regardless of whether the play is a gadget play or not a gadget play, I don't even know a gadget play is. I mean, is the reverse a gadget play? Every team in the league runs them, so is that? I don't know. Where do you want to draw the line? We've all seen the flea-flicker that we ran. We've all seen that before, too. So it's not like nobody had ever seen that play run. Again, where do you draw the line? For us defensively, all of those plays fall into a certain category and there is a certain responsibility that has to be handled in order to stop the play. Offensively you run plays that you think will work, whether it's what you would consider a gadget play or whether it's what you consider the most basic play in football.

If it's a good play, it's one you want to run. So when do we run them, how do we run them? I mean, the answer is really the same for every play in situations against looks that we think they'll be successful against. I know it's hard to imagine but we don't really want to call a bad play. That's not the idea. When that happens, then either we've put the players in a situation where they can't be successful because of the look or the defense or the play or whatever is was, just matches up poorly against what we had called, or we don't execute it properly and there's a breakdown somewhere and that's what happens. But we don't have intentionally any of those - that's not what we're trying to do. We're trying to have good plays.

Q: You must work on plays like the flea-flicker throughout the course of the whole season but how do you know when it is the right time to use something like that? Is there a specific answer to when to determine using something like that?

BB: No, not really. I mean the time is whenever you think that time is, and that can change from obviously week to week, or by your personnel depending on what the play is and so forth. I mean look, it's not the kind of play you can run three or four times a game, so you know, you pick your spots on it. Part of those plays are the timing of when they're called. Any play can be a bad play if it's called at the wrong time, and a lot of plays can be good plays if they're called at the right time, so some of it is timing. Obviously a lot of it is execution, which had some difficult ball handling there and timing and getting a certain sell to the defense, and then being able to take advantage of that and so forth. It's not an easy play to execute but it was very well done. That's an important key to it. Again, drawing a play up on paper is one thing. Being able to go out and execute it at a high level against a good defense is a whole other story, too.

Q: How do you monitor a player's energy during such an important game?

BB: That's a very challenging situation because there is so much leading up to the game. It's such a long game between pregame, the start of the game, halftime, TV timeouts and so forth. It just extends longer than what it normally does including the pregame part of it. We just try and pace ourselves through that. Some of that is nutrition, hydration and things like that. Part of it is an understanding of what it's going to be like so you don't get surprised and get into the middle of the game or the middle of the third quarter. That's kind of when the game would be ending but there's still another 20 minutes to play or so. I think understanding that and making sure that the pace of the game for each individual, which is different, for an offensive line or defensive line, the pace is a little different than receivers or defensive backs that are running 30, 40, 50 yards to cover. It's the difference between boxing and distance running.

Then, you have a lot of guys in between. It's definitely challenging but it's the same for both teams. It's the same environment. Everyone needs to try and maximize all those things I just talked about. Their rest, attentiveness and pace so they don't burn out too soon. It's a challenge. This game is unlike any other that way.

Q: How did you game plan for the Atlanta Falcons in the Super Bowl?

BB: I'd say it's more than in our head or certainly my head. My memory isn't all that good now. I think you go back and look at other games. We critique each game. At the end of each game, we talk about the things ourselves. What we did well, what we didn't do well, what we could've done differently. If we were playing this team again, all the things that might have happened in the game that were noteworthy and so forth. You reflect back on a game like that. Whether it's against the same team you were playing, the same coordinator or a team with a similar playing style. Sure, we look at those notes and sometimes it pops right back to you. Sometimes, maybe you need to go look at it, examine it a little more carefully and see what you did and didn't do. How it matched up against that particular scheme. The players are probably going to be different but from a scheme standpoint, what you were telling about a read or what you were telling a guy to key and that type of thing.

How doable that was and how effective that was or wasn't. You go back through your notes on those things. You go back and look at them and say that that was a good idea. Sometimes you look at it and say that it was good for them but this was different or a different situation and we don't want to do that. Somewhere along the line, it all comes together when you sort it out. You add somethings, kick somethings out and end up where you are. Hopefully it ties together. They interface with each other and disguise well. All the plays complement each other offensively so you know how to scatter a play here, a play there, an idea here or an idea there. It all fits together in a good comprehensive game plan. That process takes some time. It takes some time individually and collectively as a staff. When you put it together and evaluate the practice plays on the field, you modify it a little bit further from there.

Q: How much time in practice do you guys spend on improving your communication?

BB: Every play. Yeah, every play. We work with the noise home and away depending on which side of the ball we feel that noise will be coming from. Particularity against Atlanta offensively, they have a lot of different formations and variations and personnel groups and there's quite a bit of motion, so they force the defense to react and adjust to what they do more than most teams that we play. That's challenging right there, even if there was no noise whatsoever. Then when you add crowd noise, and long drives, and guys getting a little bit tired or not as alert on the 10th play of the drive as on the first play of the drive, then that just stresses the communication a little bit more. So you start piling all of those things together, a long drive, crowd noise, degree of difficulty with formations and personnel groups and motion and those kind of things, some of which we haven't seen before. They're going to have some looks that we're not going to be able to practice. Coach [Kyle] Shanahan is probably drawing them up right now. I don't know if he knows what they are yet, but it'll be things that are designed obviously to give us a problem, so the communication against this team - we've got to stress it on a lot of levels.

Q: Do you find it to be easier to communicate with the coordinators when they are down on the field as opposed to how some teams have them up in a booth?

BB: Either way we have communication with the booth that is important, and we have communication on the field that's important. I've done it both ways personally. There are advantages to one, there are advantages to the other. There are problems you have to solve if you're one place or the other. It's just a question of which ones you want to solve. Both can work, there's a lot of different ways to do it. It's just trying to find which one is best for the way that your team and your staff is set up and that could certainly change. It's changed for me within the same organization, but you move a couple of people around and maybe you feel it's advantageous to do it a little bit differently.

Q: What is the advantage to having Josh McDaniels on the sideline as opposed to up in a booth?

BB: Well, again, it's everything. It's the combination of our entire staff and our coordinators and the players that we're working with, how we feel like it's most efficient. Any of those could work, especially now where you can have a coach-to-quarterback communication from the press box. I'd say without that it would just be another step from the coordinator making the call from the press box to the sideline, and the sideline making it into the signal caller. Now that step has been eliminated, but even with that step I think it still was very doable. I mean I did it so it was definitely doable. That was back in the prehistoric days; yeah.

Q: With two weeks to prepare, is your game planning any different? Is it more of a working document?

BB: I'd say it's the same as a normal week. It's just spaced out a little bit more. Instead of seven days, call it 10 - like we weren't on Monday where we would normally be on a Monday because we didn't know who we were going to play [until Sunday]. Normally, we know who the next opponent is so all the work is done on that team, so when we open the book on Monday morning, it's all there. [You're just] adding in the game they just played the day before, let's call it, right. In this case it wasn't, so we had to get all the information on Atlanta and that took a while to compile all of that, so once that's done, it's done. We have a couple days at the end of the week in Houston that are a little different than our normal two days before the game, so we kind of get squeezed on one end or the other. Let's call it 10 days in the middle instead of six or whatever, nine instead of six. It's just six but spread out. We have to travel and there are some other obligations that just kind of cut into a normal preparation time, but we have more time to do it. What was tough was the one-week game because then you have all of that crammed into a normal week of preparation. When that happened, I was involved in that in 1990 when we played Buffalo, I was with the Giants, but we had played them in December. Then of course in 2001 we had played the Rams in the middle of the season so it helped that short week in terms of - from a coaching preparation standpoint.

4

X'S AND O'S

Q: How difficult is it to take advantage of a particular look or formation when you've already put it on film and the other team has seen it?

BB: I'd say it's a pretty common problem. Anytime you put something new out there that you haven't done before, it's hard to know exactly what you're going to get. A lot of times what you practice against is different than what actually happens in the game. Sometimes they have trouble getting even to what they want to get to because it might be new or something they haven't seen before. So you have to be ready to handle whatever it is they do. You have to just run the play out and have the quarterback or whoever the person is that has the key reads on the play read it out, and based on what they see make the right decision. If you've shown something, and like the example you're giving, where you show something and then you come back to it the next time, it's sort of the same thing. They know what you've done. If they don't stop it, maybe you go to it, but if they do stop it, then you need to have another option somewhere. Once you can hit multiple options on the same type of thing, then you've really got the defense in a tough spot. If you can only do one thing, then any good defense is going to take that away as soon they see what you're trying to do. So, you've got to be able to have some type of complementary play to go with it or some complementary play that takes a coverage matchup – if they take away one guy that you have somewhere else to throw the ball.

Q: What's the difference between a West Coast running game and a traditional running game?

BB: I'd say that's all kind of changed. When you go back to Paul Brown, that is the offense. What the running game was in the 70's when he was in Cincinnati, late 60's and 70's when he was there, what it was throughout the league is a lot different than what it is now. Even in San Francisco when [Bill] Walsh was there, it was a lot of two backs. Now most every team has one primary runner in the game. Very seldom do you see two runners and so that has obviously been a big change. So it just depends on where you want to draw that line. We're going back call it 30 years of West Coast, Ohio River offense, whatever you want to call it, and that running game has changed. I think what has probably stayed more consistent is the passing game concepts and then whatever running game you have, then you adapt that with that kind of Ohio River passing game, whether it's zone runs, whether it's gap runs, whether its 12-personnel runs, whether it's 21-personnel runs. But the pass concepts I would say there is a lot more carryover. When you go back to what Coach Brown did, Coach Walsh, those are primarily two-back sets with some one-back sprinkled in there. Now you see teams that have West Coast background, even when Mike [Holmgren] and Andy [Reid], but they've kind of transitioned as they've gotten further into their careers, they've kind of transitioned into more one-back offenses as well. But I think in the passing game, I think those core concepts kind of have stayed more constant than the running game.

Q: You guys have been using a lot of motion right before the ball is snapped. What is the advantage of doing that?

BB: Usually when you put a player in motion it's to either gain an advantage somehow on the defense or it's to force the defense to communicate and adjust after they've already made their call and you've come out of the huddle and lined up. I'd say it would fall into one of those two categories. Sometimes you do it just to force the defense to deal with something, change of strength or a tight split or a wide split that goes from one to the other, where the tight end aligns, which we know is important when teams are setting their front, their linebacker locations and trying get ready to set up their gap control. If you're trying to gain an advantage, that's one thing. If you're trying to in general force the defense to communicate and be ready to play one thing when you're actually going to snap the ball and do something else, then there's some subtle advantage to that that's hard to measure, but you know from experience that it's taking place and it puts more stress on your opponent.

Q: Do you defend a receiving tight end like Jordan Reed differently than you would defend a more traditional tight end like Jason Witten?

BB: Each player has their own individual strengths and weaknesses, whatever those happen to be, and I think you always want to be aware of what the player's strengths are and take those away. If you can gain an advantage where you feel like you have an advantage in that matchup you want to take advantage of that when you can or if you can. Again on that side of it, sometimes when you're on offense, you keep players out of situations that you don't feel are strengths for them. That's what good offensive coaches do with their players. Reeds' case, I think he's obviously one of their best players. They have a lot of confidence in him. They go to him in a lot of critical situations, he comes through. They move him around, he's all over, he at times plays receiver positons where he's split out and detached from the formation. That's fairly common. He's in close more than he's split out, but he's split out more than a lot of tight ends are. When you face guys like that, you've got to figure out the matchup that you want to be in that you feel comfortable with.

And he's made plays down the field. He's a very crafty route runner, knows how to get open in tight coverage. He's a big target, catches the ball well, has got a big catch radius, so you can kind of put the ball away from the defender where he can get it and the defender can't, and he can come up with it. He's good in the red area, good on third down. He has quickness to separate from man coverage. Yeah, it's just trying to find the best matchup, but again, a lot of times it's hard to jam him or disrupt his route because he's extended as opposed to being in-line. But yeah, he does a lot of things well. I'd say in their running game, they use their tight ends but a little differently than say the Dallas offense as an example in the way they block. A lot of times they don't force players, or extended players, so that's really compatible with the skills of an athletic tight end. It's similar to [Tyler] Eifert when Jay was at Cincinnati. I think Reed is kind of Eifert in the Cincinnati offense if you will.

Q: Generally speaking, the more mobile a quarterback is, the more threat there is on the edges. But guys like pocket passers, the more you can get through the 'A' gap, the more that player will be distracted because he's not as laterally mobile. We haven't seen that a lot with Tom Brady. He's not the most mobile guy. Is there a counter than your offense uses to that pressure? Is there a reason teams don't use that 'A' gap pressure in the middle.

BB: We see it.

Q: What's a general counter to that? Is it stuffing the middle?

BB: Well, basically what it comes down to in pass protection is if you keep – you can protect with five, six, seven or eight guys. The normal would be six. So the five linemen plus somebody else is your sixth guy. So that would handle six potential rushers. If they bring seven, then you're either hot or you'd need to have a seventh guy in protection – tight end and the back or two backs in the backfield or something like that. It just really comes down to a numbers game. Whether they put the guy in the 'A' gap, the 'B' gap or bring him outside, wherever he is, if it's a sixth guy then somebody has to block him. The question is, is that sixth guy on your back or is he on one of your linemen? If he's on one of your linemen, then you get your back out. If he's on your back, then your back stays in, then the guy who is covering the back, then he comes too. Then they add in. It's really, I think it's more how many they bring than where they bring them.

Where they bring them, you have to block them, but the question is how many they bring. So, if you have five in protection, then the sixth guy potentially is a problem depending on whether or not that sixth guy – defensively, you don't know if that fifth guy that you bring, you don't know if he's going to be blocked by the line or not. If he's blocked by the line, then you have to cover all the receivers. If he's blocked by a receiver, then you gain a guy somewhere, you gain him in coverage or you can add him into the rush. So that's kind of the protection part of it. From a gap control standpoint, there's really, when you rush a passer, you have six gaps you have to control. There's five linemen right? So, it's a total of six gaps. So if you rush four, then theoretically, you have two gaps that are free. So, the quarterback can step up and find that gap if he wants to quarterback or if he scrambles or whatever. If you rush five, then you technically only have kind of one gap free, if he steps up and finds that opening... But that's the problem with rushing four guys against a mobile quarterback. You kind of have two dead gaps there. You bring two guys on the outside to contain him, and then you have four gaps on the inside [where] you only have two rushers. So it's a lot of space for them to defend. If you bring five, then you can restrict that space a little bit, but then that creates problems on the other end.

Q: Are the linebackers in between, where they have to drop, but also pay attention to those gaps?

BB: It depends on what coverage you're in. If you're in man-to-man coverage, then they're assigned a man. If you're in zone coverage, then you have vision on the quarterback. So there are advantages to being in zone coverage against a mobile quarterback in terms of vision.

Q: Often third-and-1 plays make a big difference in the game in terms of them stopping you or you stopping them. What's the specific challenge of that play in particular?

BB: I mean, in the end, it usually comes down to fundamentals. You've got to block them, or you've got to defeat a block and make the play. The numbers are the numbers. I mean, nobody's going to run a play and cut a guy loose in the hole, so the guy that you let go is usually the guy furthest away from the play. It doesn't mean he's out of the play, but it's usually the guy furthest away who has the point of attack. Whoever knocks the line of scrimmage back is probably going to have an edge on the play. The passing game can factor in there, too. Sometimes if you don't need a lot of yardage, you're kind of reluctant to go through putting the ball in the air, protecting, running routes and all that when he can just hand it off for a yard, but you've got to be able to make that yard. We've got to obviously do a better job of coaching it and a better job of executing it and be better in that situation. I mean, that's a key situation. If you can't get a yard in this league, then that's going to eventually catch up to you. It already has, but it will continue to be a problem if we're not able to get that yard offensively. Defensively, percentages are with the offense in that situation, so a stop there is a big stop. But, realistically, you're not going to be 80 percent on defense in that situation. Offensively, that's where you'd like to be.

Q: On short yardage situations, is that more on the players to get the yards needed?

BB: Well, again, it's the coaches' job to put the players in the best situation that they can be in. So, if you put a guy in a bad situation, then it's hard for him to succeed. If you put him in a good situation, then you just have to execute the play and it will be alright. I mean, I think we need to do a better job, they need to do a better job. I mean, we've got to block better, we've got to run better, we've got to coach better. I don't think it's just one thing. We all need to improve on it. It's a key situation.

Q: What are the challenges of defending a pick or rub route by the goal line?

BB: Well, there are certain fundamental things that you have to do. You have to do them collectively as a team. You have to work together because there's more than one person involved on running those plays and defending those plays. And, if you don't execute them well, if you don't play the technique properly, then you get beat, and we've got to do a better job of coaching it and we have to play it better. It shouldn't be nearly as much of a problem as it was. But, we obviously aren't coaching it or playing it very well.

Q: How important is communication post-snap on defense in defending route combinations?

BB: Yeah, I'd say on defense it's almost always an awareness or a visual communication or recognition. You see a player crossing, you anticipate that based on the call maybe somebody else will take that guy. You kind of, sometimes you see it, sometimes you anticipate it.

We play in front of a sold out crowd here so the idea of me yelling routes to you and you yelling them to me – that might happen on the practice field, it might sound good, but the reality of it is, you're not hearing much on Sunday. So, you have to be able to visually communicate it without actually saying anything or in some cases, even doing anything. Just by your teammate's body language or by the reaction you anticipate and then once you start to see that then you know that it's happened the way you had practiced it or had talked about it happening then you're able to adjust to it. There are a lot of different levels of communication. There's the verbal communication, there's certainly the signaling before the snap, whether it's on defense or offense relative to crowd noise and so forth. On the road offensively, at home defensively, so the communication is kind of always an issue. It just depends on which side of the noise you're on. Then there's a post-snap communication between a quarterback and a receiver, a quarterback and a tight end [or] running back, running back and an offensive lineman, a pulling guard. Then the same thing defensively, with pass rush games, linebackers, defensive linemen, secondary players, linebackers that when you see something happen the way you've anticipated it then that's kind of a communication if you will that then your assignment corresponds to that.

If it doesn't happen that way then that can sometimes be a little bit of a scramble or a void somewhere along the line somewhere that then you try to adjust and react to. But that whole process is really in the end, that's the backbone, that's the spinal cord of football is all that process which can be emphasized differently depending on exactly which part of it you're talking about or where the noise is coming from, where the communication is coming from. But in the end, when you put it all together, that's really what connects everything on the football field is communication, understanding, anticipation, reaction, being able to do all that at a high level, at high speed, in a short amount of time. That's the hard, that's it. If you can't do that, it's going to be a long day. If you can do that, then you have a chance to play at the speed, the game speed that you need to play at to win.

Q: What does the three-tight end look do for your offense?

BB: It just puts another personnel group out there for our opponents to defend. If we feel like we can take advantage of it, then that's what we'll try to do. I mean, it's not a lead formation for us, but if we can gain an advantage with it in some way, we will. If we can't, then it probably wouldn't be that big of a part of the package that week.

Q: What are the challenges of defending two running backs?

BB: You just have to be disciplined in your reads. There's only one runner back there. If he's back there with a tight end or a fullback or something like that, I mean, you know who the runner's going to be. I mean, it could be a pass, but you know who basically is going to carry the ball. With two guys back there, then misdirection plays and reading your keys and making sure that you defend your responsibility, because there's more than one guy that can carry it, becomes more critical, which is the way it was when I came into the league when there were two running backs.

So the halfback blocked, the fullback ran. The fullback blocked, the halfback ran, and your keying system was, for linebackers, much more difficult then because of the different combinations of plays that they had. As that's evolved to a one-back set, again, for the most part, we know who's going to carry the ball, and so that's just changed a little bit. When you put two guys back there, especially if you're not used to doing it, understanding that there's probably not a lot of one guy is blocking for the other guy plays - there's more of one guy runs here and the other guy runs somewhere else, which guy has the ball - you have to defend both of them as opposed to having lead blockers. I wouldn't say that that's featured, but when you have two guys going in different directions, then that can slow down the defense.

Q: When you came into the league, would you have matched that set with base defense?

BB: No, I think the match is based more on the receivers. I mean, it's hard to match on running backs. I mean, it just is because the formation is still how many blockers do they have, and it's hard to treat a back as a receiver unless he really is a receiver. I mean, if he's in the backfield, you can treat him as a receiver, but I'd say that's a hard thing to do because that's not - like linebackers don't see receivers in the backfield unless it's truly a receiver in the backfield, and that's rare and usually with a very specific purpose. When you have two backs back there, it just changes the run keys and the awareness that the linebackers have to have in the inside running game. I mean, look, if a guy runs a toss sweep or runs a reverse, that's a perimeter play. I mean, that's one thing. When it's an inside play, it involves a blocking scheme and a linebacker fit on the ball, then that's a whole other issue. Yeah, I'd say the majority of the matching comes with the number of receivers the team has on the field. Now, there's some tight ends that are receiving tight ends, so you could treat that receiving tight end as a receiver, which that's pretty common in this league, but I'd still say it falls into the receiver category.

Q: Across the league, teams have leaned more towards a ten-yards-and-under passing game - why do you think teams have gone in that direction?

BB: I don't know. I think there are a lot of good offensive players, a lot of good offensive coaches, and a lot of good defensive players. I think each week, offensively, you just try to find the best matchups you can and try to find a way to be productive offensively. Certainly, with the quality of defensive linemen that are in this league, and particularly, the ones that are on Miami's team, it's hard to stand back there and hold the ball all day and wait for a lot of plays to develop as opposed to getting the ball out before they get to you, risk negative plays and getting strip sacked and all of that. Teams that have good pass rushes make it tough to hold the ball and extend plays.

Q: Does the number of different schemes you see increase once you reach the playoffs?

BB: Well, it just depends on who you play. Whoever you play, look, the best team that we face is the next team that we play. They'll be a team that's in the playoffs and has won a postseason game. So whatever they do, they'll probably continue to do a very high percentage of it because it's gotten them this far. It will have gotten them a playoff win next weekend. Whatever that team does then we're going to have to deal with the elements of them not only doing it, but doing it at a very high level and very successfully. We'll just have to wait and see who that is and what their points of emphasis are and who their dangerous players are, but we know they'll have some or else they wouldn't be playing at this time of year and they wouldn't be able to win next week without those elements in place. We won't know that until we know the team, but we know they'll definitely be there. It'll be a big challenge for us to get ready for that once it's identified.

Q: How much value is there in the screen game if the yards aren't there or aren't there consistently?

BB: Well, I mean any plays you're not making yards on, it's hard to get excited about those. Our screen game hasn't been as productive as we need it to be. We need to, obviously, coach it better and execute it better. We're not getting enough out of it. It's disappointing.

Q: It would seem that you have the personnel to execute it, so is it something consistent holding it back or is it just a breakdown here and there?

BB: I think it's a combination of things. We've run a lot of different types of screens – receivers, backs, tight ends, quick screens, slower screens. We're just not doing a good job. I've got to do a better job of coaching them and we've got to do a better job of executing them. It's as simple as that.

Q: Can it still be a positive influence and force the defense to slow down a bit despite not gaining the yards you'd like?

BB: I don't know. Based on what we're gaining on them, they should be happy every time we run one.

Q: Do you consider the short passing game an extension of the run game and, if so, are you seeing a growth in that aspect of your offense?

BB: Well, I think that our offensive system has always utilized the backs in the passing game, which a lot of those plays I think you're referring to are to the backs. Not all of them - there are wide receiver screens and things like that, so it's not exclusively. I think that's just part of the passing game that we use and, really, most teams in the league use to attack the defense at all three levels. I don't think you want to just throw all bombs. I don't think you want to throw all your passes behind the line of scrimmage or within a couple yards of the line of scrimmage and I don't think you want to throw all your passes at, call it, 12 to 15 yards. So, there's a place in the passing game for plays I think at all three of those levels. The design of the plays can vary quite a bit as we see every week, not just from our team, but throughout the league.

But, there are ways to attack the defense throwing the ball at all three levels. That changes the timing of the passing game. It changes the timing of the pass rush.

It changes the way that the defense can try to stop that part of the passing game because they have to defend all three levels, not just one or two. If they can eliminate one or two, then that makes it easier for the defense, whether they're playing man, or zone or some combination. It doesn't really matter. If you can change the levels of your passing game and the timing of your passing game, then that can be beneficial to everybody. So, again, some of those plays are reflective of what the defense is doing. Obviously, if the defense is taking away or doing a good job of taking away passes close to the line of scrimmage and are going to challenge every throw and make it hard to complete a three-yard pass, then it's probably a good opportunity to try and throw the ball behind them in the deeper areas of the field and vice versa.

Again, I think the quarterbacks job and Josh [McDaniels]' job is to try and create plays that give us options. Some plays are designed to go in a certain area, to go deep or to go short. I mean, obviously, a screen pass is a screen pass. It's not a deep ball, but with the exception of a few of those types of plays, the majority of the plays attack the defense at different levels. They're kind of all-purpose plays so that depending on what coverage they give you or if they pressure, where the quarterback should go with the ball based on what the defense does. Tom [Brady] does a great job of that and Josh and the offensive staff do a great job of designing plays to facilitate that, so that's really what happens. It's not like we go into the game saying, 'Well, you know, we've got to complete 15 short passes.' I mean, if the short receiver is covered on that play then that's really where we don't want to throw the ball. Like I said, there are some plays that are designed to go to a certain area, but the majority of the plays have options and then those options are executed based on the way the defense handles the pattern.

Q: Is there a concern about the lack of tight end production outside of Rob Gronkowski, and how will it be addressed if it is a concern?

BB: Well, I mean, look, our job offensively is to move the ball and score points. So, however we can do that, that's what we're trying to do. I'm sure if we threw the ball to a bunch of other guys and didn't throw it to Gronkowski, we'd be asking why Rob didn't get more targets. So, I don't know. I mean, if he's out there and he has a good matchup, then Tom's [Brady] going to give him a look and he's going to get some throws. There may be another player that's - we had that on a couple plays yesterday. There's more than one guy open on the play, and the quarterback went to where he thought was the best place to go, which I wouldn't second guess him on those, but it doesn't mean that other guys weren't open. It doesn't mean other guys weren't part of the play, but there's only one ball and the quarterback has to throw it to the spot that he feels is the best spot for it.

Q: What were you trying to accomplish by going hurry-up on the first-and-goal prior to the pick-six?

BB: It was the same thing that happened when we scored a touchdown in the same situation – trap their dime defense on the field at the 1-yard line. We obviously didn't execute the play well, let [Malcolm] Jenkins run four yards in the backfield unblocked. That's not what we're trying to do obviously.

Q: How important was it for your offense to get the ball to some guys out in space to help negate some of the effectiveness of their defense up the middle?

BB: Right. Well, yeah, I think it was a combination of both. Look, sometimes it's a lot easier to get the ball out in space and let the back make some yards as opposed to having to block seven or eight guys to get him into that same space. The advantage to handing the ball is you should gain some yards, whereas an incomplete pass – that could be a no gain. To make yards in the running game, any significant yards, you've got to create some space for the back and that means in the Titans case blocking an extra guy in the box because they didn't play a lot of split-safety coverage. You've got to block six, seven, eight guys depending on what personnel group you're in, in order to get the running back into space where he can do that in the passing game and he can make a lot of yards, like that screen pass that we threw to Dion [Lewis]. It would have been hard to hand the ball off and get him into that much space. You'd have to make a lot of, not good blocks; you'd have to make a lot of great blocks to get everybody that far out of the way so the runner could attack the field like Dion did on that play. To answer your question, yeah, getting backs into space in the passing game or in the running game, however you do it, and there's different ways of doing it but sometimes it's easier to throw him the ball into space than it is to, like I said, block seven or eight guys and try to create that same situation.

Q: When you decide to go up-tempo on offense does their have to be some kind of coordination between you and Josh McDaniels or you and Matt Patricia? Do you guys take into account the defensive workload when you decide to go with the hurry up just based on if it doesn't work out then those guys may be on the bench for just a short time?

BB: Right. Yeah, that's a good question. Certainly there's an element of game management involved between the offense, the defense and the kicking game. I don't want to minimize that. It does come into play. Sometimes how you play defense is a factor on how you're playing offense or how you're playing in the kicking game and vice versa for the offense. Those are definitely considerations, but that being said, the reason why we put the offense on the field is to move the ball and score points. If we wanted to punt it then we'd send the punt team out there. We're trying to move the ball and score points and defensively the reason we put the defense out there is to stop the offense from moving the ball and get the ball back for our offense. That's really the job that those units have to do. Our offense can't play defense and our defense can't play offense. They have to go out there and do their job and the best thing for them to do is to do a good job at their job. I don't think anybody would object to our offense going out and scoring a 70-yard touchdown in 10 seconds and giving the ball back to the other team. That's what they're supposed to do. That being said, there is an element of game management and I think that comes up at times, but if you're looking at overall percentage, it's probably maybe in the 10 percent range, somewhere in there. The other 90 percent of the time the offense is trying to move the ball and score points and the defense is trying to get the ball back to the offense, whether that's causing a punt, or if they've already got the ball in field goal range just keeping them out of the end zone, or obviously turn the ball over. Those units have to do what their job is. They can't overplay to another unit. Again, unless there's some specific situational football play that's involved, which that could come into play. Similar maybe to offensively if you're a fast break team and there's maybe some point where you want to just throw the ball down and give everybody a chance to catch their breath. There might be a series or part of a series sometimes that we say, 'We just need to get a first down here. Don't worry about tempo. We need to give our defense a chance to get organized on the sideline,' or vice versa.

Q: What went into the decision to use the screen game a little more last night? Do you feel that there has been an improvement in that area over the course of the year?

BB: Well, I think we've had success with our screen game this year and through the years. We've also not had success with it. We've worked harder on our execution. I think there is some evidence of better execution, better timing and more production last night. We could still improve but we had some positive plays on that which were good. It's the type of play that it's a complementary play. You can't run your offense on screen passes. You've got to have a lot of other plays, but it's a complementary play that if it hits at the right time and is executed well that has a chance to complement some of the other things you're doing. So, if you're throwing the ball a lot, as we were behind - I think everybody knew we'd be throwing the ball a lot in the fourth quarter there - that's the type of situation where that complementary play could have a chance to be affective.

Q: What are your thoughts on favoring the pass offense in the second half last night and the overall balance differential between the run game and pass game as the game wore on?

BB: Well, the biggest problem with the running game is the production. I mean, nobody around here minds calling running plays if we're gaining yardage on them, but when we're not gaining yardage it makes it hard to call. Combine that with the score and our inability to convert on third down, it's kind of a spiral that you don't want to be in and we were in it last night. We couldn't run the ball, couldn't convert on third down, so don't have another set of downs to try to get it going again to make enough positive plays in the passing game to avoid third down, or in some cases to get it close enough to have a reasonable chance to convert on third down. So, some of the negative plays in the running game are like sacks. They come up with second-and-14, second-and-13. On several of those plays we had everybody blocked on paper but didn't execute the blocks so then we had a negative play. It wasn't like we had a guy that we didn't have accounted for. We accounted for him but something happened and we weren't able to get him, so we ended up with a negative play and now we're in long yardage, so it was a lot of factors that went into it. Bottom line was we didn't have a good night offensively in really any area and we were probably fortunate to have the points that we had with a couple of big plays and gained a lot of yards in a few plays.

That was probably the best thing that we did, but our overall consistency in the running game and in the passing game wasn't at a winning level. That's obvious.

Q: Coach sometimes you bring the defense together and map something out on the chalkboard. Do you do that with your offensive coordinator, so he can do that with the offense?

BB: No. As a coaching staff you are looking for your most efficient operation. One of the things that is important there is communication. You have communication between the coaches, and then you have communication between the coaches and players. No matter how you set it up with every staff I've ever been on there is always some sort of discussion as to what is the best way to set things up on that individual staff relative to the players that you are working with and what their experience is, or how the communication goes within that group of players. However you set it up there are disadvantage and advantages. Obviously you see more from the press box, and you see less from the field. Communication is quicker on the field than it is from the press box. That's the way it is. However you are setup, you have your advantages and disadvantages and you try to weigh them out. This is a case where we have done it the other way for a couple of games. Now we did it this way, and we'll take a look at the advantages and disadvantages of doing it both ways.

We'll talk about it and try to decide which is the best way to do it. Defensively, in this particular case, although it has been done before, me being in the press box is not an option. It's been done before. There have been head coaches in the press box. I'm not considering that as an option. That is clear cut. On the other side of the ball, when I was a defensive coordinator I called from upstairs and I called from downstairs. I think there are advantages and disadvantages of doing it both ways.

Q: Do you have a guy that you consider an assistant defensive coordinator?

BB: We don't have an assistant defensive coordinator.

Q: Do you have a guy you talk to a lot during the game?

BB: There are certain jobs that have to be done during the game. Somebody has to do them. There are certain jobs that have to be done from the press box and certain ones that have to be done from the field. Wherever the people are, then that's the job that they do. If you were to switch them, then they would have to switch jobs. You can't really identify the other team's personnel from the field. It's just too hard to see the congestion across the field. It's much easier to spot that from upstairs. Whoever is upstairs is going to be looking at personnel. Whoever is upstairs is really in the best position to chart the plays and study the tendencies. It's a hard thing to do, especially at the end of the year when it's raining and cold and all that. Trying to write and keep charts in inclement weather, that's been done before too, but I can tell you first hand that it is tough. So those are the kind of things that you do upstairs. The communication that needs to be given to the players is a lot easier to do face to face than it is to always be doing over the phone, it has to go from coach to coach to player. The same work has to be done, it's just a question of how you want to do it. Should we poll the fans and see which way they would like us to do it?

Q: The wildcat formation on offense was a big factor back in 2008 when you played Miami at Gillette Stadium. Was that kind of a fad that has phased itself out of the league now?

BB: I mean you see it from time to time. Yeah, all of those things - the wildcat, unbalanced line - things like that; I mean you've always got to be ready for them.

Q: What did you learn from that game in 2008 about it and how your players reacted to it?

BB: I mean it's really just a lot of elements of the single-wing offense. We just missed some tackles. Obviously didn't have it coached very well. [We] didn't coach it very well, didn't play very well. It's not unstoppable. We just didn't do a very god job on it that day.

Q: That formation was prevalent with the Arkansas Razorbacks at the time but did it come completely out of the blue that week in the NFL?

BB: Well, again, the coach for the Dolphins [quarterback coach David Lee] was at Arkansas when [Darren] McFadden ran it. Again, no matter how you slice it up it's just putting the quarterback into the equation into the running game which creates another gap, if you will. So, if you play eight-on-seven or seven-on-six then once the quarterback is part of the play, now you're eight-on-eight, you're seven-on-seven. There's no extra gap. You've got to account for him. That's what Mike Shanahan did with the Broncos offense with all of the bootlegs. You had to account for him, so even though you could be eight-on-seven, once you accounted for that bootleg guy now you were seven-on-seven, or whatever the numbers were. You always lost a guy. It's really just a numbers game and those teams that run those type of plays - it seems like Navy that run a lot of option, run a lot of quarterback plays like they did with [Keenan] Reynolds. You run out of guys on defense. You can't outnumber them. You just run out of people. There are different versions of it but it's all the same concept. It's adding another guy in the running game that the defense has to account for that you lose a gap, which was the single-wing offense.

5

STRATEGY AND SITUATIONS

Q: Does field position dictate more than anything at the end of the first half whether you want to go down and do everything you can to score, as opposed to not giving them a chance at the end of the first half?

BB: I think field position is part of it, but so is everything else: time, timeouts, how you match up in that situation. I think it's all part of it. I think there are a lot of factors in that, in what you call and what happens in the sequence of plays that you call. Each one is different. Obviously, there are some common threads, but I think each situation each week is different based on the matchups and based on whatever the specific situation is: time, timeouts, field position, playing conditions, etcetera.

Q: When you're facing a good third-down team, what are the keys to attacking them?

BB: I think a lot of their success on third down is related to their success on first and second down – strong running game, again a lot of the West Coast passing style along with some bootlegs and moving pocket plays and that kind of thing. They get on track a lot – second-and-four, second-and-three, second-and-five – and then you're looking at having two downs to pick up four or five yards – that kind of thing. I think it all starts on first down to get a team into third down and longer type situations where they have fewer options in the passing game, like everybody. But they do a good job of running the ball and they do a good job of hitting a high number of percentage passes so they stay out of a lot of long-yardage situations, haven't been sacked very much, so they don't have a lot of bad plays.

Q: Does that put some pressure on you guys to avoid third-and-longs and typical third down situations?

BB: Believe it or not, we always try to avoid third-and-long. We never go into the game saying, 'Let's see how many third-and-longs we can get into. Let's see how many of those we can convert.' We never try to do that. That's an emphasis point every week, just like turnovers. We always want to protect the ball; we always want to stay out of long-yardage. That's basic offensive football: don't give them the ball and move forward.

Q: What's the biggest challenge in trying to defend an offense when they put multiple receivers into a bunch formation?

BB: Well, I mean, defensively, first of all, it depends on what the situation is and depends on what you have called or if you want to change your call against a certain formation. If you're in man coverage then it could be a traffic problem. If you're in zone coverage then all of the receivers close together, getting the right matches in the zones because they're there quicker than they are if they're spread out, but some of that is situationally based. Who are they? Which group of players is it? What down and distance are we talking about? What field position are we talking about and what's the defensive call? So, there's a lot of variables that depend on really the specifics of the formation and the call and the situation.

Q: What variables go into being able to execute successfully the way you did at the end of the first half, with Brady's scramble and then setting up a field goal with seconds remaining?

BB: Right, well, there's a couple things that could have happened on that. The first would have been if we had gotten the first down on the play, then we could have clocked it on first down and, I think, had plenty of time to kick the field goal. When we didn't pick up the first down, we had already made - I mean, obviously, another option would have been to throw the ball away or throw an incomplete pass so that the clock would have stopped and then send the field goal team on. That, obviously, didn't happen. So, before the play, we made the decision as to whether or not we would go for the field goal if the clock was running or we would run another play offensively if the clock was running because we wouldn't have enough time to get the field goal team on. So, we have to make that decision before the snap so that we know what to do, so if we were going to run another play offensively, then the field goal team wouldn't go on the field and we would just line up and go for it on fourth down, as opposed to trying to get the field goal team on, which takes just a few seconds longer. So, it's a close call, close play, but I thought the players did a good job. The offensive team got off the field. The field goal team got on the field. We had time to set up and have a clean operation there, so they did a good job on that.

Q: It seemed like you averaged about third-and-7 over the course of the game. Is there a reason you had more success converting on third down early in the game, or was your 50 percent conversion rate more a result of needing longer yardage to pick up a first down?

BB: Right. Well, there's no doubt that first and second down have a lot to do with third down. So, you just look at the numbers in the league, the conversion percentages on short yardage are different than medium yardage and they're different on long yardage, so there's definitely a correlation there. A couple of the third-down stops were in the scoring territory where we ended up with field goals instead of touchdowns, so those third downs in the red area, which are tough to convert because of just having less space to work with, and that kind of field position, that's a little challenging, too. But, I mean, New Orleans changed things up on us. They mixed the coverages and they ran some three-man rush, they ran some five-man rush, four-man rush, mixed in a little bit of zone. So, we hit them on some and we didn't, so that's usually the way it goes against a team like that that will do a good job of making adjustments and changing it up on you. We do that ourselves. Sometimes they hit, sometimes they don't. They don't all hit. Hopefully they don't all miss.

Q: How important is it to get off the field on third-down? And how key is the play of special teams?

BB: Third-down is always critical. If you look at the turnover plays themselves, because there is an exchange of possession depending on how third-down goes. And in the kicking game, field position and of course scoring opportunities, points, they're always important. Field position is always important in a game like this - in every game - but particularly in a game like this with two good teams. The two best teams, being ready to play 60 minutes and being expected to go all the way that a few yards here or there - as we saw last weekend in a couple of the other playoff games - how a couple of yards can make the difference between field goal range and not field goal range. It's kind of hidden yardage that can show up somewhere else; on a punt or on a punt return or on a kickoff or something like that. But then as the ball moves and those few yards become important, in terms of field goal range or percentage of accuracy in field goals, that can be critical. We saw a couple of big plays in our game, kicking the ball and punting the ball inside the 10-yard line, inside the 5-yard line, putting the opponent on a long field. Again, we saw that in multiple playoff games last weekend. So, those are big plays. Statistically, those are worth points. You've got to play defense, you've got to get the ball back, you've got to convert it, but statistically, those plays create scoring opportunities. So, yeah, sure that'll be important

Q: In using the new tablets on the sideline, did that provide any sort of new feedback or enhancement in the sideline coaching experience?

BB: So, the first home preseason game for each team they use the video component of the Surface tablets, so since this was our first home game we used those last night. Coincidentally, as it works out, we'll also use them in the Carolina game because that will be Carolina's first home preseason game, too. So, we'll actually get to use them twice. I'd say it's probably like a lot of things that are new. The concept is good, when it works it's good, when it doesn't work then it doesn't work. It's not something that we're going to use during the season. It's more of an experimental thing that you're probably looking for feedback and how to improve it or how to, I don't know, I mean it's not approved for use this year, but it's approved for use in just that one preseason game situation that I just mentioned. That's what it is. It's probably a concept that may have some possibilities if the functionality is good or can be improved or whatever.

Q: Since the rule changed, you guys have consistently deferred to receive the second half kickoff. What are the factors that go into that decision?

BB: We talk about it each week, every game. It's one of the things we discuss prior to the game as a staff and we try to do what we feel like is best for that particular game and that particular situation. Again, all the factors that you would think would go into it go into it. Sometimes we withhold that decision until we actually get and see what the field conditions are for that particular game, like last night or like Thursday night, a game like that. Obviously if you're playing in a dome in Indianapolis, we don't need to get that information. But games that are weather games, that could affect that decision, too. How you want to start the game, what your offensive or defensive game plan is, not talking about the first play but in general, here's how we want to try to start the game – maybe that affects it. There could be a lot of factors, so we try to consider them all and do what we think is best.

Q: It was reported that there were some issues Sunday with the sideline technology like the headsets and tablets you use. Does that affect the

number of plays you guys may be able to call and how does it affect any potential adjustments that you would make over the course of a game?

BB: As you know, there are multiple communication systems on the sideline. As you probably noticed, I'm done with the tablets. I've given them as much time as I can give them. They're just too undependable for me. I'm going to stick with pictures as several of our other coaches do as well because there just isn't enough consistency in the performance of the tablets, so I just can't take it anymore. The other communication systems involve the press box to the coaches on the field, and then the coach on the field, the signal caller, or the coach-to-quarterback, coach-to-signal caller system. Those fail on a regular basis.

There are very few games that we play, home or away, day, night, cold, hot, preseason, regular season, postseason, it doesn't make any difference; there are very few games where there aren't issues in some form or fashion with that equipment. And again, there's a lot of equipment involved, too. There are headsets in the helmets, there's the belt pack, that communication, there's a hookup or connection to internet service or that process and so forth with the coaches and the press box. So, there are a number of pieces of equipment, there is a number of connections that are on different frequencies. Again, not that I know anything about this but as it has been explained to me there are a lot of things involved and inevitably something goes wrong somewhere at some point in time. I would say weekly we have to deal with something. Dan Famosi is our IT person and he does a great job of handling those things. This is all league equipment so we don't have it. I mean we use it but it isn't like we have the equipment during the week and we can work with it and 'OK, this is a problem. Let's fix this.' That's not how it works. We get the equipment the day of the game, or I'd say not the day of the game but a few hours before the game and we test it and sometimes it works, sometimes it doesn't.

Usually by game time it is working but I would say not always. And then during the game sometimes something happens and it has to be fixed, and first of all, you have to figure out what the problem is. Is it a battery? Is it the helmet? Is it the coaches' pack? Is it the battery on the coaches' pack? I mean you know, again, it could be one of 15 different things. So, I would just say there are problems in every game. There were problems last week but there were problems the week before that, too. Some are worse than others. Sometimes both teams have them, sometimes one team has them and the other doesn't have them. There's an equity rule that's involved there on certain aspects of the communication system but not on all aspects meaning what happens on one side then the other team has to have the same. If ours are down then theirs has to be down and vice versa, but it's only true in certain aspects of the communication system; not everything. Overall there is a lot of complexity to the technology. There is complexity to multiple systems and there are a lot of failures, and so I know on our end Dan does a great job to fix those as quickly as possible. He has very limited access. I don't know how much urgency there is on the other part from the league standpoint.

However much urgency there is for them to have everything right, I don't know, I'm not involved with that. But yeah, it was a problem last week. It's basically a problem every week. The degrees aren't always the same but we're usually dealing with something. But as far as the tablet goes, I mean there was an experiment in a couple of the preseason games. It was one preseason game. We actually had two because it was our home game and Carolina's home game where we had video on the tablets. But for me personally, it's a personal decision, I'm done with the tablets. I'll use the paper pictures from here on because I've given it my best shot. I've tried to work through the process but it just doesn't work for me and that's because there's no consistency to it. Long answer to a short question; sorry.

Q: In a Sound FX video of you from last week's game, you remained pretty stoic on the sideline after each touchdown. Is that normally how you react when your team scores?

BB: Yeah, I don't know. I mean, I'm happy when we score. I'm really happy when we score, but there's a decision to be made on the next play and the next play and the next series. Now the game has changed. Either we narrow the gap or widen the gap or whatever it is. So, then there's something that has to be done going forward. That's really a big part of my job. So, we have a lot of fans that come to the game. They cheer. They do a great job. I feel like a big part of my job is decision making and planning ahead for the next play, the next series, the next situation. There is, sometimes, a little bit of time between a score and the kickoff when you go out on defense or how you're going to kick the ball off or so forth that I feel like I need to do a good job at that. I don't want to let the team down in the responsibilities that I have.

Q: If something has worked for you offensively in the past against an opponent, will your revisit it until they can prove they can stop it or is it more assumed that they will be keying on that aspect of your offensive attack?

BB: Yeah, I mean, that's always an interesting game plan question. You have to make a decision on that. There's usually more than one game to look at though. Unless you're the only team that runs a certain play, there's probably other plays to evaluate besides yours that have a similar, if not the exact same play, a similar concept to it. Maybe they've made an adjustment to a concept or maybe they haven't. You'd probably make your decision on that. You can usually get more than a couple looks at something that you want to get a look at, whatever it happens to be. It might not be the exact same thing but you can usually get an idea of conceptually what they're trying to do and how you would want to formulate the play to take advantage of a weakness that you might have identified.

Q: When a player is a healthy scratch for a game is his status for the next week purely dictated by what he does in practice that week?

BB: No.

Q: What are some other factors that would contribute to his availability the following week?

BB: What's best for the team. So, throw everything into that conversation and that's what it is.

Q: What went into the success that your offense had on third-down and do you think that helped negate the fact that you lost the turnover battle?

BB: Sure, yeah, well I'd say unfortunately the turnovers really weren't offset. We didn't get them and then the ones that they got, they scored touchdowns on, so we didn't really have the offset to that. I'd say on the penalties, the third-down conversions helped on some of those where we put ourselves in long-yardage situations with penalty infractions and then were able in a couple of cases to convert on third-down and overcome that, or on one case I think we overcame a sack that got us into a long-yardage situation and then converted on third-down. So, those third-downs got us out of a couple of negative plays that we had on earlier downs which we've got to do a better job of avoiding. The turnovers, we've got to cut those down period. That's just the bottom line. We can't turn the ball over as much as we have the last two weeks and expect to win consistently, but fortunately we were able to score enough points or hold them to - other than those two turnovers - really not very many points in order to win, but that's going to be hard to do every week. We probably aren't going to be able to count on that. We're going to have to do a better job of taking care of the ball.

Q: How long would you say you keep trick plays in the holster throughout the year before deciding to use them and what goes into the decision process of when to deploy those in a game?

BB: Yeah, I don't know about the first question. We run the plays when we feel like it's the right play to call at the right time. That's what play calling is.

Q: Were you surprised when the neutral zone infraction was called on the fourth down play?

BB: No, I wasn't because I thought that [Brynden] Trawick entered the neutral zone and Geneo

[Grissom] reacted to him. We practice that play every week and if it's that kind of situation – fourth and less-than-5 – and the player enters the neutral zone then we want to react to it and force the penalty and not allow them to get back and reset and not have the opportunity for it. I thought it was a heads up play by Geneo to react to that. That's what he's supposed to do and that's what he did. I thought we did the right thing. He definitely entered the neutral zone. I mean, at least what I saw. I thought Trawick was in the neutral zone, so assuming that we agree on that, if he did that then the player on the offensive side of the ball – if he reacts to that then the penalty is on the defense.

Q: Can you speaking about capitalizing on that ensuing offensive drive after the neutral zone penalty?

BB: Well, that's what football is. Football's about taking advantage. It's about making plays and taking advantage of opportunities that are there. Yeah, offensively, as you said, it wasn't one play. We had whatever it was – 80 yards to go – or whatever it was, a long way to go. So there were a lot of plays that had to follow that, but it gave us an opportunity to possess the ball. I think it was a 15-play drive or 16-play drive, whatever it was. That strings a lot of plays together and that's hard to do against the Titans. They're a very good defensive team, well coached and they make it tough on you to score in four or five plays. They make you string those long drives together and that's why they're such a good defensive team because it's hard to do.

Q: I was under the impression that if the player entering the neutral zone doesn't make contact that he has the chance to pull back out?

BB: Nope. Well, he can pull back out, but if the offense reacts to the defensive player in the neutral zone then the penalty is on the defense. Otherwise, you're going to have the whole defense flinching and the whole thing we went through a decade ago with everybody on the defensive side of the ball flinching with the silent count, crowd noise on the road and all that. You've got all the defensive players flinching but not entering the neutral zone to get the offense to false start. The league took that – they changed the rule so that A), it's illegal to flinch and B), if you don't flinch but if you try to time up a blitz or if you try to beat the count and you get into the neutral zone then, no, you don't get a chance to get back if the offense moves. If they don't move and you get back then everything resets and there's no infraction. But if the offense reacts to that then the penalty is on the defense.

Q: Do you guys sit down and look at the NFL rule book to try to take advantage of some of the rules?

BB: Well we try to know the rules and teach them to our players. It's a pretty thick book, but each spring that process starts with the league office and going through rule changes and interpretations and points of emphasis and so forth. Of course we, along with the league presentation, which they do in training camp, and as those things kind of get updated weekly with points of emphasis or specific situations that come up in games that Dean Blandino identifies, then of course we pass those along to the team and try to make sure that we know how to play and what's allowable and what isn't.

Q: Do you guys put a lot of time into that?

BB: Yeah I mean I don't know what other teams do so there's no way I can compare what we do to what somebody else does. I'm not in anybody else's building, so I just know what we do.

Q: Is teaching players the rules an ongoing practice throughout the season, and do you have to teach all new players the rules because it seems a lot of players across the league are unfamiliar with the NFL rulebook?

BB: I think it's a really good question, but it would entail probably a pretty lengthy answer. There are so many different levels that that question encompasses. Let's start with rookies coming into the league. The first thing we do is teach them the rules in the

National Football League and in particular make them aware of the changes between the college rules and the pro rules, which there are a significant number. And we don't really assume because we have no way of knowing how educated or uneducated they are on the rules, if they even are the same between the two – between college and professional football. So, it starts there. The NFL comes in and they go through all the rules changes with the team and the coaching staff, they meet with the coaching staff in the spring, which is a very informative meeting, and then they meet with the team in training camp and go through the rules changes and it's usually done during the time when the officials come to work the few days of training camp that they do for each team. So, that's also good. It creates a good dialogue between the officials, the players and the coaches, and gives coaches and players an opportunity to ask questions. Sometimes the dialogue goes back and forth – how's this being coached, how's this being officiated and so forth.

All of that is done with the intention of trying to get everybody on the same page. Each of our position coaches devotes a significant amount of time in the spring and then also in training camp, particularly in individual, one-on-one-type drills where a lot of times there are only two or three guys on the screen instead of all 22 so you can really get a good, close-up look at a lot of rules like that – the holding and illegal contact and offensive pass interference, defensive pass interference – all those kinds of things. So that's covered very much on an individual basis, specifically to that position. Obviously, the offensive guard doesn't have to know everything about pass interference and vice versa, but it's important for them to know the things in their position and how the game is being officiated. And then those things are also pointed out in various other team or individual settings as they become pertinent over the course of the year, whether it be a particular play or particular opponent or that type of thing.

And then I talk to the team on a regular basis on situational plays, which involve officiating, timing, utilization of timeouts and so forth and so on, so that's probably on a regular basis from training camp all the way through the end of the season – call it once a week or something like that – somewhere in that vicinity. Sometimes it's more than that, but always trying to keep our team aware of situations, and a lot of times we change the situation a little bit just to extend the conversation about a play. So this is what happened, but if something else or if they hadn't had timeouts or if the ball was here, or the ball was there, just try to understand and comprehend totally what we're doing from a team standpoint or an individual situation. The whole sideline, ball security, whistle, all those kind of ball possession plays, those are very important for everybody to understand and we stress those a lot. Any time the ball is loose, like it was in last night's game, try to make sure everybody

understands what they can do, what they can't do.
And of course once you get into the kicking game,
you can multiply everything that happens on offense
and defense exponentially because you not only have
the possession plays, but then you have all the plays
that happen when the ball is kicked, and those rules
sometimes are, well they are different than plays of
possession like a runner or a receiver or a returner
who's carrying the ball.

There is the whole handling of the ball and the kick
and did it cross the line of scrimmage and so forth
and so on. It's a lot for the officials to understand, it's
a lot for the coaches to understand, and it's a lot for
the players to understand. But in the end we try to
look at the rule book as a useful tool, something that
can benefit us if we know what we have to work with,
how to make the best of a situation based on the way
the rules are written and try to maximize our
opportunities there. But that being said, there is still a
lot happening in a short amount of time. It's
challenging for all of us – players, coaches and
officials. I don't know if that really answers your
question. We could probably talk about that one for
weeks.

**Q: When your team gets a safety, how do you look at
that from the standpoint of how quickly it can
change the flow and opportunity to build on that
momentum during the game?**

BB: Sure, yeah it gives you a chance to kind of go on a run which is hard to do in football. But that's how you do it, is scoring on defense or creating really good field positon. Like for example on kickoff coverage and then if you can get a stop and get the ball back, and then you have good field positon or a turnover. You need something like that. You need a turnover, you need a safety, or you need a good field positon play and three-and-out to have that kind of field positon to be able to string a couple of scores together like that. It's a great opportunity defensively, well as a team, but set up by that defensive score to try to go on a run and go from behind to ahead or go from ahead to two or three scores ahead, that kind of thing. Unfortunately we haven't had the kind of returns off of the two safeties the last two weeks that would really enhance that. Getting the ball back is good. If we could've turned those returns into a little more production that would've helped us. But yeah, it's a great opportunity, sure.

Q: Are there examples that come to mind from the past where you've been able to get a safety and turn that into a nice run that sort of catapults the team?

BB: Well, I think when you look statistically, to me I would kind of put that into the bonus points category. You go into a game and you think 'Alright, well how many points are we going to score offensively? How many points are they going to score offensively?' And that's, you know, kind of the way the game normally flows. When you get points from a defensive score, points from a special team's score, whether it be a blocked kick, or a safety, or a defensive return, something like that - I mean you can't count on those points. You can't go into a game and think 'Alright, we're going to get seven points on a defensive score.' Over the course of the year that maybe happens two or three times a year, whatever it is. I mean you know one team might have a bunch of them like Alabama has this year but that's unusual. Just the normal team, the normal stats on it, you get two or three of those a year so you can't really count on those, so when you get those in a game then that's pretty significant. I think the overall statistical advantage to scoring a non-offensive touchdown is pretty heavily - that team is going to win more games. You put turnovers in there, you recover a fumble on the one-yard line - that's not a defensive score - but if that ends up being a score you kind of have a similar result. So those turnovers - that's why the turnovers are so important because they aren't always point-plays but they usually result in points, especially if you get them in good field position then you're already in the scoring zone. But a safety is part of that. Yeah, it's definitely part of that conversation because even though its only two points it is possession so it's a little bit of an added benefit.

Q: To what extent does the success of one unit correlate to another unit, either directly or

indirectly? How can the success of the defense help the offense or vice versa?

BB: Yeah, that's a good question. I mean, they work together and there's definitely – one influences the other. The degree of it, I mean, I'm not sure. I don't know how you quantify that. It's an important interaction. It's an important relationship between the three units on the team and they certainly help each other. To what degree, I don't know.

Q: I guess we look at it as three different things but in a sense there is continuity between how one unit's actions can play a role in another.

BB: Yeah, I agree completely. But again, to kind of quantify it is a little hard to do. It's kind of a feeling that you get. I mean, obviously it relates to field position as one group gets the ball for the other, or takes the ball from the other group. Where that happens on the field, that plays a part of it. But whatever unit is out there has to go out there and do whatever it is they do – kick it, or move it, or stop the other team, whatever it happens to be. Where that happens on the field and the impact plays that come from those units and how they set up the next unit, there's definitely a lot of interplay there. How you quantify it, I don't really know. I think we all know it when we see it. I don't know if I could sit here and give it a definition.

Q: How much does the defensive approach change later in the game if you have a substantial lead? Does the emphasis change based on the situation?

BB: However, you want it to change.

Q: Is there more of an emphasis on draining the clock?

BB: It depends on the situation. Yeah, there's a place for all of those. Once you get into an extreme situation, there's no question about that. As the situation moves through that, let's call it grey area, from light grey to dark grey, it changes. It depends on what point you're talking about. Look, the game changes on every snap, first down, second down, third down, first down is at another field positon, ball exchanges, do it all over again. Every play really is a situational play. Once time and score become a factor, time at the end of the first half and then time and score become a factor at the end of the game then, obviously, that overrides a lot of things, too. A lot of times, really, from a coaching standpoint you are really only coaching three quarters. The fourth quarter a lot of times is defined by the situation, so at that point you're playing whatever the situation is. It's usually not defined too much before that. Sometimes, but not usually, but whenever it becomes defined or whenever you feel like it changes, then now you're playing situational football. But again, every down really is a new situation.

Q: How have you been able to perform so well at the end of the first half throughout the season and get points in those final minutes?

BB: Look, I attribute all of our success to good players and good execution. I mean, in the end, the success that we have is based on players going out there and executing and performing well in those situations. So, whether it's on the goal line, or at the end of the half, or on third down, or in the red area, or on the punt return team, or whatever it is, those are the guys that go out there and make the plays. If we make good ones, it's because they make good ones.

Q: How would you describe the way the team has approached its work this year in regards to tuning out some of the outside noise that goes on around the team?

BB: I think I'd really just answer that question as it relates to our play. Overall, we've done a lot of good things this year. I think our record reflects that, but it really doesn't matter. We're in a one-game season now, and so we'll turn all of our attention and focus to having the best performance we can have on Saturday night.

Q: Does the team ever use any of the media negativity as fuel to help propel them towards their ultimate goals?

BB: Yeah, what we're going to do is utilize the time that we have to structure, and practice and prepare as efficiently as we can to be ready to go on Saturday night against the Titans. That's what we're going to do. I know everybody in this organization is committed to that. We've worked all year to put ourselves in this position. Now we have after the Wild Card weekend. Things have been reseeded and we know what our challenge is. We know it's a big one and we're going to do our best to meet it. That's what we're going to do.

Q: Is this another 'ignore the noise' situation?

BB: It's just get ready to play the Titans. That's what it is.

Special Teams

Q: What adjustments do you make when you have injuries on special teams?

BB: I'm telling you though, when you're a special teams coach and you lose that first guy, like alright so this player is out, now we make our move on the punt team, on the punt return team, on the kickoff team, on the kickoff return team, maybe the field goal rush team or wing on field goal, whatever it is, OK. Now, if something happens to him, who's the backup on the next play? And again you don't know when that's going to happen, so you could be sitting there on third down and there's the guy out there and now he hobbles off the field on third down and now you're out there on punt return or punt team or they score and now you're in a kicking situation. So, forget about all the X's and O's, forget about all the situational things that come up in the kicking game, the one-play-type situation things, all the other things, personnel management on special teams is a huge part of the responsibility of that position. I know that's a lot more than you wanted to know about this. We could make that long answer even longer if you really want to. Joe [Judge], Scott [O'Brien], those guys, and Joe as Scott's assistant or Bubba [Ray Ventrone] as Joe's assistant, those guys, you've got very little time to work fast and a lot of times you're trying to make those substitutions and a guy might already be on the field. Somebody is out, alright what are we going to do, and you look out there and that guy's out there playing defense or he's out there playing offense or he's with the coaches about to go in or out in those situations, and kind of getting all that straight.

Q: Does field position become an even more important factor in November football?

BB: Absolutely, but we always want good field position so I don't want to say that it's not important at some other time because it's really always important. Just like we talked about in terms of field goal range, I'd say the game is being played a little bit differently than what it is in September. Field position is critical and that really starts with the kicking game and then of course turnovers impact it tremendously, but the kicking game overall is a big start to that. I think last week's game against Buffalo was a good example there of the advantage we had in field position. We got a good punt return from Danny. We got a couple good punt coverage plays and then we got a strip fumble by Brandon King on the punt. That was a big field position swing that involved a turnover. Those plays are huge and we've just got to keep working to get our offense and defense the best possible field positon because that always works in your favor. You've still got to go out there and play, but it definitely helps the whole field position situation – I mean the opportunity for the offense and defense in their field positon.

Q: What are some of the differences in what you're looking for when it comes to punt returners versus kick returners? How do you differentiate between the skillsets for those two return jobs?

BB: Phil [Perry], that's a good question. Of course, the easy answer is if one person does both, then that makes it a lot easier and it also makes the roster question a lot easier. I mean, the big difference, of course, is on kickoff returns, you get a chance to build up your speed, you get a chance to handle the ball cleanly, there's nobody on top of you when you catch it and you're able to run and set up your blocks and hit things full speed through that point, usually between the 20 and 30 yard line, where the coverage and the blockers in a wedge all sort of come together and the returner gets a chance to set those blocks up and hit them and try to get through there. The punting game is a lot more situational. Mostly on kickoffs, the ball is always kicked from the same place.

Rarely is there a difference. There are some, but they're minimal - after a safety or that type of thing. But punting, the ball can be anywhere, so the situation that they're punting in can be quite diverse and sometimes complex. Punters are very good at directional punting and kicking different types of punts - the end-over-end punts, spiral punts, spirals that don't turn over and so forth, so the ball handling is a little more complex and you have to deal with players around you as you're catching the ball sooner or later. I mean, sometimes a punter will outkick his coverage, but the majority of the time, there's some decision making involved, whether to catch it and try to make the first coverage player or two miss to get the return started or fair catch it or to let it go and not catch the ball or to let it go over your head and let it go in the end zone for a touchback. So, there's a lot of decision making on just whether to catch the ball and whether to catch and run with it or whether to catch it and just fair catch it that are played different than the kickoffs.

And then, in addition to that, you deal with defenders and coverage players that are on you a lot quicker on punt return, so sometimes you only have a yard or two or a couple yards to get into space, make a guy miss, break a tackle, whereas the kickoff is much more of a build-up play. Because they're so different, a lot of times you don't have the same player doing both. And, a personal opinion is because they're so different, I find the two plays very fascinating and intriguing and a great part of the strategy of football, just because the plays themselves are so different and the teaching, the rules, the skills and so forth. And so that's why I'm not in favor - I take an opposing view to the people who want to eliminate kickoffs from the game and try to have as few kickoffs as possible. I think it's an exciting play, it's a unique play and one that is a big momentum play because of what happened the play before - the score or, possibly, the two times at the start of the half where it's kind of a tone setter or a pace setter for that opening play. So, yeah, they're played different and, of course, the same thing in the blocking.

You get a chance to set up a return, whereas on the punting side of it, you have an option of trying to pressure the punter and block it or return it, but you kind of have to return it from the line of scrimmage. You can't drop off too far because of the possibilities of fakes, so you have to keep enough guys up on the line of scrimmage to ensure that the ball is punted. And, you have to ensure the onside kick that you don't get onside kicked to, but again, that's much less frequent and the rules are in the kick returner team's favor on the onside kick. So, it's a big gamble for the kicking team to do that as a surprise tactic. So, the blocking patterns and techniques of blocking are quite different on the punt returns compared to what they are on kickoff returns.

Q: Because of the decision making involved in the position, is the returner position worth a roster spot on its own?

BB: Well, I mean, I'd say the ball handling is critical. I mean, it's like the long snapper. How many plays is the long snapper in for a game? I mean, I'd call it 10. I don't know, somewhere in that neighborhood, eight to 10 - field goals, punts and extra points. But, everybody carries a long snapper. Between kick returns and the punt returns, maybe a couple less than that, but I'd say the difficulty of those jobs and the importance of them and quick ball handling - I mean, there's not much that will lose the game quicker than that. So, I think it's a high priority for everybody. When I say everybody, I'm saying every team I think that's a high priority for. It certainly is for us. So, we'll have to see how it turns out, but it's not an afterthought at all. It's a priority item.

Q: Could there be any carry over for a kicker who is maybe practicing a different technique on kickoffs?

BB: I think they're definitely different. I don't think there's any question about that. It would be like a golfer. You've got to be able to hit a sand wedge, you've got to be able to hit a five iron, you've got to be able to drive, you've got to be able to putt. That's what kickers and punters do. There's plus-50 punts, there's field goals, there's kickoffs, there's back up punts, there's punts against a heavy rush, there's punts against a six-man box where both of the gunners are getting double teamed. And just like golf there are wind conditions and not wind conditions and so forth. It's not like they're standing out there on the driving range and banging the ball away every time. Especially on place kicks, you're dealing with a center and a holder and timing on the play so it's not like you're just placing the ball down there on a tee and kicking it like you are a golf ball or a kickoff. Yeah, they're definitely different. Whether it's a punter or kicker you're talking about, they have to master different skills, different kicks, different types of kicks, different things that are specific to their position just like every other player and every other athlete for the most part has to do. If you're a basketball player you can't just shoot free throws. You've got to be able to make some other shots, too. That's part of the position. Being able to do the things that are required of that position, and yeah, they're not all the same. But I don't think they're all the same for anybody.

Q: Do you coach players to score if they have a chance on an onside kick?

BB: Well again, it depends on the situation in the game. In that particular situation with the Colts out of timeouts and the amount of time that was left in the game, all we had to do was kneel on the ball, so you don't want to take any needless opportunities or chances in trying to advance the ball. Ball possession really wins the game in that situation. But again I think that play was a little bit unusual because Rob was moving forward. He kind of made the play on the run so it might have been a little more awkward for him to go down than to just catch it and keep moving forward. The most important thing in that play is obviously just ball security, is securing possession of that ball. A lot of times it's going to the ground and securing it, but on that particular one it was probably actually easier for him to do it the way he did, and he handled it very cleanly. Those are the plays we talk about a lot. They don't come up all that frequently for any individual team. Maybe if you watched all the games over the weekend, you'd probably see a couple of them every weekend, but for your individual team, when that play comes up, it's kind of a game-winning play. It's kind of like the Hail Mary pass that goes into the end zone – if you defend it you win and if you don't you lose. The onside kick is maybe not quite that dramatic, but it's pretty close so if you can make that play then you can run out the clock and end the game and if you can't make it they have that chance to score and you've got to stop them on defense. The execution of that play is critical when it comes up. It just doesn't happen all that often. But when it does, everything you've done in the previous 59 minutes all hinges on the execution of that one play.

Q: In retrospect, would you have gone for two in the same situation?

BB: Look, at that point, if you had told me that those were going to be the final points scored in the game until a minute to go in the game, it just didn't look like that's the way the game was going at that point. But as it turned out, whether you're up by 12 or you're up by 13 with less than two minutes to go in the game, it doesn't really make any difference. You'd be better off to be up by 14 than up by 13 or 12 for that matter. If you know there's not going to be any more scores, that's why I'm saying the closer you get to the end of the game, the more you can rely on the chart, the more time there is remaining and the more opportunities there are for scores if you don't make that two point conversion. Again, going back to the Denver-Cleveland game from yesterday, it was a good example of when Cleveland went for two to make it 22-16 and they got stopped, so now it was 20-16, and then Denver scored and now it's 23-20 instead of 23-21, and now you've got the field goal to tie instead of the field goal to win. But without that touchdown, a six-point lead and a four-point lead is the same thing. But then as soon as Denver hit that long pass, now the whole chart changes again and you're on the wrong side of it. Like I said, the less time there is, I think the more you go with the chart. If you have that same score differential in the first quarter, a lot of times you just take the higher probability of an extra point and play the game out. If that is going to be the last score until the final minute of the game, then you're better off following the chart. But again, if you have a play you really like and you feel confident about the play, there is really no reason not to run that play. If you feel 95 percent about that play, then you could run that any time because it's always good to get two points.

Q: For players who excel as gunners on special teams, is there a correlation between the ability to make a special teams tackle after a downfield sprint and being a good open-field tackler on defense?

BB: Yeah, there's certainly some carryover. It's a little bit different, though. On special teams, on punt and kickoff coverage, you're running, usually, quite a ways to get to the runner. Generally on defense, you're not running quite that far - maybe a free safety coming up to the line of scrimmage, call it 15 yards or so, plus the lateral distance that he covers - but it's usually not the same or not as frequent. You maybe have one or two of those plays a game defensively, hopefully. Hopefully, you don't have any, but those kind of tackles that you're talking about that occur in the kicking game aren't that common on defense. They do occur, but they're not that common. But, regardless, we work many, many different tackling drills. They have many different components to tackling. A lot of it is leverage and position and getting to the right spot relative to your angle on the runner and your proximity to another defender or sideline and things like that. And then there's the whole technique of actually tackling - of wrapping up and getting the runner on the ground and dealing with things that runners do to try to break tackles, like stiff arms and spinning out of contact and lowering their shoulder and things like that. So, there are a lot of variables between a runner and the final tackle, but we try to work on all those things.

Q: Do the Texans special teams units do things similar to the way you've done them with Larry Izzo as the coach?

BB: Well, I think Larry [Izzo] has done a good job. They're a very good rush team. They put a lot of pressure on your kickers, field goal rushes and punt rushes. Even when they return they do a good job of rushing. A lot of times they rush guys like [Whitney] Mercilus who are hard to block no matter who's blocking them. They've had explosive plays in the return game. [Tyler] Ervin had a big play against the Raiders called back, but I think you could see pretty quickly what he can do. [They have an] excellent kicker. [Nick] Novak has had a great year for them.

[Shane] Lechler is a field position guy. He can change field position on one play and he does that. They're solid in that phase of the game. We know they're well-coached. Again, you've got to be ready for game plan adjustments or for them to do something that's going to attack you. You've got to be ready to deal with it or adjust to it during the game. They're well-coached in all three phases of the game. I don't think there is any question about that. They do a great job of making it hard on their opponents. We'll have to do a good job preparing and I'm sure there will be in-game adjustments that we'll have to deal with like we always do with them.

Q: How much emphasis is placed on creating big plays in special teams when you go into a season and how much do those plays swing the momentum either for or against a team?

BB: Well, sure I think those big plays are always good plays for momentum and, you know, just put a little spark into the team. Honestly we're always trying to make them. We've never tried to do anything but make plays. I'd just say the more playmakers you have out there then the better chance you have to make them. Sometimes you end up with players who are just fulfilling a role out there, which you need that, but when you actually have playmakers, guys in the return game that you can count on to make blocks, or you can put one-on-one to make blocks on their good players, or in coverage guys that can't be single-blocked and have to be double-teamed. If you only have one of those guys then they double team him and you're back to kind of treading water. If you have more guys than they can handle then whichever ones, one or two they might double, then you've got good opportunities with other players. So, returners that can make plays with the ball in their hand, blockers that can block good players, coverage players that have to be double-teamed and then obviously good specialty play from the snapper, kicker, punter, and punt returner or kickoff returner; those are all the keys.

Q: Is there a common denominator in terms of their mentality that allows certain guys to excel on special teams?

BB: Well, I don't know if it's a mentality. I mean it is to a degree, the aggressiveness, trying to make plays as opposed to just trying to stay in your area of responsibility. I'd say that just the instinctiveness of being primarily a space player, recognizing how much space there is between you and the runner or how much space you have to defend from the guy you're blocking to where he has to get to the runner, can you get around the guy to the backside to make the play, do you have to go to the front side, or do you have to go through him? Obviously, the combination of speed and explosiveness, their strength, is the combination that you're looking for. So, if you have to take people on you can take them on and if you can run around them or avoid them you've got the speed to do that as well. So, it's a combination of space ability, speed, power, explosion, quickness, and just judgement in space which is different than making inline judgements or close quarter type decisions. Those space judgements are your speed, their speed, the angle, what's between you and the guy, whether you're blocking or covering. Those are all kind of instinctive qualities that we coach, we have guidelines on, we try to explain fundamentally what you want to do but each situation's a little bit different. The player has to make that decision as to whether he can make it or not make it and so forth. So, it's a lot of instinctiveness on all of those plays because each one of them is different. You just have to have a good sense and a good feel for where you can get to with your skills versus what obstacles you encounter along the way.

Q: What are some of the measures you use to try to determine how effective your special teams are? I'm guessing yards gained or saved in the punting game and things like that. Are those measures you guys keep?

BB: Yeah, sure. I think that absolutely really comes under the whole category of hidden yardage, if you will. For example, fielding a punt and fair catching a punt that's say 37 yards versus not catching it and it rolls another 13 yards and now it's a 50-yard net or a 13-yard change of field position. So those 13 yards don't show up in the stats. It's not a sack, it's just if you had handled the ball, you would have had it at midfield, but you didn't handle it so you have it at your 37. Those plays are definitely hidden yardage in the kicking game. Things like penalties, they're generally at the spot of where the ball was caught most of the time, in the punting game. So if you return a punt for 10 yards and get a penalty, it's really a 20-yard loss of field position as opposed to a 10-yard penalty. So the penalties in the kicking game, generally speaking, result in more yardage than they do on normal scrimmage plays.

For example, in one game, Don Jones got a block in the back call, and so they lost the return yardage and they had the penalty on top of it, so it wound up being 20 percent of the field or 25 percent of the field. So it was a huge field position play penalty. We track all those. We try to, obviously, stress the importance to the players of those decisions and those situations because of what's at stake there from a field position standpoint. I mean another huge stat in the kicking game is missed field goals. I mean really missed field goals are almost the equivalent to a turnover. Not only do you get the ball, but you get it plus seven yards. There's a real cost to a missed field in terms of field position, particularly on a longer one, obviously. But if you miss it from the 15, it's not that much different than if you had punted. But you know what I mean. If you miss a long field goal, that's really like a turnover. There's a lot of hidden yardage there.

There's a lot of different ways to calculate it and measure it and all that. The bottom line is as a coach, what you want your team to do is make the most out of each situation. Like, we saw a play in our game where we mishandled a kickoff in the end zone, but the ball didn't come out of the end zone so we downed it. We saw a play the other night, similar play, where the ball did roll out of the end zone. Things like that, which again, it's not really a stat play, it is but it isn't, but it's certainly a big field position play. Like I said, the goal for us as a coaching staff is to try to get the most out of those plays, whatever it is. Do we measure it? I mean, yeah, we do. But the most important thing is to try to make sure we do it right and get the most out of it. When we don't, we need to make sure players understand and we all understand how important those plays are.

Q: What did you see from the missed extra point last Sunday? Was the whole timing just thrown off due to the snap?

BB: Yeah, well, there are several things that could've been better on that play, obviously. It's the National Football League. We've got to be able to execute that play better than we did. Obviously, need to coach it better, need to execute it better. We've just got to do a better job on it.

Q: In general, have you been satisfied thus far with that operation on your team?

BB: I think we've had a lot of really good plays there. That wasn't one of them. Again, we've just got to do a better job of coaching it, preparing the players for that type of situation and being able to execute under not perfect conditions but, as I said, we're in the National Football League. We've got to be able to execute that play.

Q: What is the learning curve like for a player like Jacob Hollister on special teams where he is being asked to make tackles despite being primarily an offensive player throughout his football career?

BB: Look, that takes a lot of work, takes a lot of extra work. [Matthew] Slater was in that category, [Brandon] Bolden, guys like that, that played in the kicking game for us. Hollister is in that category. Yeah, you keep working on those things in practice and leverage, breaking down the actual technique and fundamental of hitting the guy, and hitting the runner and wrapping him up, closing space, taking the proper angle when you close, maintaining that leverage, understanding where people are around you. We do tackling drills every day and we watch a lot of film on tackling. We practice it, especially with a player like that who, as you pointed out, doesn't really have very much experience doing that. Some things come more naturally to some guys than others. I'd say in Jacob's case, a lot of things that he didn't do, which was almost everything, he's picked up relatively quickly. I'm not saying he's got it all down.

I'm not saying that at all. But I'd say he's picked up a lot of things at the tight end positon, which as we've talked about, is not the easiest position in our offense to learn and in the kicking game. He's involved in all four phases on that – kickoff, kickoff return, punt and punt return. Each one of those kind of has some unique aspects to each of those units. But yeah, he's worked hard at it. He's come a long way. He can still improve and get better at it but he learns every time he walks out on the field and especially in those areas that, as you said, he doesn't really have very much experience with.

Q: How much time is dedicated to special teams in practice? Is it equal to offense and defense?

BB: Oh no. No, but look, we try to prepare for the game the best that we can. We have a lot of things we have to get ready for. We try to balance that out and we put a lot of time into everything - situations, offense, defense, special teams. But, no, it wouldn't be split equally, but we do what we feel like we need to do to be prepared. Players work hard at it and Joe [Judge] and Bubba [Ray Ventrone] do a great job of teaching it. It's about what it's been in the past.

Q: What are some of the things you saw overall from your special teams units last night?

BB: Well, I would say it's overall pretty similar to what we could say about our whole performance on offense, defense and special teams. We had our moments. We did some things well. You mentioned some of those. We missed an opportunity to down the ball with good field position. I'd say we missed some opportunities in the return game. We were close on a punt rush, but didn't have a lot of production in the return game in the end. I thought the onside kick recovery was obviously one of the big plays in the game, probably the most important play of the game on special teams, even including the blocked field goal because of when it happened. I mean, that play is always a critical play. I thought our punt protection against a good punt rush and field goal rush team for that matter, our punt and field goal protection were both pretty solid, which is as I said, a real challenge against that team; Baltimore. Nobody's blocked more kicks then the Ravens have in recent years. There were good things and there were individually a lot of good things even on some of the plays that didn't go well. We've just got to keep working at it but that was a good special teams unit that we faced, and as you said we made some, they made some. We'll just keep working to make those plays. That group works hard. The unit works hard. I thought our three specialists gave us a lot of good plays.

Punt/Punt Return

Q: With Australian punters coming into the league, has the teaching and philosophy of when to field punts changed, or do you still tell your returners to

stand on the 10-yard line and if it goes over your head let it go?

BB: That's a really good question and I think there are a lot of factors that go into the coaching of that positon and that situation that you described, but among the things that the returner has to consider is where the ball is being punted from and how close the coverage is to him and how apt they are or what kind of position they're in to be able to down those balls. We've all seen a lot of plays where the returner runs out of the way and the coverage player comes down there, turns around and catches the ball on the three-yard line or whatever. I think it's definitely a challenging situation. First of all, it's a lot different when a punter punts the ball from his own 40 and the ball is carrying 55 yards and hits on the five-yard line from when he's on your 40 and the ball is being punted straight up in the air and it comes down on the five-yard line.

The trajectory of the ball and as you mentioned the technique of punting it where it has a backspin if you will or kicked in a way that it's less likely to bounce forward, then you've got to think about catching the ball inside the 10 as opposed to letting it be downed on the one or two and the chances of it going into the end zone are probably not very good. So, there is that whole situation. I think a good returner can tell by the way the ball is traveling, not that you can predict at 100 percent, but you can get a pretty good idea if it's going to bounce or if it's going to kick backwards based on the way the ball is spinning. So that can play into it. The wind can play into it. And then there is the whole philosophy like we talked about before with kickoff returners that if you have a great returner, and you handle the ball, assuming that you don't fumble it, that you handle the ball in that kind of situation, what's the risk and what's the reward. You might lose a few yards of field position versus giving that player an opportunity to return a kick and possibly make a big play.

So are you willing to trade a few yards of field positon for an opportunity at an explosive play and handling the ball, and I think that a lot more returners are given the green light on that maybe than what they were in decades earlier let's call it. I think that's part of the equation, too, taking your returner out of the game just because the ball goes inside the 10-yard line, not saying that's wrong, but it's also a decision you're making to limit the playmaking ability of potentially one of your explosive players. Long answer to a short question, a lot of different factors, I think every team probably gives their returner certain guidelines. I think the more trust and confidence and experience that player has, the more willing you are to let him make the right decision based on the actual kick and what happens on that play as opposed to just a generic set of rules. And then there are some situations that are cut and dry, depending on the score, time and situation of the game, there is not really a decision to make. Here's the way it is and we follow those rules. But it's certainly an interesting point of discussion, and I don't know that there's any right or wrong answer to it other than whatever has been identified and communicated to the returner by the team. But there is certainly variability on that subject.

Q: What goes into playing the punt protector role that Nate Ebner played on your punt unit?

BB: Yeah, that's one of the toughest spots to play. It doesn't come up every play. I'm not saying it's - it's kind of like playing quarterback, but you play quarterback for, call it 60 plays a game, 70 plays a game. You only punt five to 10 times, let's call it - somewhere in there. But, there's a lot of different variables. You know, if it's eight-on-eight, then it's getting the right eight-on-eight. Now, if you split your gunners out and a guy comes in from the outside, now they have nine-on-eight, and that creates some problems. You also want to try to be able to maximize your coverage, so let's say there's only six guys rushing and you have eight blockers, right - seven plus the personal protector.

If you can block those six with six and then have two free guys going to the ball, particularly if it's the two guys that are your best coverage players or two of your best coverage players, there's some strategy there, too. So, identifying the rush, identifying the return - sometimes you can tell what the return is based on the way they align - or if there's a double team on the gunner or not a double team on the gunner, a lot of times the wind plays into that. Sometimes the situation plays into it. Teams that like field returns are bound to return in certain situations, or middle returns in certain situations, like plus-50, things like that. So, there are a lot of variables there, but a good personal protector takes all those into consideration, just like a quarterback does, and A, protect the punter, B, he's the last line of defense. So, a lot of times, even if your protection is not right on the front, if that guy gets the right guy and does the right thing, you still could possibly save a blocked punt by just him doing the right thing, even though somebody else has made a mistake in the front of it. So, that decision making is a key part of it there, and the whole cadence and communication between the snapper, the punter and the gunners if we directional punt - if we're trying to punt the ball one way or the other, making sure that everybody knows where that is and if it changes, which sometimes it does based on the look that they give you. So, there's a lot of different things that go in there. It's not an easy job at all if you want to do it right and get the most out of it. So, we've had a number of guys do that - Pat's done it for us, Jordan's [Richards] done it for us, obviously Nate did a great job of it. Those guys all meet together and work together, just like the quarterbacks do. They all learn the same things so that they all understand what the options are, and what's a good option against one team might be a bad option against another team.

It frequently is. We wouldn't always necessarily do it by the book. It would depend on what the look was and who the people are on the other side of the ball, who we're facing. So, the plus-50 punting game where they leave their defense on the field and don't put a punt return team out there, that creates a whole other set of problems that you have to deal with on the punt team. The size and the type of player that's rushing is a lot different than, a lot of times, the player that's on the punt return team and the rushers they would use would be different. So, that creates another element of it, too. A lot goes into that position. It's a tough position to play, as I said. I'm not trying to say it's like playing quarterback. You don't do it 70 times a game, but the times you do it, it could be a team like Buffalo that gives you some different looks, Miami that gives you a lot of different looks. It's challenging.

Q: Is punt returning one of the toughest things to simulate in practice since you can't account for some game factors?

BB: Like tackling?

Q: Yeah and crowd noise and other game day circumstances.

BB: Well, I mean it's the same with everything. We can turn the music up just like we can turn it up for the offense. I mean, look, practice is practice. It's the closest we can get to simulating a game. It's not game conditions but it's as close as we can get. Players that can perform in practice I think have a chance to perform in the game. It's still another level. It's another step, but if you can't do it consistently in practice then it's pretty unlikely it's going to happen consistently in a game. That's really true of every positon on the field. I can't think of one that wouldn't fall into that category. You do what you can do. You make it as realistic as you can make it, or in some cases maybe you make it a little bit harder where you can in some areas and then the game is the game. It's a different speed. It's a different level.

Q: Is there a longer list of guys on this team that may be able to return punts than we think or have seen ourselves?

BB: There probably is; yeah. I mean look, [Julian] Edelman never returned punts. He was at the top of the league for pretty much every year that he's done it. It's like a lot of other skills. It can be developed. It can be improved. It doesn't mean it happens with everybody, but it could if a player has good skills for it, if he has good judgment, can handle the ball. I mean that's the biggest thing, is the ball handling. Kickoff returns, there's nobody on you for the most part, so you have plenty of time to catch the ball.

You're not under pressure to make a decision as to whether to fair catch it or catch it. You might make a decision if you want to bring it out of the end zone or not, but that's different than actually handling the ball with guys around you and having to deal with them almost as soon as you touch the ball. Catching the ball and judging the ball, especially here - we're not playing in a dome - so every kick is a little bit different based on the wind and the way the ball comes off the punters foot and so forth. They're all a little bit different. That's a big skill for a punt returner, is just ball judgment, and ball handling, and decision making, whether to catch it, fair catch it, let it go, so forth, plus-ten, plus-five, depending on the hang time and conditions and so forth. There's a lot. A lot more decision making involved there. So that really is experience. The ball handling is, I'd say, not a natural thing because it can be improved, but to some degree it's a natural thing.

Q: Your team is at the top of a lot of the rankings in punt coverage. How much has the overall speed of that unit contributed to the success that they've had?

BB: I mean it's really such a team play. Obviously the punter is a very important part of it. Ryan [Allen]'s done a good job for us. The snapper is an important part of it. Joe [Cardona]'s done a good job for us, the other nine guys, the coaching, and all of the situational plays that come up in the punting game.

Again, it's not like standing there on the driving range and just banging them out there. I mean every punt is different. There's a six-man box, there's a seven-man box, there's an eight-man box, there's an overloaded box. Who are the edge-rushers? What's the field positon? What's the down and distance? Who's the returner? The wind, the return tendencies based on are they vising the gunner, are they vising both gunners? Do they have a key guy that sets the return that's kind of the point of attack guy in the return game? Are we going to kick away from him or whatever the case might be? Who are their game plan rushers? How do we handle the guys coming off the gunners? The corner roles, the fake corner roles and all of that. The personal protector is a critical guy in all of that. Nate [Ebner] - he's done a great job for us. Definitely being strong down the middle there from Joe to Nate to Ryan is important, but everybody up front being on the same page, being able to pick up all of the different twists and having to involve a guy with his head between his legs as a blocker, especially when they put good rushers on that guy. I mean that's usually where you get one of their best guys so the challenge of snapping and blocking but also helping that guy with his block because he can't see and if they twist when he's snapping the ball, which they do, then other people have to come in play there. So it's really a great team play.

The gunners not only making tackles but downing balls and playing with proper leverage and getting the ball to the other coverage players so they can be effective. I think it's the whole team really that has done a good job on that. We've had a lot of consistency there, a lot of the same guys lined up in the same spot week-after-week. Joe [Judge] and Bubba [Ray Ventrone] have done a good job of game planning that. It's a game within a game. It really is. It's a one play situation but so many of those situations are so - if you punt seven or eight times in a game probably five of them are going to be unique. One or two might repeat. You might have a second plus-50 punt or a second backed up punt with the same direction or the same wind or whatever it is. But there's a lot of variety in those plays and the later it goes in the game then the more it becomes really a situational game. And a lot of time honestly the yards aren't that important. Whether its 35 or 40, you know, it's nice if its 40 but that's not the most important thing. The most important thing is that it's not minus-20.

Q: What has made Ryan Allen so efficient in punting the ball with all of the different weather conditions that you get in New England?

BB: Well, Ryan's gained a lot of experience since he's been here. He's operated in those conditions in practice and in games. I know he's learned from those opportunities to kick in various weather situations repeatedly. So, you do it and you learn from it and the next time you try something a little bit different and maybe some part of that works, maybe some part of it doesn't. The next time you continue to build off of it over a period of time and then heat, and cold, and rain, snow, crosswinds, wind in your face, wind at your back, so forth and so on. You just get used to it. You learn what you can do, what you can't do, how much is a problem, how much isn't a problem and try to combine all that with game plans and the strategy of the situations in the game, but in the end it comes down to being able to hit good balls, make good punts, whether those are long, or high, or in a direction; whatever it happens to be. Ryan's a smart kid. He works hard. His game is important to him. He's very coachable. He takes corrections and understands what you want him to do and tries to do it. He's gotten better in a lot of areas. He'll continue to work hard and hopefully continue to improve.

Q: Are there certain things that you coach a punter on throughout the week regarding technique?

BB: Yeah, absolutely. Yeah, definitely. Again, there's a lot of different techniques depending on the type of punt that you want to hit, whether it's for distance, for hang time, for both, directional, plus-50, to a single gunner, accounting for the wind and so forth. Those techniques change depending on the type of punt that you're trying to hit. Sometimes your timing changes based on how much of a rush there is, or if you have to bring a gunner in and maybe you can't block everybody, or you need to get the ball off before a player that's not blocked gets to the punter; things like that. So, there are a lot of different situations in punting and therefore there are a lot of techniques that go with those particular individual punts that have coaching points with them or corrections that go with them.

Again, it's sometimes easier. Sometimes when you do it you can know what you did wrong, know if you made a mistake right away. Sometimes it's easier when somebody else is watching you that's not involved in the mechanics of the operation. They can observe it and sometimes they see it a little bit better than you do. There's a give and take on that, too. A lot of times when you're coaching those guys you see something. Sometimes it's a fine line. It's hard to see it, but the player can feel it and he can tell you kind of, 'This is what happened on this.' Sometimes he knows how to fix it. Sometimes he might need some help from the coach to help him fix it or help him correct the mistake. Those are very fine-tuned skills. Again, it's a lot like hitting a golf shot. The difference being, of course, there are guys running at you and you have to handle a snap and all. You can't just put the ball on a tee and swing. But, the mechanics and the technique and all that, on a golf swing it just doesn't take much for a good shot to be a real bad shot and punting and placekicking are a lot like that, too.

A couple of inches one way or another, or the tilt of the ball or something like that - an inch or two on the step or an inch or two on the ball placement - those kinds of things can make a huge difference in the result. [You're] trying to work for that level of consistency, and timing and execution that's the same over and over again. That being said, it never really is the same because each punt is different. Each snap is a little bit different. You start moving all of those situations into the equation and they look the same but there are subtle differences. They're important differences and good players are able to make those adjustments. Ryan's done a good job of that. It's great to be sitting here on Tuesday talking about all this punting. It's great. You don't get a chance to do that. Actually, you know, I really enjoyed [coaching punters]. I enjoyed coaching [Dave] Jennings, [Sean] Landeta, [Tom] Tupa earlier in my career. Those guys were all right-footed punters and they were all good and could really - they could do a lot of good things. We've had a lot of left-footed punters recently. You just kind of have to look at it a little bit differently, but still the fundamentals are the same. I've been fortunate.

I've had a lot of guys that have had good hands, could handle the ball and could place the ball pretty well at those positons throughout the years. It's been a good thing. The kickers, really, you go back to [Matt] Stover; he was pretty good. Obviously, Adam [Vinatieri] and Steve [Gostkowski] here. I've been real fortunate to have good specialists, good guys at that position. Same thing with snappers - Lonnie [Paxton] - Joe [Cardona]'s done a real good job for us. Lonnie was great. It's nice to put your head on a pillow and not have to worry too much about those positons.

Q: What have you seen the last couple of games from the kick and punt coverage units?

BB: Those guys have done a pretty good job all year, all the way back to training camp, as well. We put a lot of work into that. You know, you have to be able to protect the punter, and that comes up from time to time. If you don't do a good job of it, it will come up a lot. But if you do do a good job of it, then you're in a coverage game. We just, I think this year, maybe allocated a little bit more time to individual coverage techniques, and Joe [Judge] and Bubba [Ray Ventrone] have done a real good job of improving the individual players with their leverage and technique, but also as a unit everybody working with each other and making sure that we're sound in our field coverage responsibilities. You know, the first guys down are important, guys like [Matthew] Slater, Jon Jones and guys like that. And then the next layer of coverage, kind of the lane coverages, is important to be disciplined and to maintain leverage on the ball. You know, I thought we faced a good returner last night who ran hard and had good vision, was a strong runner. And then the third layer of coverage – kind of the safety, one or two safeties, depending on what the scheme is – those guys are in position to prevent a long play, and a lot of times they end up making tackles not that long after the returner's got the ball.

They can attack when inside the 25-yard line on kickoff or something like that. A lot of times it clears up for them and they're able to fit in there and make the play. You have to have good kicks, of course, but the coverage team has to be well-coordinated, and we have a lot of guys that have experience that are working together. Some of the players that don't have as much experience on our team, even though they have experience in the league – guys like [Marquis] Flowers and [Cassius] Marsh that have been a big factor for us in the kicking game – they've worked in well with their other players.

Q: Is Dave Jennings in that conversation about best punters as well?

BB: [Dave] Jennings? Yeah, absolutely. Yeah, no absolutely. Yeah, and Dave - Dave could throw. He had very good directional placement on the ball. He was a clutch punter when you needed one. I still remember in the Dallas game being backed up inside our 10-yard line. He hit a 55-yarder out of the end zone that eventually got us into the playoffs, so it's not just average. It's like golf, it's not can you make a putt. It's making them when you've got to make them, so the same thing with kickers. Yeah, I'd definitely put Jennings in there. [Sean] Landeta - no question. But you're talking about an athlete with [Johnny] Hekker now - he's a little more athletic than Landeta, just to pick a name. I would say Ray Guy - Ray kicked for great average but these guys lead the league in punt coverage. They lead the league in gross punting, lead the league in net punting, lead the league in inside-the-20, and lead the league in punt coverage. I mean if you're in front in one of those categories you're pretty good. Last year they led the league in all three. They're right up there this year, plus he's a threat on fakes and stuff like that. He's pretty good.

Q: Can you speak to what you have seen from Ryan Allen this year in terms of situational punting?

BB: Yeah, sure. Punting is such a situational play, and it's not just standing there and kicking it as far as you can. It's making the right kick in the right situation. So, sometimes part of that's the rush, sometimes part of it's the coverage, sometimes part of it's the field position and game situation, time left and so forth, and certainly the elements and field conditions come into play there, too. But, overall, he has done a very good job for us in those not just situational punts, but last week when he was backed up and had to hit for distance and coverage, field position, into the wind, he did a good job of that, too. Ryan works hard and he's really a guy that pays a lot of attention to his job and all the little things that we ask him to do. When those situations have come up, he's done a good job of executing them.

Q: We know that certain positions have their own positional coach. Where do placekickers turn for that level of expertise? Do the special teams coaches have a level of knowledge about placekicking despite the fact they themselves may not have been kickers in the past?

BB: I certainly get where you're coming from. I don't think that's the case here. I can't speak for other teams. I think Joe [Judge] is very knowledgeable about the techniques of kicking. I know when I became a special teams coach and coached special teams for many years as an assistant coach and I continue to be involved with it as a head coach, but for many years as an assistant coach that's one of the things I had to learn. I had to learn how to coach those individual specialists; the snappers, the kickers, the punters, the returners. I don't think it's any different than coaching any other position. Things you don't know you need to learn and the things you do know you need to be able to teach to the players, however you've acquired that information. And some of that certainly comes from the players, especially when you coach good players at the position that you're coaching. You can learn a lot from them just like I learned a lot from many of the players that I coached going back to people like Dave Jennings as a punter or Carl Banks or Lawrence Taylor or Pepper

[Johnson], guys like that as linebackers for the Giants. However you acquire that information you acquire it. You have to be able to convey it and teach it to the players and recognize technique or judgement. I mean look, there's a whole host of things that go into performance but all of the things that are related to those, but you know, be able to figure out which ones are the most important, which ones need to be corrected and so forth, but I think Joe is very knowledgeable in that, as was Scott O'Brien. I've had a lot of experience with that myself. But that's what coaching is. If you don't know it then you've got to find out. Nobody knows everything. I mean no coach knows everything about every position. Maybe if a guy has played it for a decade he might be well-versed in that position but I'd say for the most of the rest of us that haven't done that, things you don't know you've got to learn. You've got to find out. You've got to figure it out.

Q: I read that Denver had brought a left-footed punter into camp and worked him out. I'm curious about the history of left-footed punters, with you in particular. Is there an advantage to it? It seems like it's become more commonplace in the league recently, but what is the thought process behind that. Is there a difference over the course of the season in having a left-footed punter?

BB: That's a good question. There's definitely something – a left-footed punter, right-footed punter, the ball spins opposite and what you get used to when you go to the other foot it's reversed. I think there's definitely something to be said for that, practicing that way. I know going back to when we were at the Giants and I was the special teams coach there, we had a right-footed punter obviously with [Dave] Jennings and then with [Sean] Landeta and when we would face a left-footed punter, we always kind of just wanted to get the returner to handle those balls, which was [Phil] McConkey. It was several different guys, but I definitely remember McConkey and how Phil would talk about how that would, even though he'd done it before, it was just good to get familiar with it prior to doing it in the upcoming game. [Phil] Simms would punt to him. Even though Phil [Simms] does a lot of things right-handed, he punts left-footed, believe it or not, and actually punts pretty well. So, we would do that. I had a lot of right-footed punters. I had Jennings, I had Tom Tupa in Cleveland, [Brian] Hansen and then when I came here, we had a left-footed punter with [Lee] Johnson and then it just was [Ken] Walter and [Josh] Miller and it's just kind of evolved that way. Now we had [Todd] Sauerbrun for a while, half a season or a third of a season, whatever it was, but for the most part it's been left-footed punters since I've been here in New England. That's not really by design. I'd say it's just more kind of worked out that way. But it is kind of a long coincidence of that. But it was probably just as much a coincidence that it was the other way. I don't think it really makes any difference in terms of the punting because there's nobody else involved. The snapper and then the punter, it's not like you have a left-footed kicker where you have to flip your holder and the operation is a little bit backwards. With the punter, it's just the way he does it and it doesn't really affect anybody else. But I think there is something to the returner getting familiar with those balls. I don't want to make a big deal out of it because I don't think it's that big of a deal, but I do think that there's no question it's the reverse spin and the reverse reading of the ball.

Kickoff/Kickoff Return

Q: What is the thinking behind kicking off closer to the sideline as opposed to the middle of the field where the returner may traditionally line up?

BB: Well, I think what most teams try to do on the corner-type kicks is to force you as the return team to either take the ball right up the sideline where you catch it, which means you have a limited amount of space to work on, or to bring the ball all the way across the field which means you're doing a lot of running without gaining yards and there's the potential that you could really get caught inside the 10 or really get pinned down there deep if somebody's able to cut off the returner before he can get all the way across the field. And if you put hang time on that ball that makes it tougher to come across the field with. On the return end of it if you know

where the balls going to go then you could set up a
boundary return even though you're running into
pretty tight quarters there, but you could set it up and
get the blocking angles the best that you can and just
try to take the ball up the field the shortest distance.
But if you're not sure where it is and if the kick goes
away from where you think it's going to go, so if you
set up a boundary return one way and the ball ends
up getting kicked the other way, now you've kind of
got all of your guys out-leveraged, and again, your
choices are to either take the ball straight back up
field with not enough blocking or bring it across the
field to where your blocking is but you've got a long
way to go. It definitely can put you in a tough
situation on that. That happened to us in the Carolina
game where they kicked it over to the corner
and James Develin had to field it and he obviously
was our short returner, not the primary guy, so it
kind of limits what you can do if they can get the ball
in the right spot or in a tough spot. It really limits
your options for the return team. Obviously, the best
option for you in the kickoff return is that the ball is
straight down the middle of the field with not very
much hang time. That's the best returnable ball. The
toughest returnable ball just on the kick alone - forget
about the coverage, that's a whole other discussion - is
a ball with good hang time that pins you in the
corner. You just have a lot fewer options there.

**Q: Statistics have shown that a large number of the
kickoffs for your unit that are returned by the**

opponent are resulting in them being stopped inside the 20-yard line. How much of an emphasis do you put on that for your kickoff unit?

BB: Well, I think that's a very big play. Obviously, there's only two times when you kickoff. One is after you score and the other is at the start of a half, but good play in that situation is really kind of a momentum play and it sets up the coming series for the defense. It's hard to go on a run in this league, but that's one way to do it, is to score, have good kickoff coverage, good field position, make a stop on defense and now the offense is in pretty good position to score again. So, the kickoff coverage really gives you an opportunity to possibly string a couple of points, some points together if you can play good complimentary football. Our guys take a lot of pride in it. Joe [Judge] and Bubba [Ray Ventrone] do a great job of coaching it. We have a good kicker, we have good coverage players. They work together and we do take, as I said, those guys take a lot of pride in it and they put a lot of effort into it and it certainly helps us. I mean defensively, the thing you hope for the most as a defensive coach is good field position. Sometimes you get it, sometimes you don't. You've got to go in and play regardless of where you go in at, but it's always good to have good field position. It certainly gives you a lot more options defensively in terms of play-calling and game management. That's where I think it becomes very helpful for the defense. Obviously the same thing is true in the punting game and our coverage in both phases this year has been good. The return game's been another story but yesterday was the best we've had on that so hopefully that's heading in the right direction.

Q: Is there statistical analysis that has shown that an offense will have a tougher time starting with the ball on the 20-yard line as opposed to the 25-yard line, and is that why with the change in touchback rules this season there has been a bigger emphasis on those lofty kicks that are designed to force the return team to bring the ball out of the endzone?

BB: I think that's part of it. Yeah, I do. I think that's part of it. I'd say, you know, also part of it is just the matchup with your opponent and what they're strength is in the return game and so forth. You know, I would say over the last couple of years because of fewer and fewer kickoffs were returned, it made decisions tougher for teams, made it tougher for teams to carry guys on the roster whose strength was on kickoff or kickoff return, whether that be the returner, or a coverage player, or a wedge guy or something like that because you just weren't getting very many shots at it. And so if you have a real good kickoff returner, how many times are you going to get to return it? In some games you're probably not going to get to return any. Again, especially depending on where some of those games are being played, a little bit less of an issue where we are because sooner or later those balls aren't going to be touchbacks but if you're kicking in a dome or you're kicking in the south consistently, those are pretty heavy touchback games. That's one thing there, so I'm just saying that explosive kickoff returner that maybe could make a handful of plays during the year that would change the game, can you really afford to carry that guy for the number of opportunities he's going to get? Overall, generally speaking the level of returner in the league has probably declined a little bit on kickoffs because the opportunities that they have and so it's become more of a punt and punt return game. Not to digress, but when I came into the league on special teams you had six phases. Every phase was very competitive, so field goal protection, field goal rush, kickoff, kickoff return, punt, punt return - now that's really down to just two phases; punt and punt return. Field goals - it's very hard to block a field goal because of the rules. You can't hit the center, you can't jump, you can't overload, you can't do much of anything. You just have to make a great play to somehow split the coverage or have a bad kick or both to really affect that play. It's not impossible but it's hard, so field goal protection isn't what it used to be and the field goal rush has really been taken out of the game. Then when you start touch-backing the kickoffs you take the coverage players out of the game because you and I could cover a lot of the kickoffs when they're nine, 10, 11 yards deep in the end zone. You don't need anybody to cover them and the same thing with the return game. They don't block because there's no return, so it's become a punt and punt return game and that's where a lot of the emphasis now has to go in the kicking game because that's where most of the plays are. As the kickoffs I think are coming back into it, at least it seems like they are this year more, then that increases those opportunities and probably the value of some of those players that play in that phase of the game. It will be interesting to see how it goes. We're only a couple of weeks into the season. We'll see how it all plays out, but in looking at a few other games it looks like there are a lot of teams that are doing some of the directional, corner-type kicking with good hang time. Just kind of popping the ball up in the air and making teams bring it out, which isn't surprising. That's exactly what happened with the college rule.

Q: It was interesting that the first rule change in 2011 to the kicking game didn't entice teams to do these lofty pop-up kicks.

BB: Right. Well, I think the 25 - getting the ball out to the 25-yard line is obviously harder than getting it out to the 20 and those touchbacks that put it on the 20, I mean I know it's only five yards and five yards is five yards, but it just seems like it's a lot easier for teams to just touchback and put the ball on the 20, whereas now there's just a little more incentive to make them return it to the 25 as opposed to just handing them the ball on the 25-yard line. And I think there are really a lot of teams where if the ball is a yard or two yards deep in the end zone, they're pretty content to just touchback it and take it on the 25. I think that extra five yards has enticed the return teams to do that more.

Q: Has it now become a part of situational football to decide whether or not to kick the ball off for a touchback or try one of those pop-up kickoffs to the goal line? Would your decision on the final kickoff to pop it up have been different if the touchback brought it out to the 20-yard line like in years past?

BB: Yeah, it might be. I don't know, I don't really think of it in those terms but I understand your question Mike [Reiss]. I can't sit here and say "Well what would we have done last night if the touchback was at the 20, at the 22, at the 18, at the 17," you know? There's some breaking point in there, wherever that is, but I think what ended up happening on that play [is] we kicked off and [Patrick] Chung and [Nate] Ebner made the tackle I think around the 16-yard line, but then with the penalty [against] **Jonathan Jones** it put the ball around the eight. And so the difference between the ball being on the eight and the 25 on that last field would've been pretty significant. I think at that point last night we kind of had the mentality of "Our kickoff team - it's their job to do go down there and get them." We're going to make them earn however many yards they get. We're going to make them earn them. We're not going to give them a quarter or 25 percent of the field. We're going to make them earn every yard that they get the ball out to. They're going to have to block, and run, and break a tackle, or whatever, to gain those yards, and the players - they made great plays. [Matthew] Slater made a great play that helped free up Ebner, Ebner made a great play coming off of the block, Chung sliced in there and made the tackle and **Jonathan Jones** was the first man down. They had to hold him to block him so that he didn't get him sooner. All of those guys were a part of it but would it have been different if the rule had been different? I mean at some point it probably would've been. I can't tell you exactly where that is.

Q: On the kick to the up-man, what do you look for from the guys that are back there in that position?

BB: It depends on what scheme you're trying to run and really what you're trying to do. I'd say they're not all the same. Some teams have big offensive and defensive linemen back there. We've had them back there before. I'd say that's more of a wedge-blocking scheme. There is certainly an element of ball handling that goes on back there like what happened on that play or squib kicks and things like that. I think depending on what kind of returns you're running, also obviously what personnel you have available, but what type of returns you're running and what you're trying to defend in terms of the types of kicks you're getting, how much movement is involved are all considerations as to who you would put back there.

Q: Do you prefer to kick with the wind if you scored on the third down play? How much did you think the wind was a factor?

BB: Yeah, we were on the one-yard line there, inside the one, so if we would have scored there then we would have had the kickoff with the wind. Of course, it didn't work out that way. The wind, I thought it gusted, so there were times during the game I thought it was more of a factor than others. It wasn't a constant, just a steady factor. It kind of came and went at times. I think it was more a factor in the kicking game than in the passing game though.

Q: Earlier this week you were shown on Patriots.com breaking down film with Scott Zolak. You were discussing on kickoff coverage why the unit was sort of bunched together. Could you elaborate a little bit on that and what kind of challenge that presents to the opponent?

BB: Well, again, there's a lot of different ways to do things and there's no, I would say, right or wrong way. When you put a lot of players together it's less defined for the return team who's where. Who is the five? Who is the four? Who is the three? Who's the safety? And also possibly sometimes those alignments of players play into the direction of the kick. Some teams have a kick side, five guys on the kick side, five guys on the backside, so again, depending on how those players are distributed may give keys to the return team ahead of time. If you just line up straight across - 'Here we are. Come and get us or we're coming to get you,' - that certainly takes some of the mystery out of who's where. It's easy to sit back there and identify 'I've got the three. You've got the four.' Who's playing the five? Is it a speed player? Is it a size player? Who is it? So, the movement can disguise that a little bit. We see that from a lot of teams in the league. We do it some, we don't always do it. There are some advantages on the kickoff team, again, to just lining up and 'OK, we know where they are,' and get a good read on our keys. We see where their players are lined up and where they go when the ball is kicked and we react to them, or we can be on the move and maybe make it a little cloudy for the other side but maybe it's not quite as defined for us either. Again, there are advantages to doing it both ways. And we do it and I would say there are a lot of teams in the league that it might be more of one than another, but I'd say most teams have some element of both. I think there's a place for different alignments on the kickoff team.

Q: Have the rules, or perhaps the responsibilities of your players, changed at all on the kickoff return due to the change in the league rules?

BB: Well, whatever your rules are, they are. That's not the returner. It's the other people involved with the returner, the short returner, or the wing guys, or whatever it is. But yeah, whatever your rules are, they are. You can make them whatever you want them to be and ours change from game to game. We don't necessarily do the same thing at every single game. So, if you were to say 'Well, don't do this. Don't do that. Don't field a punt in this area. Don't bring a return out in this area,' well unless you know what the guys being told to do then I don't know how you would know that. Again, I know we have a lot of smart people out there analyzing the game so I respect that. It's still hard for me to understand how they would know what people are told to do in those situations because there's a lot of different ways you can handle it.

Q: What was the risk-reward calculation on the first onside kick? Why did you think that was a good time to do it?

BB: Well, I mean there wasn't a tremendous downside to the play. It was like when they mortared their one over there and [Michael Williams recovered it]. It was different, but it was kind of the same thing – kicking it to dead space.

Q: What was the thinking on the onside kick when you were up 14-0?

BB: I think everything we did, we're trying to do what we think is best.

Q: Why did you have Nate Ebner kick twice and Stephen Gostkowski only once on the three onside kicks?

BB: Because we thought that was the best thing to do.

Q: Who handles the play calling on surprise onside kicks?

BB: We make all the decisions.

Q: Specifically on the drop kick, was he supposed to put air on the ball so it's a jump ball or was he supposed to hit it on the ground like a typical onside kick?

BB: We don't have time for all that.

Q: What makes a good consistent kicker?

BB: Well, it's a little different than punting. You have to have an operation. There are two other guys involved in the whole operation whereas in punting it's a little bit more of a one-man band, if you will. So it's an operation but he's a talented player. He gets good height on the ball and he's accurate. He's got a strong leg.

Q: How did you feel about the kicking game yesterday and the impact the conditions had on it?

BB: Right, well, the field goal was a huge kick for us, obviously, and put us in position after we were able to make a stop on defense to come back on the final offensive drive to go ahead. Really, I thought the conditions were good. I thought the field was in great shape. It was a plush field, good, thick grass and kind of like Cleveland, where we played there last year. But, it was good. There was some light rain early in the game, but that let up. I didn't think it was bad at all. The wind was not much of a factor. So, I thought Ryan [Allen] got off a couple good punts. I thought they kicked the ball pretty well. You know, the big thing, I think, for us is just in the kicking game, on kickoffs, those extra yards that we gained on the kickoff, we had good field position on our kicks. And, even that last kickoff, getting them on the 20 instead of touchbacking it on the 25 might have made a difference on those final couple of plays after the long catch-and-run by [JuJu] Smith [Schuster]. But, I thought our kickoff coverage team did a good job and our kickoff return team, even though we didn't break any long plays, we were able to punch the ball out there a little bit further than taking touchbacks. They were forcing us to return the ball, so we were getting it out there to decent field position. It was a big play by [Matthew] Slater downing - Ryan had a real good punt on that - of downing the ball on the 3, 4-yard line, whatever it was. I think we got some good field position plays on it in the game, and every yard's important in a game like that. Just it shows up sooner or later. I thought our kicking game played - you know, we were competitive on special teams. Certainly, there were plays that could have been better, I'm not saying that. But overall, I thought we did a decent job.

Q: I'm not sure this was the league's intention, but now that you've had time to monitor it do you feel like the new rules to the kickoff have made that play a more competitive and strategic play?

BB: Yeah, maybe a little bit. We'll see. I mean we'll see when all of the numbers come in and all of that. Again, I know for us we look at each situation every week and we're not in a controlled environment here, so there are some variables even though we haven't really had any bad conditions but potentially there are some variables here that other teams don't have to deal with. They could override any rule that you put in or anything like that. But it'll be interesting to see what the league-wide numbers are and all of that. I'd say last week was a good example though of some of the big proponents of 'We want more touchbacks.' We saw a pretty big concussed play with a touchback. So part of the touchback is 'Well, we think it's going to be a touchback so everybody's really not playing at the same speed because we think it's a touchback. It's going to be a no-play.' But then as a coverage team you don't know for sure the guy isn't coming out or not so you're playing it at full speed, so some of the concussions and some of the injuries look to me like they come on touchbacks. So we want more touchbacks - is that really solving the problem here as it's been presented by the competition committee? I mean I think you know how I feel about it. We'll see how smart some of that has really been to address the problems that we think are being addressed. I don't know. It seems like football - we've got a pretty good game here. It's been that way for a long time. It seems like the kicking game has been a great part of our game. But I guess we have a lot of people that feel like the game needs to be changed, so I don't know. We'll have to see where all of that turns out. I don't know what all of the numbers are. I couldn't tell you for sure.

Q: How have you seen the kickoff coverage unit grow during the course of the season? How have you seen their communication develop as they've all gotten more used to each other?

BB: Right. Well, there really is a lot of communication on those plays. Not a lot of it is verbal. It's just visual recognition so that two or three of us running down the field together, we see the same thing and we know how we're going to react to it, how I'm going to react to it, how the guy beside me is going to react to it so that you have the lanes covered and you defend the return they're trying to set up. There's definitely a lot of, let's call it visual communication on those plays. Yeah, we have had some different combinations of people in there. Steve [Gostkowski] has done a good job. He's given us a lot of good kicks, a lot of great kicks to work with. Several of our touchbacks have been on balls that were a yard or two deep in the end zone whereas a lot of times you see those returned, but the aggressiveness of the team is probably a factor there. The players that are on that team - Joe [Judge] and Bubba [Ray Ventrone] have done a great job with them and given them the awareness of the blocking schemes and the types of returns we're going to face and given them opportunities to work off of each other to try to create space in the coverage so that we can get down there and try to penetrate. Those guys have worked hard at that. They do a lot of extra things on their own. That's a group that has had that communication that you just refereed to. They've played well for us all year. Our field position on those plays has been outstanding.

Q: Beyond accuracy on field goal and extra point tries, how valuable is it to have a placekicker that can pin teams deep on kickoffs?

BB: Right, yeah. Again, the kickoffs, that's an important play. In a lot of cases, as it relates to the field goals, I mean, there is no kickoff if you don't make the kick. So, kicking the ball through the uprights is No. 1. Kickoffs is not to say a distant second, but it's definitely second to kicking it through the uprights for the kickers. But, both plays are important. Our kickoff coverage unit certainly has benefited from the excellent kickoffs that Stephen

[Gostkowski] has given us all year, so not only the location, but the hang time. And, he's put a lot of pressure on those returners when they catch the ball right there on the goal line, 1-yard line, whether to bring it out or stay in. You know, they're looking down, they're trying to make sure they make the right decision instead of being aggressive sometimes with catching the ball and looking at the blocking scheme and so forth. So, there are a lot of little things that come into play there, but Steve's done a good job of all those and our coverage team has taken advantage of those opportunities and created the good field position for our defense. So, there's nothing better defensively then going in there on a long field and having them backed up. We just defensively have to do a good job to take advantage of that.

Q: What stands out to you about Jacksonville's kicking game and special teams coach, Joe DeCamillis?

BB: Good at everything. Good return game. [Jaydon] Mickens, Grant - really explosive players. Good coverage team. They do a lot of directional kicking, put a lot of pressure on the ball handling, good rush team - field goal and punt rushes. Good situational football team - like the onside kick they had against San Francisco, plays like that - well-executed, end of the game plays. Well-coached, got a lot of good players. They're big - big on special teams. They have a lot of big, physical type players. A few speed guys, but they have some size, more than most teams do, I'd say, in the kicking game. They're well-coached and they have a lot of explosive players. They've had a lot of production. They're aggressive - fake punts, onside kicks, plays like that. Yeah, got to be alert.

Q: How important is vision when returning kicks?

BB: Yeah, very important. Vision is part of it. Setting up blockers or setting up blocks is a big part of it, too. In this league you can't just get the ball and run. There's too many good players. You have to help your blockers make the blocks. You have to set up blocks in order to get into space. Once you get into space then the back's instincts can take over, but getting there is not always that easy. Sometimes the backs have to have good vision on the play. Sometimes they have to take the defenders and put them where the blockers can block them and set those plays up. That comes with experience, and working together, and blockers and the runner being on the same page in certain blocking relationships.

Two Point Conversions

Q: Has the two-point conversion turned from a novelty play to a more mainstream, and do you practice more to stop it?

BB: We prepare for them every week so there is not a week that goes by that we don't look at that, but in the end, it's like a lot of situations we prepare for – some and some come up and some don't. I thought that our game with Buffalo and the missed extra point, that led to some point differentials that are not as common and then that probably prompted those tries for Buffalo, and the score kind of got out of sync a little bit there. I don't think that's a bad thing for the game. Just like I said before, I think it just makes the play a little more competitive. It's still a very high percentage play, but it's just not the very, very close to 100 percent that it was. So, I personally think that is good, that's why we supported it.

Q: Do you like seeing more teams go for two?

BB: Yeah, whatever they decide to do, they decide to do. We don't have any control over that. If it comes up, then we have to stop it, just like we always have.

Q: Does the fact that they are more willing to go for two-point conversions affect the way you need to game plan at all?

BB: Well, I mean it'll be a game management thing. We'll see what the score is and what the situation is and that may affect our decision making. Sure, it's possible, yeah. But again, they're good at that. They've done it this year, did it a lot last year, were successful in it in '14, so yeah we've got to be prepared for it.

Q: The Steelers have been outspoken about being advocates of going for the two-point conversion after touchdowns and have done it a few times this season. Do teams typically have specific play packages set up for those two-point conversions and as a defense does it require you to do more prep work this week against an opponent like that?

BB: It'll definitely require some extra preparation. And again, they've had a lot of success with doing that. I think they did more of it last year but we know they kind of like to do it. They've done it so we've got to be ready for it I'd say more so than an average game. This game there's more of an element of that. I think you've seen a little bit of a shift in the two-point play, so it's a really good question Bob [Socci]. Overall I think there are generally two philosophies on the two-point play. One philosophy would be to run a red area play that you would run with that field position anyways just as if it was fourth-and-goal on the two [yard line], if you will. The other philosophy was to run a play that the defense had never seen before; unusual formations, some type of play, you know, the play that they couldn't possibly be working on because only – and I'd say the Steelers are a team that used to like to do that especially under Coach [Bill] Cowher. They were very successful in doing that in some of their critical situations; put Hines

Ward somewhere or run a reverse and throw off of it or things like that. And there wasn't any downside to doing that. I think the issue now is, you know, with that play being a defensive play as well, so an interception or a fumble or something, if the defense got the ball they'd be able to score on that play, so I think we've seen a little bit less league-wide of kind of the once-a-season type of play in that situation. You see it occasionally but for the most part it looks like the philosophy has gone more towards a red area play. Something that we're good at, something that we've repped a lot that we've seen with multiple looks and we have a lot of confidence in, and the teams are taking more of that type of philosophy towards it. In the past on a two-point play we're always kind of having in mind, and especially to alert the defensive players, there's a good chance you're going to see something you've never seen here before, whatever it is, and either personnel group or formation or a type of play that this team has never run that we can't work on. We have no idea if they're drawing it up themselves. But I'd say that that's become less prevalent in the last couple of years. At least it seems like it has to me. Definitely extra preparation for that situation this week.

Q: On the two-point conversion play that failed it looked like D.J. Foster's initial responsibility was to stay in the backfield and help in pass protection. Is there a general rule of thumb that states how long

he should do something like that before releasing out to become a receiving option?

BB: That's really a long conversation, but to try and give it a short answer, if the [running] back has blitz pickup responsibility and either as he's going to block his responsibility or if his responsibility leaves and he really doesn't have any responsibility, you know, you'd never want to tell the back to run by a free player. Say the back is supposed to run a route and his linebacker doesn't come so he starts to run his route and in doing that he sees a free rusher coming that's not his guy, well just instinctively - backs - they just know to block those guys. There is no sense in going out for a route if the guy is going to run in there and hit the quarterback. Those are kind of plays that backs have to make a reaction to and good backs will make the right decision as to whether he needs to block the player or doesn't and can get out in a pattern. He doesn't want to run into a guy that's being blocked and take himself out of the route, but at the same time he doesn't want to go out into the route and let a player who's running at the quarterback, run at the quarterback. Again, those are kind of things that come with experience and those are quick decisions that backs have to make because it's not really their man. Technically, they'd be right to just ignore him and go on but in terms of having a successful play that's not always the best thing to do. It's a long answer but again, it's an experience thing. Could it maybe have been a little bit better? I don't know. He certainly wasn't the primary guy in that play.

Q: On James White's successful two point conversion, was that a good check at the line of scrimmage by the quarterback or are you not really doing things like that right now?

BB: I don't want to get into the specifics of each play. We could be here all day talking about that. Again, any time that you run the ball basically you just want to have I'd say a fair fight. You want enough blockers for the defenders and you've got to block them. Any time you can outnumber them then that's a big advantage. It doesn't happen very often. Any time they outnumber you, unless you're only looking for a couple of inches, it's hard to count on making yards against unblocked players in this league. There's a point where you don't want to run a bad play, but not every play is just going to be [a situation] that you have a great advantage on. You're going to have to block them and then they're going to be sitting there and they have to defeat blocks. I'd say in that situation you feel OK about running the ball.

Q: After reviewing the film, what did you see on that fake punt play?

BB: Well, I think the play was a version of the swinging gate play. I don't know exactly how it was supposed to work. That's something you'd have to ask them about. They brought the gunner in to snap the ball so he would've been an eligible receiver, so we had to cover him. I think basically you want to try to, on punt formations you like that, it's just a numbers game. You want to have enough guys to match to the smaller numbers, and as many guys as you can to match to the larger number where they were over-shifted. We certainly knew that the punter could throw. He's done that before. He's thrown passes to uncovered guys on punt formations, and we saw him run against Tennessee, so we were aware of those things. So it's just kind of everybody making sure that they take care of their responsibility on the shift and make sure that we can defend the formation and know who is eligible. I think it's something that every special teams coach goes over. The same thing could happen on field goals with the swinging gate. You see teams line up for an extra point with everybody over on the hash mark and if you don't have it covered they flip it out to him and if you do then they come back in and kick the extra point. It's that type of a play.

Q: How impactful of a play was that for your team?

BB: Well, it was a good alert play by our punt return unit and Coach [Joe] Judge and Coach [Ray] Ventrone for having those guys well prepared. It gave us good field position, and then we were able to capitalize on the field position and turn that into seven points. Any time you get that kind of field position, whether it be on a turnover or in this case on downs, whatever it is, you want to be able to take advantage of it. That was the most important thing and we did that, so that was the best thing about it.

Q: Did Jamie Collins make the decision to jump the line on his own to block the extra point, or was that something that was called in from the sideline? How impactful of a play was that for your team?

BB: It was an interesting situation. When we scored the touchdown after the fake punt, there was strong consideration given to going for two there, and as it turned out that would have been the right thing to do to go for two. Now there was quite a bit of a time left to go in the game and that one point swing the way it turned out, it would have been better to go for two the way the game turned out, but had there been other scores, like what happened in the Cleveland-Denver game yesterday, with time left that can change the equation a little bit so we elected to kick it and make it a 13-point lead given the amount of time that was left in the game. So, the blocked extra point led to it being a touchdown game instead of a six-point game which as it turned out didn't make any difference, but had they recovered the onside kick then it would have made a world of difference. I think any time you run a play like that you need some kind of coordination. I don't think you want a player to do that on his own because you could have one of your interior lineman making the move into a gap where he is trying to get through and then you run into each other and that kind of thing. So, I don't really think that's what you're looking for. If you want to try to run that type of a block, I think you need it coordinated. Otherwise, you're probably asking for something to go wrong and then you have a good play and you screw it up because it's just not orchestrated. We definitely didn't want anybody running where he was going to go.

Q: What goes into the decision to go for two in a moment like that when there are so many things to consider?

BB: The less time there is to go in the game, the fewer possessions there are, then the more I think you want to just stick to the chart. That gives you the best mathematical probability of doing the right thing. The problem is that if there is enough time to go in the game, those numbers can change. Of course if you make it, it's always the right decision. If you don't make it, like again what happened in the Denver-Cleveland game, had Cleveland kicked the extra point and not gone for two going back to whatever the score was there, then they could have potentially been kicking a game-winning instead of a game-tying field goal at the end. If you just want to go purely by the chart, you can do that. Again, sometimes that can get you into trouble if there is enough time for there to be multiple scores and then the numbers change. Again, if you feel very confident in your two-point play for whatever reason, if you like the matchup or the look you're going to get or whatever it is and you make it, then that's always the best decision. But percentage-wise, it's a lot higher probability that you will kick the extra point than you will convert the two-point conversion if it's just strictly a statistical comparison.

Red Zone

Q: How important is it to maintain poise and composure on defense once a team reaches the red zone? Does it require a certain mindset to hold firm there?

BB: Yeah, look, the game changes on every play, so field position, down and distance – those all chang. Once you get into the red area it's a different game. It's a different emphasis. There's different plays. We have different defenses. The way you defend the field is different because it's different. It's changing your mindset to what's required down there, whichever side of the ball you're on – offense or defense – it doesn't matter. It's just things change. They're different down there. You've got to treat them differently.

Q: How do you feel this group has handled those situations in the red area?

BB: Well, I mean, look, it's a long year. We've had our

moments where we've done things well. We've had other moments where we could've been better. Again, it doesn't really matter. It's what it's going to be the next time we have to do it. We'll always try to learn from the good things or the bad things to reinforce them or correct them and be ready for what comes up next, or sometimes the situations sort of grey into each other, so maybe this is one situation that we actually experience but if it were a little different it would be what the differences would be. We talk about that, too; the hypotheticals of say the ball being on the 8-yard line. If it was on the 4-yard line or if it was on the 2-yard line, maybe there's something that needs to be modified somewhat.

Q: What are the specific challenges of scoring a touchdown when the field is condensed in the red zone? Is there a specific percentage that you are looking to shoot for every year?

BB: Yeah, well, like you said, I mean we have a pretty short-term look at it so every time we're down there we want to make the most out of the opportunity. In most cases you want to score. Sometimes at the end of the game there's something that might not be exactly the same situation but, yeah, we're always trying to score touchdowns. Some of it is what you do. Some of it is what they do. It's a combination of those things - your matchups, the schemes they run. I don't think you can just run the same play against every defense. I don't think you want to do that. We try to attack the defense where they're weak. They try to disguise them. It's a lot of very contested plays down there because you don't have a lot of space in the passing game. There's extra guys to block in the running game. Safeties, linebackers are down there because they're pretty close to the line of scrimmage as soon as you get into the lower red area. You're basically nine against 11. You just run out of guys. You have to decide who you're going to block, who you're not going to block and the backs have to make some tough yards.

Q: Do you have a rule for your players when it comes to handling the ball on the goal line and whether or not to extend the ball out to cross the goal line?

BB: Yeah, we talk about it. We talk about everything that's football related, so situations, ball security, all of those things. We go over all of the situations. There are a lot of different ones. They're not quite all the same, but we cover them and make sure that they understand what we would want them to do in different situations. As I said, there are many different things that could happen on the types of plays that you're describing.

Q: On the final offensive drive of the first half did you decide to go up-tempo once you reached the red area to prevent Jacksonville from getting its goal line defense on the field?

BB: Right. Yeah, well, there wasn't a whole lot of time left at that point. I don't know what they would've done. I don't think they would've put goal line out there unless we had put our goal line out there. I mean, I don't know that for sure but I don't think they would've done that. We just felt like there was an advantage to moving quickly on that. Josh [McDaniels] did a good job of getting the situation set up. Tom did a good job of executing it and getting things set up to the line of scrimmage and making sure we had a good play when the ball was snapped. Sometimes when you go fast on a play like that you can end up running right into something as much as you can end up running away from it. Just really pretty well executed all the way around and James [White] made a good run. But I don't think they would've been able to or would've even wanted to sub in their goal line unless we had done it first. Remember, in the two-minute situation there's no defensive match, so any subs you make in a two-minute situation you're on your own, whereas at any other time – the other 28 minutes of each half – the umpire will step in there and give the defense the opportunity to match the subs, right? In a two-minute situation there's no match, so trying to sub a goal line unit on if they're not subbing, if the offense isn't subbing, is kind of a risky thing to do. You could do it anyway and struggle with the tempo of the play, but with no hold up at all by the umpire, just the ability of the offense to go right to the ball and snap the ball, to go to the line and snap the ball, that would really make it tough. That could really make it tough to make that substitution. That's what it looked like to me.

Q: Devin McCourty spoke about the job Brian Flores has done as the defensive red zone coordinator. How would you assess his performance in that role?

BB: Yeah, Brian does a good job, works hard, has a lot of experience. He does a good job of analyzing what we do, what our opponents do, trying to put it all together. He helps Matt [Patricia] and the defensive staff. I think that's kind of the way it is on most staffs. The coordinator is obviously in charge, and then each person on the staff has a different area that they kind of do a little extra research in – red area, goal line, short-yardage, third down, big plays, however you want to break it up.

Q: Is the red area coordinator usually the same as the goal line coordinator?

BB: No, I mean, it could be. But no, not necessarily. A lot of the time the goal line and short-yardage is the offensive or defensive line coach. But, it could be however you want to do it. It's just hard as a coordinator. You look at everything. You put everything together, but say, like right now, to go back through a whole season, let's say, of the Jets and look at all their short-yardage plays or all their red-area plays – that's pretty time consuming – all of their third-down plays, all of their big plays, all of their negative plays. Again, however you want to break it down. One of the other people on the staff kind of breaks that up and then they come back to you and say, 'OK, well I've looked at 60-70 plays of X, red area, 15-yard gains. Here's the theme. Here's what we got to do,' or 'Here's what they've had trouble with,' something like that. The same thing on the offensive side of the ball. It's just kind of a way of getting more detail on it. Early in the year maybe it's going back and looking at all of last year's stuff if you haven't done that in the offseason; something like that.

Q: Having been in the game as long as you have, do you like that particular rule from Sunday that overturned the would-be touchdown catch by Jesse James?

BB: Well, I think that's really a conversation for people like Al [Riveron] and the league and so forth. But, there's always been a philosophy in the league and it's gone back several decades of philosophically whether you want to have a catch and a fumble or an incomplete pass, and the philosophy has always been incomplete pass. Otherwise, you'd have a million catches and fumbles. I agree with that. The catch in the end zone is very clearly stated, so you've got to complete a catch. It's pretty clear. Whether there's a better way to do that, I don't know. It's a tough rule. It's a bang-bang play. It could go either way, so I think you have to have a philosophy and whatever philosophy you have then there will be people on the other side with a different philosophy and then it really gets back into that whole discussion. I think if you've got a better way to do it, suggest it and let somebody take a look at it and we'll talk about it. I don't know.

Q: What did you see from your red zone defense and your third-down defense especially early in the game?

BB: Well, you know, most all of those plays really revolve around team defense. Malcolm [Butler] made a good play on the interception and kind of used his body to box out [Antonio] Brown and make the play. But it's team defense. You've got to stop the run, you've got to make the quarterback uncomfortable, you've got to get on the receivers whether it's man or zone. We had our moments, but yeah, certainly in the end the red area was a huge difference in the game. In a close game those points amount to a lot. Again, team defense.

Q: Do you ever decide to sort of sacrifice the pass rush to ensure that the team defense is going to be solid against a particular weapon?

BB: Well, again, it comes back to team defense. We always try to do the best we can to defend whatever it is we're defending in that particular week or in that particular situation. How many guys you rush affects how many guys are in coverage and what coverage you can play to a certain degree. Some of that is a function of their personnel, their style of play, personnel and the situation. I think we used all - about everything along the way. But based on each game and each situation we try to do what we think is best. I mean we're not trying to sacrifice anything. We're just trying to win that down, win that situation.

Q: In reference to the James White screen play that you mentioned, is it a little more difficult to call a screen play like that down in the red area due to the compacted space that you have to work with?

BB: I mean that's a good question. I think it depends a little bit. But you know, for the most part on the screen once you get past the - maybe call it the first five to eight yards from the line of scrimmage to five-or-so yards down field - that's really where all the action takes place. You get the ball to the screen back and then you have one or two blockers, three blockers, whatever it is to block two or three guys whether it's a slip-screen to a wide-out or a back-screen. You've got a couple of blockers, you've got a couple of defenders and say whether the ball is on the 20-yard line, their 20 or your 20, it's probably going to be about the same space where those blocks occur. How much the deep guys get run off, I mean not as much obviously in the red area, but they're usually not the main factor on the play. The main factors on the play are the guys that are close to the line of scrimmage. Like the play that [Ryan] Shazier made, I think it was in the second quarter, we actually kind of had two blockers there. We couldn't quite get him. He made a nice play. He kind of knifed in between us and broke it up, but had we gotten him I think it would've been quite a few yards on that play. Again, it's usually really about getting the runner started and getting them I'd say, once you get them more than four or five yards down field then a lot of the rest of it takes care of itself. It's getting them to that point cleanly.

Q: Do you look at some of the struggles on defense in the red-area as a concern or is simply too small of a sample size?

BB: We're a third of the way through the season, so I mean look, we try to improve on everything every week. That's where we are. We're in September to early October. Nothing probably is as good as it's going to be, at least I hope not, as good as it's going to be over the course of the year. Hopefully we'll continue to improve in every area; running the ball, throwing the ball, defending the run, defending the pass, situational football, special teams. I mean you name it. There are a lot of things we need to work on. We all have things we need to do better, coach better, improve on and everything's in that category. Statistically some things are better than others but regardless I think we try to continue to improve in all of those areas. It doesn't really matter what the stats are or aren't. I mean it matters; they're somewhat relevant. But I think improving in every area is important, so yeah, we're going to address it regardless in everything.

Q: What changes for a defense inside the twenty-yard line?

BB: Less field. Offensively everybody's closer to the line so the safeties are linebackers; linebackers are in a lot of cases borderline defensive lineman. Everything's just compressed. So, there are a lot of things you have to handle differently. Routes are different, coverages are different.

Q: Do the physical matchups become underscored when there is less field like that in the red zone?

BB: They could; they could, yeah. It depends, again, on the matchup but generally you see more size in that area because there's less space so speed is less of a factor. It's always a factor but less of a factor. There's only so far you can run. Technique is important, coordination offensively or defensively is important, the proper spacing, the proper leverage, using the space that you have and of course everything happens so much quicker down there because there's less space and less time so throws and catches have to be good, a lot of tight coverage, a lot of catches away from the body into a short space. Defensively you're fighting for every inch, every yard. It's critical. Two yards at midfield is one thing. Two yards on the five-yard line is 50 percent of the length; 50 percent of the field. So, it's all heightened, it's all a little bit more urgent and there are definitely some personnel and scheme factors that - there's a transition period in there but once you get down there low like inside the 10-yard line or inside the five-yard line you're talking about real tight space.